PLATO'S
PHAEDRUS

**Purdue University Press Series
in the History of Philosophy**

Adriaan Peperzak, *Editor-in-Chief*
Arion Kelkel
Joseph J. Kockelmans
Calvin O. Schrag
Thomas Seebohm

PLATO'S
PHAEDRUS

The Philosophy
of Love

Graeme Nicholson

Purdue University Press
West Lafayette, Indiana

Printed in the United States of America

Library of Congress Cataloging-in-Publication Data
Nicholson, Graeme.
    Plato's Phaedrus : the philosophy of love / Graeme Nicholson.
       p.   cm. — (Purdue University Press series in the history of
philosophy)
    Includes bibliographical references and index.
    ISBN 1-55753-118-8 (alk. paper). — ISBN 1-55753-119-6 (pbk. : alk. paper)
    1. Plato. Phaedrus. 2. Love. I. Title. II. Series.
B380.N53 1998
184—dc21   97-46404
                                                              CIP

For Luke

The lunatic, the lover, and the poet,
Are of imagination all compact.
One sees more devils than vast hell can hold;
That is the madman. The lover, all as frantic,
Sees Helen's beauty in a brow of Egypt.
The poet's eye, in a fine frenzy rolling,
Doth glance from heaven to earth, from earth to heaven;
And as imagination bodies forth
The forms of things unknown, the poet's pen
Turns them to shapes, and gives to airy nothing
A local habitation and a name.

CONTENTS

ACKNOWLEDGMENTS

I am grateful to Joseph Kockelmans, one of the founders of this series, who invited a contribution from me, and who did not demur when I suggested the *Phaedrus*.

Anyone who writes on Plato, I suspect, will have a particular person to thank, the one who was one's guide to the dialogues early in one's life. My good fortune was to have James Doull as a teacher, at once a profound philosopher and a classical scholar of comprehensive learning.

The footnotes to this volume will offer some evidence, though far from complete, of the debts I owe to those who have written about Platonic philosophy.

For decade after decade, the University of Toronto has been able to foster the study of ancient and medieval philosophy in an ideal climate, connecting it to every kind of philosophical inquiry, at the same time upholding the highest standards of scholarship. Here I have been able to hear wonderful expositions of Plato and read the text with very learned people. The University has been a home to me as well as a school for many years, and not a year has passed in which I have not been able to discuss a Platonic text with a group of students here.

More recently, John Sallis and John Russon have helped me come into contact with a broader international world of Plato scholars, and I must acknowledge some very recent help as well, on a number of points, from Kenneth Dorter and Eva Buccioni.

The photo on the cover of this book renders a bust of Plato that was produced in Roman times as the copy of a work made in Athens by the sculptor Silanion, probably while Plato was still living, so it is very likely a good likeness of Plato in old age. The bust is now to be found in the collection of the Staatliche Antikensammlung und Glypothek in Munich. Along with the publisher, I would like to express my gratitude to the museum for supplying the photograph.

INTRODUCTION

The *Phaedrus* lies at the heart of Plato's work, and the topics it discusses are central to his thought. It treats the human soul, not only its interior structure, but its origins and destiny as well; it offers one version of Plato's theory of ideas; and it contains one of Plato's most extensive treatments of the theme of love. It is well suited, then, to be a guide to Plato's philosophy and to play the role envisaged in the History of Philosophy Series, where a single text is to present the fundamental ideas of a great philosopher. A treatment of the *Phaedrus* will lead us quite naturally to the other works of Plato, and, in connection with the topics I have already mentioned, the soul, the ideas, and love, it is tied closely to the other dialogues that constitute the work of Plato's "middle period," the *Phaedo,* the *Symposium,* and the *Republic.*

A further dimension of the *Phaedrus* is its treatment of rhetoric. Rhetoric in theory and in practice was a powerful force in education and politics in the days of Plato's youth, while he was consorting with Socrates, and in the later years as well, when he was writing the dialogues. The discussion of rhetoric in the *Phaedrus* gives us a picture of the rival forces that contended for control of the intellectual life of Greece, the crucible in which Plato's own conception of philosophy was formed. The relation between political power and truthful inquiry—and that is what the issue of "rhetoric" involves—had always been Plato's preoccupation, and our study of it will bring to the fore another whole area of his work, invoking such dialogues as the *Gorgias* and the *Protagoras.*

So broad a range of topics does the *Phaedrus* treat that it has been seen sometimes as a virtual compendium of Platonic philosophy. That was the view of the great scholar Friedrich Schleiermacher, who translated Plato into German at the beginning of the nineteenth century. He put the *Phaedrus* at the head of his series of translated dialogues, as a kind of overture to the whole, and he also supposed it was the first of the dialogues to be *written*. His opinion on its early date of composition finds no support among scholars today, however, and even the "overture" or "compendium" model for the *Phaedrus* is an overstatement. No great writer would ever attempt to put into one work everything that his other works expressed. Although we can see reflections in the *Phaedrus* from all the other dialogues, it has its own definite character and shape as well.

It captures our attention first of all with the beauty of the scene in which it is set and then with the theme of its conversations and speeches—love—and then with the gorgeous imagery of Socrates' Great Speech on love running from 244a to 257b. It has the further advantage among works of philosophy that it left a mark on the poetry and art of the Greeks and Romans; the Italian Renaissance; and English literature in its greatest periods, Shakespeare[1] and Wordsworth,[2] for instance. The student who first begins to read the *Phaedrus,* then, may have been exposed beforehand to some of the traces it has left and so may enjoy the pleasure of recognition while reading it. Besides that, it is Plato's most mature exposition of the philosophy of his "middle" period, the soul's journey of salvation, its immortality, and its recognition of the eternal ideas, the prototype of all reality. Perhaps Plato's "middle-period" philosophy has some grip upon the imagination of all human beings!

These happy circumstances do not of themselves prove the stature of the *Phaedrus* as a philosophical or a scientific work. At times, scholars of a more academic or scholastic bent have preferred to focus on dialogues that offered them a better reflection of their own prosaic sobriety.[3] Others have been troubled by Plato's exuberant use here of the

---

1. *A Midsummer Night's Dream,* act 5, scene 1, the lines that appear on this book's dedication page.

2. "Ode: Intimations of Immortality from Recollections of Early Childhood."

3. In this connection I am led to think of Paul Natorp. His influential book, *Platons Ideenlehre,* was rather scornful of the *Phaedrus,* because what Natorp was looking for generally was a Plato who would look respectable in the company of neo-Kantian analytical philosophy professors. And that tendency in Plato interpretation is not confined to German professors or to neo-Kantians. As we shall see, we find it still today among those who write in English.

motifs of Greek mythology. One of the goals of the exposition that follows will be to bring out the serious philosophical import of a work that is at once a rhapsody and an argument. The exposition will need to deal directly with such questions as the role of mythology in Plato's text, and, on the other side, characterize what an *argument* in Plato is, what dialectic is.

Plato's Life and Writings

Born in Athens in the year that we call 427 B.C.E., Plato was descended through his mother from Solon, the great lawgiver of Athens, and was the relative of several important political figures, Critias and Charmides, for instance, who held great power in Athens in the last years of the fifth century B.C.E.[4] Plato has told us a lot about himself in the autobiographical passages contained in his letters.[5]

"When I was young," he says, "I had the same ambition as many others: I thought of entering public life as soon as I came of age. And certain happenings in public affairs favoured me."[6] Such indeed was the common expectation of young men born into aristocratic circles in the 420s, the 410s, and the 400s. Plato continues his account, referring to events that took place in the year 404. He describes the violent and subversive practices of the so-called Thirty, an oligarchic faction who had seized power in Athens at the time of the Athenian defeat at the hands of the Spartans, and then he goes on to describe the restoration of the democracy that followed shortly thereafter. And here he refers to Socrates, the most important figure both in his young life and in his

---

4. These details are recorded by Diogenes Laertius in his *Lives of Eminent Philosophers* III. Diogenes probably composed his history in Alexandria around the year 200 C.E., but because it is evident that he drew upon many early documents, his testimony on certain details, such as Plato's family and date of birth, is reliable.

5. These epistles were often believed by scholars in the nineteenth century to be inauthentic, but in our times most scholars have come to the conclusion that at least the longest and the most important one, the *Seventh Letter*, is the genuine work of Plato; even those who remain doubtful on that score will grant that the letter was written by someone very close to Plato and is therefore a reliable historical source. See *Plato's Epistles*, trans. Glenn Morrow (Indianapolis: Library of Liberal Arts, 1962), pp. 44 ff.

6. Plato is probably writing in the year 353, when he was about seventy-five years old. My running quotations are taken from the *Seventh Letter*, 324b and following, in Glenn Morrow's translation.

life as a whole, and proceeds to a narrative of the greatest crisis of his young years.

> Now many deplorable things occurred during those troubled days, and it is not surprising that under cover of the revolution too many old enmities were avenged; but in general those who returned from exile acted with great restraint. By some chance, however, certain powerful persons brought into court this same friend Socrates, preferring against him a most shameless accusation, and one which he, of all men, least deserved. For the prosecutors charged him with impiety, and the jury condemned and put to death the very man who, at the time when his accusers were themselves in misfortune and exile, had refused to have a part in the unjust arrest of one of their friends.

This happened in the year 399, when Socrates was seventy years old and Plato just under thirty. One of Plato's earliest literary works, *The Apology of Socrates,* offers his record of the great speech of defense Socrates made at his trial, in which Socrates touched on the party struggles and illegal arrests of those years, while vindicating his own life as a whole and vindicating the very pursuit of philosophy.

Plato's narrative continues:

> The corruption of our written laws and customs was proceeding at such amazing speed that whereas at first I had been full of zeal for public life, when I noted these changes and saw how unstable everything was, I became in the end quite dizzy; and though I did not cease to reflect how an improvement could be brought about in our laws and in the whole constitution, yet I refrained from action, waiting for the proper time. At last I came to the conclusion that existing states are badly governed and the condition of their laws practically incurable, without some miraculous remedy and the assistance of fortune; and I was forced to say, in praise of true philosophy, that from her height alone was it possible to discern what the nature of justice is, either in the state or in the individual, and that the ills of the human race would never end until either those who are sincerely and truly lovers of wisdom come into political power, or the rulers of our cities, by the grace of God, learn true philosophy.

The idea expressed in these lines was to become the central thrust of Plato's greatest work on political theory, the *Republic,* very likely written during the 380s. Plato goes on in his letter to tell us more of the course of his life experience around the year 388, when he was about forty. He took a trip to Italy and Sicily, visiting some of the courts of the local princes, and in particular the court in Syracuse in Sicily, and he records his disgust, in rather puritanical language, with the luxury and frivolity of the courtier's life. Several things seem to have led Plato to Italy and Sicily. He wanted to visit some of the Pythagorean communities on the mainland—philosophers living a communal life, and whose intellectual pursuits were combined with a certain amount of political influence. He was invited to Syracuse in Sicily to visit the tyrant there, Dionysius I. A young man named Dion, one of the tyrant's advisers, knew of Plato's views and wanted to offer him the opportunity to put them to work by seeing if the regime at Syracuse could be reformed by philosophy. This venture had little success, except that it led to Plato's deep friendship with Dion, twenty years his junior. There is reason to think that Plato developed a passionate loving attachment to Dion that lasted the rest of his life—he never married.[7]

After this sojourn abroad, probably lasting between one and two years, Plato used some of his inheritance to buy land and establish a sort of college in the "Academy," a park just outside Athens. The life of the Pythagorean communities, as well as the convictions he himself had formed earlier, led him to the belief that what the leaders of the future really needed was an early education, and an ongoing education, in intellectual discipline. From about 387 on, the approximate date of the founding of the Academy, Plato labored to guide the school, leading his pupils in discussions about politics, morals, mathematics, and metaphysics, while making himself known to a broader public through his written works.

About twenty years later, in 367, the tyrant of Syracuse died and was succeeded by his son Dionysius II. Dion, still in the service of the regime, prevailed upon Plato to make a second trip to Sicily, in the hope that a younger ruler might prove to be amenable to the influence of philosophy. But again, the effort did not bring much success—in fact, it provoked a hostile reaction in other political circles in Sicily. Plato had to return in haste to Athens after about ten months, and Dion himself came under increasing attacks.

---

7. See W. K. C. Guthrie, *A History of Greek Philosophy* (Cambridge: Cambridge University Press, 1975), vol. 4, p. 18.

Plato visited Syracuse for a third time in 361 with the hope, again, of helping with the constitution of the city, but again the enemies of Dion forced him out after about a year. From then on, he stayed in Athens. Dion was killed by his enemies in 354, and it was on this occasion that Plato wrote to "the friends and followers of Dion," the document known as the *Seventh Letter,* which I quoted from earlier. It was just a few years after that, in 347, that Plato died in Athens, aged eighty.

Almost all Plato's writings are in the form of dialogues, dramatic representations in which two, three, or four figures, sometimes more—always men, all Greeks, mostly Athenians, mostly real historical persons, but never including Plato himself—enter into a discussion about ethics or politics or education or mathematics. To our good fortune, history seems to have preserved all Plato's writings, though on the other hand some of the works preserved in the collection are not Plato's own. For over a hundred years, scholars have been trying to establish the definitive list of authentic and inauthentic dialogues, establish the order in which Plato wrote the authentic ones, and assign each one to a definite year or years. On the first two points, there is today a fair measure of agreement, though it has proved impossible to assign absolute dates of composition to the dialogues.

There are thirty-six items in the Platonic corpus: thirty-five dialogues plus the Letters (in addition to a few minor items written in some of the manuscripts —"Definitions" and so on—that hardly anybody ever accepted as authentic). Dialogues rejected as inauthentic by a good number of contemporary scholars include *Alcibiades* II, *Hipparchus, Amatores, Theages, Hippias Major, Clitophon,* and *Minos.* Even if Plato had written one or more of them, they would not help us much in our study of his major works: they are philosophically slight. Indeed, slightness is one argument for their inauthenticity. One need not assume that a doubter of authenticity is always right—nineteenth-century scholars carried such doubts to the point of absurdity—but such works would not matter significantly to Plato interpretation even if they were authentic, and that is the real reason why we may leave them to one side here. *Alcibiades* I is not a slight work, but its authenticity is often contested.

The other two questions, regarding the dialogues' order of composition, and the dating of each one, are still under discussion among classical scholars, and since they have some bearing upon an interpretation of the *Phaedrus,* I shall summarize current opinion briefly. Plato's dialogues certainly fall into groups that are marked by certain literary features: by length, by the style of writing, by theme or subject matter, and by the way of treating character. They are commonly divided into three groups, but I shall subdivide the first group, 1, into (a) and (b), and the third group, 3, into (d) and (e). These groups are assigned by almost all contemporary scholars to distinct periods of Plato's life.

1. (a) Eight fairly short works, between eleven and twenty-five pages each in the standard edition, represent Socrates in debate with one or two interlocutors, usually on the question of defining some virtuous characteristic such as courage or temperance: *Euthyphro, Apology, Crito, Charmides, Laches, Lysis, Ion,* and *Hippias Minor.* It is almost certain that Plato wrote these between the time of Socrates' death, 399, and the first Sicilian trip, 388.

1. (b) Five longer dialogues, between thirty and eighty pages each in the standard edition, represent Socrates in debate mostly with "sophists" or their defenders, on questions about knowledge and opinion as well as virtue: *Gorgias, Meno, Protagoras, Euthydemus,* and *Cratylus.*[8] Very likely later than all of group (a), these are generally assigned either to the period just before the first Sicilian trip or just after it, when Plato was getting his Academy started. The idiosyncratic work *Menexenus* would seem to be a sixth work of this period.

2. Four longer works united by theme—the exposition of a metaphysical doctrine, the theory of ideas: *Phaedo, Symposium, Republic,* and *Phaedrus.* These dialogues were almost certainly written during the twenty years between the founding of the Academy, 387, and Plato's second trip to Sicily in 367, Plato's "middle period" as it is usually called, when he was between forty and sixty years of age.

3. (d) Seven works of middling length, between forty and eighty pages, dealing with rather formidable technical issues in philosophy. These works are often critical in their treatment of doctrines found in the early and middle works; moreover, the figure of Socrates is not as central as in the early and middle

---

8. It is common, though, to date the *Cratylus* later than that; see Guthrie, *A History of Greek Philosophy,* vol. 5, pp. 1–2.

dialogues. For these reasons, they are generally dated after 367: *Parmenides, Theaetetus, Sophist, Statesman, Philebus, Timaeus,* and *Critias* (unfinished). The first two of this group have some things in common with the *Phaedrus* and might have been composed before the Sicilian trip of 367. The case that the *Timaeus* should be assigned to group 2, the middle period, was argued some decades ago,[9] yet the replies on behalf of the traditional late dating were at least as strong,[10] and, I think, have prevailed in the court of scholarly opinion.

3. (e) Plato's last work, by far his longest and demonstrating the tenacity of his interest in political philosophy: *The Laws,* probably including the *Epinomis.* He died leaving this work without its final editing.[11]

In all this, the point that is important for our purposes is that the *Phaedrus* can now be assigned to group 2, and indeed to the end of that period, following upon the *Phaedo,* the *Symposium,* and the *Republic.* One contemporary who has surveyed the history of scholarship on the dating of Plato's works is Leonard Brandwood.[12] All the evidence in his survey points pretty clearly to a position after the other dialogues of group 2, and in the neighborhood of the *Parmenides* and *Theaetetus,* which would place the composition of the *Phaedrus* around the year 370, when Plato was in his late fifties. That is the dating I shall assume in what follows. In my interpretation of the *Phaedrus,* however, the question of its date of composition actually will bear little weight. The *Phaedrus* is connected to Plato's other works through its characters, its themes, its setting, and its style, and these material bonds will loom large in our study, for there are points in the *Phaedrus* that reference to other dialogues will clarify, and points in other dialogues that can be clarified by reference to the *Phaedrus.* Interconnections like these, informative and illuminating as they are, do not usually depend on any particular hypothesis about dating, and they permit us to treat the col-

---

9. G. E. L. Owen, "The Place of the *Timaeus* in Plato's Dialogues," *Classical Quarterly,* n.s., 3 (1953): 79–95.

10. Especially H. F. Cherniss, "The Relation of the *Timaeus* to Plato's Later Dialogues," *American Journal of Philology* 78 (1957): 225–66.

11. Guthrie, *A History of Greek Philosophy,* vol. 4, pp. 48–49.

12. *The Chronology of Plato's Dialogues* (Cambridge: Cambridge University Press, 1990).

lection of Plato's works as a synchronous library tied together by bonds of theme, character, and style.

Love and Philosophy

Part 1 of this study will draw upon the whole of the *Phaedrus* in order to express the *idea of philosophy itself* that was guiding Plato in this text. In the various chapters of part 1, I shall look at a variety of Plato's other works, earlier and later, showing which elements are constant in his idea of philosophy and with respect to which elements the *Phaedrus* may differ. For one thing, we shall be seeing the novel position that Socrates takes as the "philosopher" toward his rivals, the advocates of rhetoric, a figure of Socrates that is rather different from the character shown in other writings of Plato. But in each of Plato's writings Socrates is the embodiment of philosophy itself. So there are differences between the guiding conception of philosophy here and the conception offered in the simpler, shorter (and earlier) dialogues of Plato. It will be abundantly clear that *this* Socrates is the creation of Plato himself, with not a great deal left to connect him to the historical Socrates whom Plato had known between 410 and 399. Part 1, then, is focused on philosophy itself as a mode of discourse, and it will reveal a denser, more complex composition of philosophical discourse than in Plato's earlier works. I call this the study of the "voices of philosophy." And there is another point about discourse. Philosophy may be expressed in speech, but it may also be written, and, as we read in the concluding pages of the *Phaedrus,* that makes a great difference. We shall treat that question in chapter 4.

Part 2 of this book consists of my translation of the central portion of the *Phaedrus,* the Great Speech of Socrates, as it is generally called, which runs from 243e to 257b, prefaced by the introductory conversation between Socrates and Phaedrus, 241d to 243e. These numbers refer to the "Stephanus" pages, the pages of the Renaissance edition of Plato's works in Greek, which I referred to earlier as the standard pagination, almost always printed in margins of translations. This speech is one of the magnificent tributes written by Plato to the passion of love, the others being found in the *Symposium,* ascribed to Aristophanes, the comic poet in the *Symposium* 189c–193d, and to Diotima, the "wise woman of Mantinea" in the *Symposium* 201d–212c.

Part 3 is an exposition of Socrates' Great Speech. It goes into detail on Plato's philosophy of love by treating the psychology of love;

its sexual character; and its social, ethical, and religious meaning. Then these chapters will bring to the fore a whole series of further phenomena, for there is a huge vista that opens out when we follow Plato in thinking about love—the phenomenon of beauty; the status of beauty in relation to the other "ideas," *ideai,* as he calls them, such as justice, temperance, and truth; the relationship of the human soul to the divinities; and the grounds of the possibility of knowledge. In these studies, too, we shall be in a position to show where the *Phaedrus* accords with other dialogues and where it differs. To offer here a rather programmatic remark, I should like to indicate what Plato's intention is regarding the relation between erotic love and philosophy. It is not an effort to condemn a love or a sexuality that fails to become sublimated into philosophy. Rather, it is a claim in the opposite direction: he wants to declare a philosophy inadequate that has not taken its start from the deep recesses of our *erōs,* our desire, and our memory. In particular, as the counterfigure of Lysias and the other sophists and orators will remind us, Plato denounces a philosophy that takes its start from the self-assertive combats of the intellectual class. It is the same for philosophy as for poetry (*Phaedrus* 245a): if it is an exercise of mere intellect and contrivance, not touched by the divine madness, it will be of no use. Philosophy without *erōs* cannot disclose true being.

A number of further points are connected to the high stature that *erōs* has in Plato's thought. There is the fact that Plato accords a higher value to homosexual attachments than to heterosexual ones. And yet— if this second point does not cancel out the first—he also praises a life of celibacy over one of sexual self-expression. The bond that ties wisdom to *erōs* is grounded through the preexistence of the soul in advance of our birth in this life, a matter we shall examine in chapters 6–8. This dialogue is strikingly committed to the soul's capacity to live independently of the body, but it is the prenatal existence of the soul that is Plato's focus here, a matter that entirely overshadows the doctrine, also presented here to be sure, of the soul's survival of bodily death. All these points, so important to Plato, and seemingly so much at odds with today's mainstream opinions, must be submitted to the closest interrogation in our commentary. These points all circulate in orbit around the doctrine that has always been seen to constitute the heart of Plato's philosophy—the doctrine that there are absolute norms, absolute ideas or forms, that constitute true reality, by comparison to which the empirical world is a secondary, imitative, dependent thing. In the chapters of part 3, I shall outline this doctrine, not concealing my conviction that it is substantially true.

There used to be a debate over whether the "true theme" of the *Phaedrus* is rhetoric or love, but many scholars today are impatient with that question (though not all: the debate continues—see the introduction to part 3). By the division of the present study, we shall be able to deal with rhetoric and other questions about discourse in part 1, and then turn to the more substantive theme of love in part 3, with part 2 connecting them: Socrates' discourse on love.

Like other English-speaking students of my generation, I am greatly indebted to Reginald Hackforth, whose translation of the *Phaedrus,* with commentary, first introduced me to the dialogue and has been my companion through the decades.[13] C. J. Rowe's translation has set a high standard of accuracy,[14] and A. Nehamas and P. Woodruff's translation has added further luster to their reputation for beauty in Platonic translation.[15] I am particularly indebted to three modern books on the *Phaedrus:* the commentary by de Vries,[16] especially rich in linguistic and philological insights; the study by Griswold,[17] outstanding for its philosophical exploration of the *Phaedrus;* and the book by Ferrari,[18] which captures so well the literary spirit of the dialogue—what I call later the spirit of holidays.

The study of Plato in the twentieth century has been a story of interaction between those who work as classical scholars and those who work primarily as philosophers. In my own case, I must acknowledge that I am only a "consumer" of the work of classical scholarship, never a contributor to textual criticism, lexicography, Platonic biography, or

---

13. *Plato's Phaedrus,* trans. R. Hackforth (Cambridge: Cambridge University Press, 1952).

14. *Plato: Phaedrus,* ed. and trans. C. J. Rowe (Warminster, Wiltshire: Aris and Phillips, 1986).

15. Plato, *Phaedrus,* trans., with introduction and commentary, A. Nehamas and P. Woodruff (Indianapolis: Hackett, 1995). The notes to their translation are also useful; as for their introduction, I shall have some comments on it in the body of this study.

16. G. J. de Vries, *A Commentary on the Phaedrus of Plato* (Amsterdam: Hackert, 1969).

17. Charles Griswold, Jr., *Self-Knowledge in Plato's Phaedrus* (New Haven, Conn.: Yale University Press, 1986).

18. G. R. F. Ferrari, *Listening to the Cicadas* (Cambridge: Cambridge University Press, 1987).

the impact of Plato in late antiquity and beyond. It was my studies in metaphysics that always continued to restore my interest in Plato, and my hope is that this book may contribute to the philosophical interpretation of Plato. It is a remarkable fact, however, that modern studies of Plato *written in English* have been very powerfully influenced by the modern philosophy that has been *written in English*. Classical scholars who work in English are usually well aware of the classical scholarship of France, Germany, Italy, Greece, and other countries and other languages, but in the world of philosophy there remains an extraordinary alienation among "national" or "linguistic" traditions, with the result that the philosophy on which English-language Platonic scholarship has drawn was almost entirely English-language philosophy. I have found that German-language Plato scholarship, nourished by over two centuries of German philosophy, has often opened doors of insight and interpretation of great value in the study of Plato. One of my goals in this book is to make some mention of the fruits of this scholarship and this philosophy, with the hope of facilitating an interaction between classical studies and philosophy that does not confine itself to philosophy written in English. Here and there, I shall be quoting from G. W. F. Hegel and Friedrich Schelling, Ulrich von Wilamowitz-Moellendorff and Julius Stenzel, Hans-Georg Gadamer and Thomas Szlezak, scholars who think philosophically in the German tradition. It is our good fortune that Paul Friedlaender's work, an integral part of that tradition, has been available in English now for several decades. At certain points where the context calls for a sharp and decisive comment, I have included some extracts from the biography of Plato by Wilamowitz,[19] an older book, as much admired outside Germany as inside it, which, despite that, has never been translated into English.

---

19. Ulrich von Wilamowitz-Moellendorff, *Platon*, 2 vols. (Berlin: Weidmann, 1917).

The Voices
of Philosophy

Socrates and Plato have left many marks upon our culture, and the strongest one perhaps is the stature they gave to philosophy by contrasting it with other forms of thought and speech. Plato's portraits of Socrates in dialogue with different characters, especially in the early works, give profile to philosophy by differentiating it from poetry, for instance, and from rhetoric and from religion. As for poetry, we see that Socrates in the *Apology* 22b–c acknowledges the impact poets have had on people, yet he says that when he wants to ask them what their poems mean, they usually cannot answer him, not in the way he wants. Something like that is enacted for us in the *Ion,* where Ion, a rhapsode, someone who would put on performances of Homeric poems, cannot explain himself or his art, or the poems themselves, to Socrates. The *Republic,* II and III, goes on to codify a sharp opposition between philosophy and poetry.

In the same books of the *Republic,* we find a division between philosophy and religion. And the earlier work *Euthyphro* has already enacted a clash between Socrates and a traditional religionist, Euthyphro, who is made in that dialogue to look morally obtuse and to be a poor reasoner to boot. Other dialogues of the early period draw a line of demarcation between Socrates and the partisans of popular political rhetoric, especially the *Gorgias,* and another line separating Socrates from the rival company of intellectuals, the sophists, the *Hippias Minor,* for one. To a considerable degree, the demarcations made in Plato's early works have lasted right down to our own day.

Yet the *Phaedrus,* probably belonging to Plato's middle or late period, is no longer engaged in drawing lines of demarcation. Socrates is still very much the philosopher here, and he continues to practice his accustomed art of questioning, the art of dialectic, but he is able to speak in other tones and accents as well, able to mix the voice of myth and the voice of rhetoric with the voice of dialectic. Plato has taken him out of his accustomed urban milieu and put him into a scene of great natural beauty along the river Ilissos, where a multitude of statues stand in honor of different gods and where demigods and river nymphs are said to sport. Inspired by the beauty and the divinity of this scene, Socrates is led into discussions about mythology, and in his own great speech he launches into a vast mythological discourse about the soul. He is bringing his dialectic into the closest connection with myths.

The dialogue also shows Socrates ready to enter into a rhetorical competition with a famous orator, Lysias, and the subsequent discussion shows a Socrates who is not nearly as hostile to rhetoric as he had been in earlier works such as the *Gorgias*. Indeed his own speech is a highly polished work of rhetoric and is so described and so praised in later pages of this dialogue. The *Phaedrus* is a dialogue in which Plato, confident of the integrity of philosophy, confident of the strength of his dialectic, does not need to resist other forms of culture, but is ready to assimilate them. A philosophy that turned its back on poetry, myth, rhetoric, and religion would never come fully into its own, for the highest topics are not open to treatment by a merely analytical philosophy or a merely dialectical one. In the *Phaedrus*, it is the polyphony of myth, rhetoric, and dialectic that is able to reveal the true nature of love. Part 1 of our study will treat each of these three voices, trying, as we proceed, to show how their polyphony gives expression to the idea of philosophy that guided Plato at that time. We shall also treat the relationship of writing to living speech and see what reasons Plato found to justify the practice of writing.

CHAPTER ONE | Myth

We treat myth first of all, a form of thinking and communicating that was far older than Plato and his philosophical text, but which he has woven into it. Myth is perhaps the most archaic sort of thinking, and philosophy, like rhetoric and history, rose up in opposition to myth in the fifth century. Yet myths are in the foreground of the *Phaedrus,* right at the beginning and throughout the whole. Why does the *Phaedrus* have so many myths, and why does it talk so much about them?

Let us look at the first myth that appears in the text. It is a beautiful scene that Plato has set in the opening pages,[1] and this is due in part to the storied past of the river Ilissos. The different altars and statues that adorn its banks are a sign that the river has been alive with nymphs and demigods since time immemorial. As they proceed upstream, 229b, Phaedrus mentions the god of the North Wind, Boreas, recalling a fragment of the old story, in which Boreas had come to carry off the maiden Oreithuia. He asks whether it was right on this very spot that it happened. This was a story of great significance for the Athenians in particular, for this girl was an Athenian princess, the daughter of the legendary Erechtheus, Athens's first king in remotest times. Boreas had come to carry her off to his home in the north country, and because of Oreithuia, he retained an affection for the Athenians. Later in

---

1. Ferrari, *Listening to the Cicadas,* has an excellent discussion of Plato's scene setting, particularly in its opening chapter, but recurring throughout the book. Charles Griswold, *Self-Knowledge in Plato's Phaedrus,* pp. 33–36, also has excellent commentary, particularly on the symbolism of the scene.

historic times, when the Persians invaded Hellas under King Xerxes and were approaching Athens, Boreas proved his loyalty by blowing on the Persian ships and wrecking them on the rocks—so the story is told by Herodotus in his *Histories,* VII, 189. In gratitude for the rescue, the Athenians built for Boreas a sanctuary on the banks of the Ilissos, on the very spot where, it is said, he had carried off Oreithuia, and they instituted an annual festival to honor him: the Boreasmi. As he and Socrates walk through a particularly lovely part of the river, Phaedrus asks if this is the exact spot. Perhaps we can imagine a counterpart to the mythical scene in Sandro Botticelli's painting *La Primavera,* for at the center of it there are Eros and Aphrodite (i.e., Cupid and Venus), and out of the trees on the right-hand side there looms the pale blue wind-spirit, Zephyr, reaching out to capture the nymph Chloris, just like what happened to Plato's Oreithuia. It is true, as Ferrari has shown, that Plato recurs to his "background," his scene setting, repeatedly throughout the course of the dialogue—far more so than in any other work—and we can surmise that this natural beauty and its mythic elaboration are germane to the philosophy of the *Phaedrus.*[2]

At the moment it is the question posed by Phaedrus, 229b, that concerns us: Is this the exact spot where Boreas captured Oreithuia? The water is certainly beautiful here, just right for maidens to be playing in. But Socrates says no. It all took place two or three stadia (about one-fourth of a mile) downstream from here. Socrates knows this because that is where the Boreas altar is, but Phaedrus had never noticed the altar. Socrates' confident answer to his question, however, leads Phaedrus to ask a second question: "do you really think that this bit of mythology [this *mythologēma*] is true?" (229c). Now he is not asking where the capture took place, but whether it took place at all, and Phaedrus's question has a scope more general than the details about Boreas. By calling the story here a *mythologēma,* he is typing it as one species of things said and things heard, and if this myth should not be true, it is not because of details peculiar to it, but rather because of something about the whole class of myths. By generalizing in this way, Phaedrus's second question has inaugurated a philosophical discussion. And he is speaking for his generation. Socrates' reply makes it clear enough that

---

2. Ibid., pp. 1–4, 21–34. Besides the crucial invocation of the cicadas at 258e–259d, I see references to the physical setting at *Phaedrus* 236e, 238d, 241e–242c, 263d–e, 278b, and 279b–c.

Phaedrus's question was a commonplace of the intellectual life of the time. A whole *kind* of speech, it seemed, might not be true.

Phaedrus and Socrates on Myths

First, let us try to express the general concept of myth that Socrates and Phaedrus are working with. It is something said (*legetai,* 229b), narrating an occurrence in the remote past (Oreithuia), which may be highly specific as to locale (229c), on which however there may be varying traditions (229d), usually involving the interaction of divine and human characters, and often fantastic creatures (229d), extended into a vast encyclopedia of memory (229d), and recognized by altars, statues, and other memorials (230b). It is a tradition passed on first to children (see *Republic* 377b); fashioned into epics and other poems; related by priests, parents, and teachers (*Republic* 364b–e); yet nowadays often scoffed at by youth (*Republic* 367b–e) and the sophisticated, the *sophoi,* as in the present passage (229b–230b) of the *Phaedrus.*

We today often learn some of the Greek myths by a conscious effort as part of our higher education, perhaps with sections and divisions (theogonies, legends of heroes returning from Troy, etc.), with the result that they all add up to a pretty thick book.[3] I do not know if anybody today could keep all this undulating, shifting mass straight in his or her memory, but in any case, it was not in the form of such compilations that the generations of Socrates and Plato learned the myths. The myths were incorporated in epic poems and in other poems and dramas, they were expressed in rituals and conversations that reinforced them every day, and they were invoked in laws and speeches and incarnated in buildings and statues. We today can approximate their experience when we sense the operation of one of the myths in a finished work of art, a Sophocles play, or a marble sculpture. It is not the whole body of mythology that is before our minds there but just one fragment of one cycle of myth. It was only one such fragment that Socrates or Plato would have had before his mind, in any particular case; the rest of the body of mythology was lodged in the unconscious memory. Claude Lévi-Strauss has shown that myths inhabit the unconscious

---

3. Robert Graves, *The Greek Myths,* 2 vols. (Harmondsworth, England: Penguin Books, 1955). A compilation from late antiquity, the Apollodorus library, is offered in Michael Simpson, *Gods and Heroes of the Greeks* (Amherst: University of Massachusetts Press, 1976).

mind in the same way that language does.[4] Where a given utterance brings words and syntax together in a single combination, the whole of the language remains unconscious in our minds. So it is when we recount the story, say, of Boreas. Certain figures and relationships are before the conscious mind, but the totality that we can call the mythology itself is present only unconsciously. And the dialogues of Plato bear this out. Socrates, for instance, in addressing an individual or a group, may invoke some fragment of myth in a setting where it is an appropriate archetype for what he is saying. Other occasions will require other fragments. In the same way he may cite a line of Homeric poetry, with the whole body of poetry lodged in his unconscious memory. Virtually all the dialogues show Socrates invoking figures from the myths in his argument and also making literal quotations of poetry. There are scores of cases, for example, *Phaedrus* 243a or *Apology* 28b–d.

If we step back to take historical perspective, we can see that the fifth- and fourth-century Enlightenment, with its critique of myths, was connected to the advance of literate culture and the decline of orality, and hence connected as well to the loss of authority of poetry—epic, lyric, and dramatic—and the advance of other modes: history, rhetoric, and philosophy. Socrates and Plato were not making a sociological study of the historical transition that they were living through, of course, but Plato's texts express an awareness of these changes with a clarity and depth that are quite unique. Thus, we find, at the very end of the *Phaedrus,* Socrates' reflections on writing and oral speech that correspond to the interest in myths that he expresses at the beginning of the *Phaedrus.*

The Greek word *mythos* and its related verbs signified in Homer a word or a speech, particularly one given in public or to a group. It could mean not only something said but something thought. But by the fifth century, it meant more often a fictional narration as opposed to a truthful one, and from this period onward the note of opposition begins to predominate: that is, whenever *mythos* is mentioned, there is usually a contrast, explicit or implicit, with something else—*logos* or *historia*

---

4. His early paper in defense of the linguistic hypothesis was "The Structural Study of Myth," in *Structural Anthropology,* vol. 1, trans. C. Jacobson and P. G. Schoepf (Garden City, N.Y.: Anchor Books, 1963). His hypothesis was applied in the multivolume work *Mythologiques,* which began to appear in France in 1964, beginning with *The Raw and the Cooked,* trans. J. and D. Weightman (New York: Harper Torchbooks, 1969).

or truth. It no longer means speech or discourse, but a specific kind of speech and discourse, contrasted with another kind. *Mythos* usually counts for less than the other kinds. *Mythoi*—stories, fables—are already false just by being *mythoi,* or fictional, as Socrates says, for instance, in the *Republic* 377a. Yet the present dialogue undertakes to investigate the meaning and value of myth.

In Plato's text, myths are a prolongation into the current time, that is, the time in which the dialogues were set, of a discourse stemming from an earlier time. By *discourse* I mean not only a particular kind of speaking, but also a particular kind of hearing and thinking. All of these forms are tied up with one kind of *life* and constitute a total form of society, oral culture or traditional society, it can be called, that was undergoing a profound transition. Some things that would fit into this discourse—gorgons and centaurs—could find no place in the emerging discourse. A mode of discourse is also a way of living, since our life and our being are suffused with our understanding.[5] Whereas Socrates in the *Euthyphro* and the *Republic* is pictured as being fully on the side of the contemporary Enlightenment, in its suppression of myth, the *Phaedrus* depicts him instead as no longer willing to follow the *sophoi* in that direction. He is happy to preserve mythic discourse.

At 229c6, Socrates' reply to Phaedrus's question regarding Boreas is so deeply wrapped in irony that it requires the closest scrutiny. In the first place, he lends no support to what Phaedrus has just suggested: that stories like this are not true. Rather, he says with some scorn, disbelieving the story is exactly what smart people, cultivated people, the *sophoi,* tend to do these days. His irony deepens as he describes the dazzling feats of scientific explanation that these *sophoi* could now produce. He proposes that they would say that what has been called Boreas was obviously just a gust of wind. There was some sort of accident with some young girls—here or perhaps on the Areogapus; apparently one of them was blown off on to a pile of rocks and killed. Stories and myths, obviously, began to circulate (you know how the popular mind works).

Who are the *sophoi* that Socrates and Plato have in mind here? On this, modern scholars are divided. Hackforth identifies them as a

---

5. See Ernst Cassirer, *Philosophy of Symbolic Forms,* vol. 2, *Mythical Thought,* trans. R. Manheim (New Haven, Conn.: Yale University Press, 1955; first published 1925). His treatment of "Myth as a Form of Thought" in part 1 is followed by "Myth as a Form of Intuition" in part 2 and "Myth as a Life-Form" in part 3.

"school of allegorical interpretation,"[6] but, as Ferrari points out,[7] what Socrates is objecting to is not allegory but a naturalistic mode of historical explanation, of the sort found at times in Herodotus. De Vries has nominated a "demythologizer,"[8] Metrodorus of Lampsacus, as the possible target here; Ferrari, in reply,[9] argues that the broad sweep of Socrates' (or Plato's) critique is obscured if we narrow in on just one target and that Plato deliberately left the reference to *sophoi* vague. Ferrari is right that this form of naturalistic explanation had become so influential among the intellectuals (Ferrari's translation of *sophoi*) that we are diminishing Plato's intent if we narrow the critique in on only one or two figures. I shall make an equivalent point in the next chapter regarding the *Phaedrus's* critique of rhetoric—it touches an entire movement, not just one or two of the figures. Yet still we can define the specific practice that Socrates is discussing here: substituting for the divine or the miraculous narrative of myth a normal and natural occurrence supposedly located in historical time. Such an approach was prompted by the sophistical and philosophical tradition for over a century. Anaxagoras had demythologized the sun and other heavenly bodies, declaring them to be just molten rock. We have no reason to think that he had investigated the body of mythology in the same spirit, but it seems that there were others who did, Prodicus and Diagoras for instance.[10] A universal system of these explanations was in fact published some decades after Plato's death by Euhemerus of Messene under the title *Sacred History* (now lost). All the gods and their deeds, according to Euhemerus, were just idealizations of historical human beings and their deeds. Generations of "intellectuals" had been at work paving the way for Euhemerus, those mentioned by Guthrie, for instance, and their approach was certainly known to Plato.

What, exactly, is Socrates' objection to such interpretation?

He observes that such *mythologēmata* constitute a system. You could not just analyze and explain away a single story like that of

---

6. *Plato's Phaedrus*, p. 26. Hackforth refers here to previous studies by J. Tate.

7. *Listening to the Cicadas;* see especially p. 235 n. 14.

8. *Commentay on the Phaedrus*, commentary on 229c6.

9. *Listening to the Cicadas*, p. 234 n. 12.

10. The evidence for these figures is scant, but Guthrie offers an integrated account of the "enlightened" approach to myth in his *A History of Greek Philosophy*, vol. 3, chap. 9, "Rationalist Theories of Religion: Agnosticism and Atheism."

Boreas and Oreithuia all by itself. As soon as you tried it, you would have to go on to the centaurs and Chimera, the gorgons and the Pegasuses, and provide an equally clever rationale for them all. You would have the enormous task of going through the tradition as a whole. The *mythologēmata,* we might say, add up to a system, and that is mythology itself.

Socrates simply has not got the time, or the heart, to take on this huge labor of reinterpretation. He has a completely different priority for his life, namely to follow the commandment of the inscription of Delphi: to "know thyself" (229e). Scientific interpretation of myth is an extraneous inquiry. But it is not as if these two kinds of inquiry—into the tradition, and into oneself—stood side by side as two equally valuable lines of inquiry. One cannot miss the condescension with which Socrates speaks of the earnest pedantry and pointless learning of the person who goes through the body of myths with a view to giving a scientific explanation of them. Instead of that, Socrates prefers to accept the myths in their standard form (230a). It is better, in other words, to think that Boreas captured Oreithuia over there by the Boreas altar than to explore the "clever" explanations for the legend.

The archaeology of these myths would have value for Socrates only if it contributed to his self-knowledge—otherwise it would be a waste of time. To judge by the words of this text, the same would hold for all studies: he is not going to inquire into anything that is at all alien or external to him (230a1).[11] In fact, this was the issue that originally diverted Socrates away from the study of natural science. We read in the *Phaedo* that he had become dissatisfied with the naturalists' causal explanations in the first place because of their inadequate explanations of his own perceptions and thoughts (*Phaedo* 96b) and his own actions and decisions (98c–99a). Self-knowledge was Socrates' all-absorbing task. And looking to the trial scene of the *Apology,* we see that this challenge, to know thyself, was precisely the demand Socrates had put to the Athenians in all its rigor and purity (*Apology* 28b–c, 36b–c), though to be sure the words of the Delphic inscription are not quoted literally in the *Apology.* And yet, even at his age and after so much inquiry and experience, he can still say in our present text that he has not achieved self-knowledge. The search for it leaves him time for little else.

---

11. Griswold, *Self-Knowledge in Plato's Phaedrus,* gives a convincing reading of the whole dialogue with reference to this text.

But what does Socrates want to know about himself? He says that he does not know whether, within his soul, he is a ferocious monster like the legendary titan Typhon, or a tamer and gentler kind of creature (230a). First of all, we must recognize that such a self-analysis on Socrates' part is a truly cognitive inquiry. It would misrepresent him to see the pursuit of self-knowledge *only* as the effort to acquire a moral virtue. It is true that in the dialogue *Charmides,* 164d, the speaker Critias makes a close link between the Delphic commandment and the specific virtue of temperance, but there that did not lead to any profound psychological investigations. Here, however, Socrates is thinking about the possibility that he might be, within his soul, so strange as to resemble a mythological monster, and the dialogue that develops will contain Plato's profoundest investigation of the soul. But second, and what is central for us, the Typhon reference shows Socrates making use of an item of mythology in his inner self-searching or self-scrutiny. This is a study that he has defined for himself, and thus he is making a free appropriation of the myth, converting it into an image or a metaphor, an intelligent and literary use of an item of myth. Socrates is free either to use a myth or not to use it, but if he does, it is with the thought that it can help him toward self-knowledge, opening up to view a stratum of his soul. Explaining the myth away is just boring.

We have not yet entirely caught the spirit of Socrates' reply to Phaedrus on the subject of Boreas and Oreithuia. It is a reply made in the holiday mood: lighthearted, free-spirited. The scholars want to probe and pry into Boreas. Soon, they will be led further on into the centaurs and the Chimera, the gorgons and the Pegasuses, and on and on in a scholarly industry that could be prolonged forever. That is not for Socrates! He will not identify with those scholars who study the centaur—he feels more at home identifying with the centaur. He wants to follow the Delphic oracle and look into himself to see if in his own soul he is really more like one of these monsters such as the Typhon. Or maybe after all his soul is really a very gentle animal. Socrates is speaking a holiday language here: myth. He does not "say good-bye to myths."[12] He will continue with the myths, "accepting them in the re-

---

12. So Ferrari puts it, *Listening to the Cicadas,* p. 11, though in the whole context of pp. 10–12 he certainly hits the right note. Robin translates 230a1–2 as "Aussi je laisse de cote ces fables" ["And I will leave these fables to one side"] but what Socrates is leaving to one side are not the stories but the learned explanations of them.

ceived version," (230a2) even though the inquiry into which he may insert them and in which he may quote them, the inquiry into himself, may never have been anticipated before. And now Socrates will proceed to express his delight in the character of this riverside spot: surely the temple to the river nymphs is most fitting here (230b). And the Great Speech, 244a through 257b, will begin by evoking the wisdom of ages past. Woven profoundly into the speech, as we shall be seeing in chapters 6, 7, and 8, are the prototypes of Stesichoros (243a–b) and the divinely inspired prophets, priests, and singers (244a–245a), and the myths that all of these invoked.

So the path on which Phaedrus and Socrates strike out at the start, pointing the reader too away from town and society, out into the fresh air where the stream flows under the shade of the tall tree, has invoked the spirit of holidays. And Wilamowitz, in his beautiful study of the *Phaedrus*,[13] invites us to think of Plato's writing the *Phaedrus* on holiday on a happy summer's day, away from his Academy, on his family's country estate. The *Republic* was a philosophy of the city, set in the nighttime in the port district of Piraeus, the climax of the great series of dramas, including *Gorgias, Protagoras,* and *Meno,* in which Socrates confronts the urban intelligentsia and the wealthy classes. There will be time enough to get Socrates back into the dust of the town and the heat of its struggles in the *Sophist* and the *Statesman.*

Socrates' acceptance of myths seems to be at odds with previous dialogues such as the *Euthyphro.* At *Euthyphro* 6b and 6c, Socrates states—twice!—to Euthyphro a skeptical-sounding question about the goings-on of the gods that is almost exactly the same as the question put to *him* here by Phaedrus at 229c. The *Republic* II discusses a great deal of the traditional mythology, and in his exchanges there with Adeimantus, beginning at 377e, Socrates has no hesitation in going through the traditional tales (*mythoi*), the epic poems, and the shorter fables recited to young children, showing that many of them are so offensive and so out of keeping with the divine nature that they could not possibly be true. These stories are pretty much the same ones that come up in the *Euthyphro.* Socrates applies a standard of purity and probability in the *Republic* that he casts off conspicuously in the *Phaedrus.* In a brief note, Hackforth suggests that this *Phaedrus* myth might be less

---

13. Wilamowitz-Moellendorff, *Platon,* vol. 1., chap. 13, "Ein gluecklicher Sommertag," p. 455.

offensive than those criticized in the *Republic*,[14] seeking in this way to make the earlier critique of myths consistent with the present text. Yet, really, the stern moralist of the *Republic* would hardly have sanctioned the present myth either![15] The fact is that Plato and Socrates have become more tolerant. This change affects not only the moral content of the stories, but their character as narrative as well. To "accept the stories in the received version" means that the accustomed diction and wording, *diēgēsis* and *lexis,* no longer need any philosophical reformation, whereas the *Republic* III seeks to eliminate much of the older *style* of storytelling as well as the content. So there was a form of expression or discourse of which the *Republic* was suspicious but which Socrates now accepts: mythology.

In the *Phaedrus,* Socrates points out that the *sophoi* wanted to reduce or translate each specific item of myth into a different discourse, history, since the latter supposedly has real truth in it. But now Socrates does not believe in that translation or reduction any more. He will take a myth as it is. And the dialogue as a whole is more saturated with myths than any other work of Plato's, not only in the conscious quotations but in the scene-setting, and especially in the great speech beginning at 244a that invokes immemorial figures and dreams and long-remembered scenes. Fully comparable in this way to the great works of Attic tragedy and architecture, it still succeeds precisely as philosophy, not driving the myths out but welcoming them under its roof. There is no doubt that philosophy, in Attica as in Ionia and Italy, was a post-mythical discourse just as its contemporaries, history and rhetoric, were. Yet Plato, among the philosophers, and the *Phaedrus* in particular among Plato's writings, sought to maintain the substance and form of the preceding mythic consciousness, integrating myth into the work.

The Platonic Myths

Up to this point we have been concerned with a small fragment of the *Phaedrus* and a small unit of myth. But in referring, now, to the great speech in the middle of the dialogue, we have entered into another as-

---

14. *Plato's Phaedrus,* p. 26. Hackforth also quotes a discussion between Thompson and Tate, the former claiming against the latter that the Boreas legend is a harmless one.

15. In chapter 6, we shall study this interchange in the *Republic* between Socrates and Adeimantus more closely.

pect of the question of myth, for Plato not only quotes bits and pieces of the inherited mythology to brighten his literary works. We see that there are passages of extended mythologizing in a number of his great works, not only the early use of myth, evident in the *Protagoras,* the *Lysis* and other early dialogues, but a sustained mythology created by himself in the *Meno,* the *Gorgias,* and the great works that followed, including the *Phaedrus.* Plato's earliest mythical passages are in the nature of a jeu, decorative additions to a conversation, a literary practice reflected by the Boreas myth of the *Phaedrus* and the witty conversation it leads to. But Plato discovered a possibility in mythical discourse for communicating a depth of thought that no other form would permit. When we find the great mythical passages concluding the *Phaedo* and *Republic,* we can no longer regard them as decorative fancies, but rather as his most sober and considered way of treating things that did not allow of dialectical treatment.

One of the contributions of Paul Friedlaender is to call attention to the thematic unity of the myths that occur in five of the dialogues: *Meno, Gorgias, Phaedo, Republic,* and *Phaedrus* (not to deny that fragments found in other dialogues, too, can be integrated into this cycle).[16] These are myths that bear upon the remotest origins of the human soul and its eventual destiny, myths that, though put in the mouth of Socrates, are attributed to "priests and priestesses" or "the wise" and so are represented as having a different source from the usual Socratic interrogations. We shall be treating them at greater length in part 3, and on that occasion we shall be able to see that the *Phaedrus* myth, in the Great Speech of Socrates, offers the most complete and mature version of Platonic mythology, knitting all the previous versions into one. Here we may quote some of the version that is very likely the earliest of them all, *Meno* 81b–d.

Socrates is replying to a question posed to him by Meno in the course of a discussion concerning virtue, and we are alerted immediately (81a) that what Socrates is about to tell him is not the product of his own reasoning but heard from others who are not named but identified as "men and women wise in divine things." They are

> priests and priestesses whose care it is to be able to give an account of their practices. Pindar too says it, and many others of the

---

16. Paul Friedlaender, *Plato: An Introduction,* trans. Hans Meyerhoff (New York: Harper and Row, 1958; trans. from the 1954 German 2nd ed.), chap. 9.

divine among our poets. What they say in this; see whether you think they speak the truth: They say that the human soul is immortal; at times it comes to an end, which they call dying, at times it is reborn, but it is never destroyed, and one must therefore live one's life as piously as possible:

> Persephone will return to the sun above in the ninth year the souls of those from whom she will exact punishment for old miseries, and from these come noble kings, mighty in strength and greatest in wisdom, and for the rest of time men will call them sacred heroes.

As the soul is immortal, has been born often and has seen all things here and in the underworld, there is nothing which it has not learned; so it is in no way surprising that it can recollect the things it knew before, both about virtue and other things. As the whole of nature is akin, and the soul has learned everything, nothing prevents a man, after recalling one thing only—a process men call learning—discovering everything else for himself, if he is brave and does not tire of the search, for searching and learning are, as a whole, recollection.[17]

Chapters 6 and 7, which deal with the soul and the gods, will have much more to say about the content of this *Meno* passage, but here we may make one or two points about its style or form. The lyric poem that Socrates quotes has a fixed text and a definite author, Pindar, but Socrates is aware that the poet is relying on sayings that have been handed down from ancient times, sayings that circulated in the form of narratives that do not have a fixed text—only the outline is preserved from one telling to another—or a definite author, for the narrative is told by wise men and women, priests and priestesses, who remain anonymous. The myth and the poem inhabit Plato's text side by side—the poem is quoted in the middle of the mythic narration, the one reinforcing the other—and together they introduce into the dialogue an atmosphere of mystery in the persons they invoke and the horizon of time they assume. In ages immemorial a sin was committed and a penalty paid; mighty kings came forth; and Persephone, Hades' Queen, took them up to the region of the sun. Most mysterious is the form of immortality. The soul, says Socrates, is immortal, but in the myth the soul does come to an end; yet it is also reborn, in a sort of punctuated immortality, interrupted by a death and then a new beginning. This is a

---

17. *Meno* 81 a–d, in Plato, *Complete Works,* trans. G. M. A. Grube (Indianapolis: Hackett, 1997).

form of time in which, according to the myth, the soul lives again and again, hard to clarify by the standards of reason—impossible, surely—and yet the argument of the *Meno* has led to it and the myth will be employed in the argument when Socrates and Meno return to the question that generated the mythical interlude: "How can you search for virtue if you do not already know what it is?" The story of preexistence and recollection lays the basis for Socrates' answer. What is the role, exactly, of this myth in this argument?—a topic that part 3 will cover.

One cannot deny the mythic character of much of Plato, but the question that presses upon us is the way in which myth is integrated into philosophy and in particular whether there are passages in which myth intrudes where we would want a purer philosophical discourse, whether a myth is sometimes made to bear the weight that should have been borne by argument alone. Opinion among modern scholars, and especially modern philosophers, is extremely divided on this point. There is one school of thought that we might trace back to Paul Natorp[18] which finds the myths an embarrassment, an evasion on Plato's part of the philosopher's obligation to be logical. Another view, more common recently, is to grant that Plato's mythical discourse has a literary justification but that he is not completely committed to the things he says mythically—the reader should allow for myths by according what they say a lower degree of credence than claims made dialectically. Thus, C. J. Rowe comments on *Phaedrus* 265b–c, in which Socrates looks back on his earlier speech (244a–257b) as a "mythical (*mythikon*) hymn of praise to love," by taking Socrates to mean that "this second speech is not, after all, to be taken seriously, except insofar as (in conjunction with the first) it illustrates a particular kind of philosophical method."[19] Rowe also notices that Socrates says the speech was made

---

18. See introduction, note 3, in this book.

19. *Plato: Phaedrus,* with ed. and trans. by C. J. Rowe (Warminster: Aris and Phillips, 1986), p. 8. In their introduction to *Phaedrus,* pp. xxix–xxxii, the translators Nehamas and Woodruff apply a similar construction to 265b–c. They add (with no justification that I can see) that earlier lines at 262a–c have a "dismissive tone" regarding the speech; perhaps they are referring to 262d, but it is to me apparent that when, at 262d, Socrates is implying that he spoke playfully under the influence of local divinities, that is a reference back to 241d–e, where he jests that his *first* speech, *not* his second, has been prompted by the nymphs. As their introduction proceeds, the translators seek further ways to diminish the Great Speech; we shall examine these references in our chapters on dialectic and truth.

in play. But neither the word *mythikon* nor the word for playful, *paidia,* should be pressed to Rowe's conclusion. Socrates does not use the word *mythikon* to mean that it would have been better to apply some other philosophical approach. It is true enough that here (265b7–8) Socrates allows that some parts of his speech might not be true (and that statement is often made where the discourse is mythical, most famously at *Timaeus* 29b–d), but Plato has in mind precisely the details of the myth's elaboration. He does not use this word to take away the speech's claim of truth, but only to prevent a ludicrously literal reading. The term *paidia* should be understood here in the sense of "festive, enjoyable, unlaborious," that is, it is a holiday speech. The highest things are the things of the holidays. Gundert has made a study of *paidia* in Plato, calling attention to its many meanings and applications, and its very dignity as a mode of thinking and speaking. He has shown that "the more [Socrates] is dealing with philosophically-minded people, the more he is inclined to describe their dialogue as play."[20] The discussions characterized as play are the *most* philosophical. Gundert cites *Phaedrus* 262d and 278b, as well as the present text, 265b–c, and also *Republic* 536c. De Vries, referring in part to Gundert, also calls attention to the import of play in Plato's whole way of thought,[21] and he is supported in this by Guthrie.[22]

A more adequate view of the Platonic myth passages has been developed by Friedlaender in his chapter "Myth." What he starts from is the question of *why* Plato wrote the mythical passages, and he notes, "When Socrates employs a myth in the later dialogues, that means that he cannot express himself in any other form."[23] Thus, in these passages Plato wanted to say something that could not have been said better in another mode of discourse such as dialectic. Far from allowing us to diminish the mythical discourse and its truth value, this fact augments the discourse, showing that philosophy has subjects to disclose for which it must implement more modes of speech than dialectic alone.

> The great myths of the soul, at the conclusion of a work, evoke
> the unknowable beyond, after the theoretical and practical order
> has first been established with a view toward eternal being. They

---

20. Hermann Gundert, "Zum Spiel bei Platon," in *Platonstudien,* ed. K. Doering and F. Preisshofen (Amsterdam: Gruener, 1977), pp. 65–98, quote p. 96.
21. De Vries, *Commentary on the Phaedrus,* pp. 18–22.
22. *A History of Greek Philosophy,* vol. 4, pp. 59–65.
23. Friedlaender, *Plato: An Introduction,* p. 176.

are variations on the same theme, each variation fitting into the particular dialogue where it occurs. For these genuinely Socratic-Platonic myths are quite different from those characteristic of the first phase in Plato's mythology in that they are not irresponsible, jestful play now and then accidentally revealing an essential point. They presuppose conceptual analysis and carry it beyond the limits set for human existence and human knowledge.... And mythology makes sense only if it can be shown that the myth carries forward the lines of argument set by the *Logos.*[24]

The mythical discourse opens a certain avenue to philosophy, playing a role for which nothing else can exactly substitute. And there are laws of composition that Plato is following as he interweaves the mythical passages into his work, assigning them one place rather than another. "As long as Plato concluded his dialogues on an aporetic note, he could not—as he did subsequently, beginning with the *Gorgias*—conclude them with a Socratic myth."[25] We must therefore reflect, not only on Plato's literary practice, but more broadly on the character of mythology as a whole before we take our leave of this topic.

Philosophy of Mythology

We shall have occasion to treat the argument offered in the *Meno,* and the role played in it by myth in chapters 6 and 7. Now our questions are more general: what a myth is, what it does, what kind of discourse it is, how it can be connected to other kinds of discourse such as rhetoric or dialectic, and how an author like Plato can both exploit old myths and compose new ones of his own—a philosophical question that must draw upon the philosophy of language and the philosophy of mind. In the *Phaedrus,* Plato has been showing us a Socrates who no longer participates in the "enlightened" flight from myth, but rather seeks to make it useful for self-knowledge and philosophy generally. In this way, Plato can be a guide to us in the twentieth century too, for, although we have inherited an "enlightenment" of our own, and lived through a vast cultural flight from myth toward reason and science, we are no longer able to participate in that flight in a straightforward way. Our times require us, not to overcome myth, but to understand it, what it is and what it does. The twentieth century has brought forth a number of outstand-

---

24. Ibid., p. 189.
25. Ibid., p. 178.

ing theoretical works devoted to those questions—I have already mentioned the structuralist theory of Lévi-Strauss, and the work of Ernst Cassirer, whose 1925 volume *Mythical Thought* shows the unity of this form of thought with a form of life, and the nature of the transition to other forms of life.[26] Such is the vast cross-cultural scope of these theories, however, that they do not highlight much of the specific, detailed place of myth within the philosophy of Plato.

The nineteenth-century philosophers explored mythology in a way that entered deeply into the Greek myths in particular, the place they assume in Plato's work, and the problem of his own mythical compositions. Hegel for one developed a philosophy of mind, or spirit, that gave a specific place to myth and religion, over against understanding and reason. Under the influence of the classical scholar F. Creuzer,[27] he attempts, in his *Philosophy of Religion*,[28] to interpret ancient Greek religion largely through the records of the Greeks' mythology. It is a program of interpretation that focuses especially on the war of the gods against the Titans, and the attributes of the particular gods—Zeus, for instance, who embodies the attributes of law, order, and rule and expresses their dignity. Hegel's program is grounded in his own philosophy of spirit. What the spirit or mind first grasps by way of pictures and mythical stories—that is, *Vorstellungen* (representations) such as Zeus—is the very truth about the spirit itself and its world, but it is not expressed in the final and adequate *form* that this truth requires.[29] This last step is to be accomplished by concepts that rational thinking formulates, especially philosophical thinking, with its understanding, for instance, of the divine character of justice. The content of a myth is *elevated* when it is reexpressed in a concept. Hegel's method may not be traditional allegorizing, such as the Alexandrian school of antiquity

---

26. *Mythisches Denken*, vol. 2 of the three-volume study of consciousness as a whole, *Philosophy of Symbolic Forms*. Vol. 1 is *Language* and vol. 3 is *Phenomenology of Knowledge*.

27. F. Creuzer, *Symbolik und Mythologie der alten Voelker, besonders der Griechen* (Leipzig: Heyer and Leske, 1819–23).

28. G. W. F. Hegel, *Lectures on the Philosophy of Religion. One-Volume Edition. The Lectures of 1827*, ed. P. C. Hodgson (Berkeley and Los Angeles: University of California Press, 1988).

29. Ibid., pp. 144–51. Griswold comes very close to Hegelianism in his discussion of myth in *Self-Knowledge in Plato's Phaedrus*, pp. 140–47, although in the following pages he moves away from it.

and the Neoplatonists practiced, but it is akin to it in its philosophical intellectualism.

Hegel's rival, F. W. J. Schelling, went a very different route. He not only examined mythology very closely, more so than any philosopher before Cassirer—he also kept his focus primarily on the Greek myths. He was an excellent scholar of Plato and the author of dialogues in the Platonic manner. In his later years, Schelling delivered several courses of lectures, compiled into the *Philosophy of Mythology.*[30] He refused to regard myths as fictions or inventions. He asserted that they are not produced by any consciousness, either individual or collective, and that they should not be treated as *Vorstellungen;* even less are they available for translation or transposition into some other discourse, supposedly superior, such as a philosophy that operates with concepts and ideas. The central thrust of Schelling's argument against rationalizing interpretations is that mythical discourse originates in a preconscious and nonrational "potency" of the soul.[31] Although scientific and philosophical discourse spring from the same soul, they express another and different "potency" of it.

And everyone's soul has these same "potencies," and therefore everyone has the capacity to respond to the myths just as the ancients did. Thus, for Schelling, philosophy and science do not appropriate the myth, but stand beside it. The myth is in this way parallel to the work of art. Schelling argues at the end of his 1800 *System of Transcendental Idealism* that there is more in a work of art than is placed there by the conscious intention of the artist; the work is only in part a product of consciousness, and, where there is genius, an unconscious "poetry" has been at work. This "potency" operates in advance of consciousness and its controls, and the work of art, like the myth, is created through the cooperation of the conscious and the preconscious potencies. In the *Philosophy of Mythology,* he writes, "The might or power that lays hold of human consciousness . . . is not accidental, nor does it express anyone's will. . . . What is deepest in the origins of humanity is the ten-

---

30. See his *Philosophie der Mythologie,* 2 vols., in *Saemmtliche Werke,* vol. 11 (1856) and vol. 12 (1857) (Augsburg: Cotta; reprint, Darmstadt: Wissenschaftliche Buchgesellschaft, 1966). I am indebted in this exposition to the excellent study by Edward A. Beach, *The Potencies of God(s): Schelling's Philosophy of Mythology* (Albany: SUNY Press, 1994).
31. See Schelling, *Philosophie der Mythologie,* vol. 2 (12), 6th lecture, pp. 108–31. See also Beach, *The Potencies of God(s),* pp. 184–85.

dency to posit a god, . . . and this takes place without our consent. . . .
The consciousness of this arises only at the end of the process."[32]
Schelling's doctrine of the interaction of the conscious and unconscious
potencies is linked to his philosophy of nature, too, for the nature that
lives within us is just this unconscious drive that enters into the artwork
and myth along with our conscious designs. His doctrine accords with
many phenomena of mythology, in that it does not promote hasty interpretations and translations. It lets the myths be; the notion of a separate potency in the soul for myth recognizes that there really was a
need for mythical expression as such. Schelling's view is particularly appropriate for grasping the place of myth in Plato's philosophical texts.
Plato found that a myth could be the best way of saying something that
he wished to say. So the question arises: Should we, can we, interpret the
myth?

One valuable point we may take from Schelling is the observation
that we today can read the myths and hear them and enjoy them just
as they stand. We too tell stories today, and it is surely true that we possess the capacity to respond to the Greek stories as well as to modern
ones, without a great heap of collateral information and theory. If our
soul is nourished through exposure to Plato's thought, one of the ways
it is nourished is through having our imagination enriched through
the stories he tells. A myth is like a jewel gleaming in its setting, and,
in the *Phaedrus,* this is abundantly true of the mythical narration of
the Great Speech. The myth that accompanies a passage of dialectic
addresses us in a different way, or rather it addresses some other part
of ourselves, adding to the instruction of dialectic the delight of narrative, and the narrative is itself instructive in a different way from the
dialectic.

Schelling and Friedlaender agree on the point that Plato would
undertake a mythical narration precisely where other discursive modes
could not soar so high. If, at some points, Plato's mythical narration
outstrips reason and dialectic, on what grounds would we suppose ourselves able to substitute a rational thought for it, to translate it or reduce it? This would be a presumption parallel to that which Socrates
criticized among the *sophoi.*

And yet, to give Hegel and the rationalists their due, it is apparent

---

32. Schelling, *Philosophie der Mythologie,* vol. 2 (12), pp. 125–26. See
also Beach, *The Potencies of God(s),* pp. 184–85.

that Plato did not want what we would call a merely "aesthetic" reading, enjoyment of what is merely fabulous and gorgeous. The myths have a meaning. Is there an appropriate route of access to the meaning?

We *never* find a myth pure and simple in any text of Plato, but always *joined* to a passage of nonmythical reasoning, whether dialectical or rhetorical. A number of key words, especially *soul* and *god,* move easily among these kinds of discourse. The fact that the myths are already set within a dialectical framework has two distinct effects. First of all, their having such a setting works to inhibit readers from adding new allegorical interpretations of their own to the myths. Indeed, to a considerable extent, it inhibits myth interpretation altogether. On the other hand, the conjunction of a passage of myth with a passage of dialectic bestows on it what we might call an objective interpretation of the myth. If the myth has a meaning, it must lie in that conjunction, which is open to our study. And such words as *soul* and *god,* which circulate between mythical and nonmythical discourse, break down any strict barriers among discursive modes. Plato's text is a tissue woven of different fabrics, or, in the principal metaphor I am relying on, a polyphony.

We need to be aware precisely of the polyphony, the voices in the text of Plato, and understand why he wrote that way. Can we give the reason for it? As we apply the thought of Schelling to that of Plato, we are drawn above all to the manifold constitution of the *soul.* What Schelling spoke of as different potencies have already appeared in Plato, especially in the *Republic* and the *Phaedrus,* as the three parts of the soul. Our question about the status of myth in relation to reason is initially a question about forms of discourse, different possibilities of language, but upon closer scrutiny it turns into a question about the composition of the soul or the mind. This will be our topic in chapter 7. Plato's tripartite soul offers the grounding for a doctrine of different modes of discourse, each an expression of the soul but not reducible to one part and one mode in the ways usually sought by philosophers of pure reason.

Phaedrus and Euheremus wished to substitute something different for myths that are not rational; later allegorists, Alexandrian and Neoplatonic, sought the hidden rationality in the stories; Hegel elevated pictures into concepts and ideas. But Schelling is closer to the Socrates of the *Phaedrus* by hearing the discourse in its own terms and *expanding* philosophical reason to accommodate it, including the myth within the philosophy. In our later chapters, we shall recur frequently to the myths of the *Phaedrus* and the other Platonic myths, and we shall explore them in their conjunction with dialectical and rhetorical speeches. We shall not seriously invoke stories like that of Boreas, but rather the stories of the soul and the gods, seeking to ascertain whether, given all their conjunctions within the total discourse of the dialogue, there appears an objective meaning of the myth, or a self-interpretation of the text.

CHAPTER
TWO | Rhetoric

A great deal of the *Phaedrus* is devoted to the discussion of rhetoric. At the beginning, Phaedrus reads to Socrates a speech written by Lysias that is supposedly the *ne plus ultra* of contemporary oratory. Then he challenges Socrates to compete with Lysias by offering a speech of his own on the same topic: love. Later, Socrates is compelled to offer a further speech, a palinode as it is called, and the rest of the dialogue will be devoted to an analysis of the three speeches and a discussion of rhetoric as a whole. Socrates, speaking as a philosopher, will express his criticisms of rhetoric. And yet there is the earlier dialogue, the *Gorgias,* where Socrates encounters the most famous of all champions of rhetoric, Gorgias of Sicily, and two of his followers, and launches an attack upon them that is about as savage as anything we find in Plato. This is not repeated in the *Phaedrus,* certainly not with the same force. In addition to that, this palinode, beginning at 244b, outlines some of Plato's most cherished teachings, but does so in the format of rhetoric! This great speech is rivaled only by Socrates' speech in the *Symposium* for its impact on the reader: it is a compendium of Platonic philosophy, in rhetorical form. We must examine, then, to what extent and in what way Plato has made peace with rhetoric.

There is no doubt that powerful and effective speech had been highly valued by the Greeks since very ancient times.[1] The epics of

---

1. On this point, and on a number of other points in this chapter, see George A. Kennedy, *The Art of Persuasion in Greece* (Princeton, N.J.: Princeton University Press, 1963). Kennedy mentions the speeches in Homer on pp. 4–5.

Homer offer numerous cases in which a leader such as Agamemnon or Achilles made an impressive oration, and we hear such speeches from the mouths of divinities like Zeus and Athena too. But we find around the middle of the fifth century, and especially in Sicily, the beginnings of a conscious art of speech construction, the effort to elaborate rules for diction and for the choice of persuasive arguments. Tisias and Corax in Sicily are the figures usually mentioned as the progenitors of the art of rhetoric. The important point is that the term *rhētorikē* does not just mean the practice of making speeches—we saw speech-making in Homer, for instance, and of course we know that people made speeches in the assemblies and courts—but rather the art, the *technē,* of fashioning speeches consciously according to norms. Likewise, the *rhētōr,* the practitioner of the art, is not merely someone who happens to be able to speak well, but one who has the mastery of a conscious art, who can explain what constitutes eloquence, and who can teach the art to others.[2]

Given the political and legal terrain in which rhetoric operated, and given the promises that it held out to the public, we have to see that it actually amounted to even more than an art. It was really the engine of a whole social movement—it carried with it a certain set of ideas and it bore a promise for the remaking of society. Gorgias found an eager clientele in Athens when he arrived in 427 and introduced himself as a *rhētōr.* The reader can see from the opening of Plato's dialogue, the *Gorgias,* 447a–449a, how Gorgias presented himself to the Athenians. His claims for his art were indeed extravagant, so much so that, if they could be sustained, the art would have a truly revolutionary force, displacing virtually every other form of discourse and virtually all the other arts of the city.

---

2. Tisias and Corax were famous in later times for their success in litigation. There is some debate over whether they had a consciousness of practicing a special art called *rhetoric.* Thomas Cole, in *The Origins of Rhetoric in Ancient Greece* (Baltimore: Johns Hopkins University Press, 1991), p. 2, makes the claim that there was no formal conception of the art of rhetoric prior to the time of Plato; the earliest documented occurrence of the word *rhētorikē* seems to be in Plato's *Gorgias,* 449a5. Other scholars, however, in addition to Kennedy (*The Art of Persuasion in Greece*), sustain the traditional view that the Sicilian Gorgias did come to Athens shortly after 430 as a representative of this new art. See Ian Worthington, ed., Persuasion: *Greek Rhetoric in Action* (London and New York: Routledge, 1994) for articles covering many aspects of this history.

One of the key elements of rhetorical culture—exceptionally pronounced in Gorgias—was the cultivation of ornamental and arresting speech. When Gorgias came to Athens from Leontini in Sicily in 427, he brought with him a number of oratorical set pieces that he would declaim and that he also circulated in written form. His ornate style of address borrowed heavily from the lyric poets, and it also featured the "periodic" style of composition: a careful, rhythmical balancing of clauses. It is this aspect of Gorgias's style that has left its mark upon later times in the very connotations of the word *rhetoric,* for nowadays it often has an unfavorable sense, meaning an excessive and florid, emotional style of address. Gorgias's "grand style" is well illustrated by *Epitaphios,* a funeral oration from which I shall quote a few lines.[3]

> For divine was the courage these men possessed, human the mortality; often they set gentle equity above stubborn justice, often rightness of argument above strictness of law, believing this the most divine and most universal law, to say and not to say and to do and leave undone what was due at the right moment; they practiced above all two things men should, mind and might; the one in deliberation, the other in execution, tenders of those in undeserved distress, chastisers of those in undeserved success, stubborn in accordance with expediency, good-natured in accordance with propriety, with wisdom of mind checking the folly of might; insolent towards the insolent, restrained towards the restrained, fearless towards the fearless, terrible among the terrible.

Another staple of the rhetoricians' trade was paradox, to entertain their Athenian audiences, and paradox mongering had genuine social effects, in Plato's view. A number of illustrations are preserved from Gorgias. One of these was his famous oration—now lost, alas, but preserved in summary form—on the nonexistent.[4] We could say that it mocked not only some of the previous generation of philosophers, but, very likely, human reason itself. Gorgias was the author of another disturbing and paradoxical speech that came closer to the interests of most Athenian citizens—his "Defense of Helen [of Troy]," referring to the woman whose desertion of her husband Menelaus was blamed in the tradition for the outbreak of the Trojan war. It lifts the blame from

---

3. I quote the translation by C. Carey published in his *Lysias: Selected Speeches* (Cambridge: Cambridge University Press, 1989), p. 7.

4. A fuller discussion of Gorgias's oration "On the Non-Existent" can be found in Guthrie's *A History of Greek Philosophy,* vol. 3, pp. 192–200.

the shoulders of Helen by showing that she exercised no choice at all: perhaps it was the gods who made her do it, and so the blame should rest with them, yet there are other inexorable powers, too, that may sweep away all human choice, and one of them is rhetoric, the power of speech. Gorgias's oration is preserved in fragments.[5] It was in the spirit of the rhetorical movement (and its companion movement, sophistry) to sweep away ancient ideas of responsibility and obligation with the invocation of irresistible external forces. What is specific to Gorgias, however, is to view his own rhetorical practice in that same light. "The Defense of Helen" continues with a celebration of the powers of speech.

It does seem that the life of those times gives some confirmation of Gorgias's point, showing that his rhetoric, at least, provides evidence of the power of words—they left their mark. For instance, there is the tragic drama, *The Trojan Women,* written by Euripides and produced in Athens in the year 415. The action takes place in Troy after the Greeks have conquered it and killed the Trojan fighters. As the women of Troy are bemoaning their fate, to become slaves to the Greeks, the victorious Menelaus comes to claim Helen—but will he kill her? Will he let her live? The Trojan women persuade him to let Helen speak in her own defense. Helen's case includes the following arguments. Lines 915–22: it was not *her* fault but that of her seducer, Paris, or, really, not even *his* fault either but that of his mother, Hecuba, who brought him into the world; lines 930–40: it was Aphrodite's fault, for making Paris so susceptible to beauty; lines 945–50: she can't say *why* she ran away at all; who knows what makes people act? Zeus himself is a slave to love! Can't you forgive me, Menelaus? she pleads. "Would you be stronger than the gods?" (964). This is argumentation that Euripides had learned from the rhetoricians and the sophists.[6]

But Plato was suspicious. When he wrote his *Gorgias* he took the opportunity to sketch the effect of this kind of rhetoric upon the temper of the city, though it is notable that he treats the old gentleman, Gorgias himself, with some kindness, granting him an attractive dignity. For in the dialogue, he is accompanied by two other characters

---

5. There is a version published in Philip Wheelwright, *The Presocratics* (New York: Odyssey Press, 1966), pp. 249–50.

6. Guthrie, *A History of Greek Philosophy,* vol. 3, discusses the influence of Gorgias on Euripides, p. 192.

who come off much worse, making the teacher look quite sensible in retrospect. Gorgias presents himself as an omnicompetent man, not so much *vain* as *complacent*. His art of rhetoric seems to be a universal art: he says he can make every kind of speech—for example, both short and long—and discourse on all subjects and teach that skill. But he is also shown to understand Socrates' questioning and to be able to free himself from the mannerisms of his art. It is to Polus, Gorgias's pupil, or rather teaching assistant, that Plato gives the most effusive speeches of the *Gorgias* (e.g., 448c), at the same time presenting Polus as perhaps the stupidest of all interlocutors with whom Socrates converses throughout Plato's works. After the portrait of the professor and the assistant professor, the longest portion of the dialogue, beginning at 482c, features the politician and lawyer Callicles, who studied with the two rhetoricians, not to become another professor but to advance his political career through the rhetorical art he acquired from them. And it is in this figure that we sense Plato's deepest reservations about the rhetorical art—its lack of a substantive moral and political ideal. The Callicles-Socrates encounter is a bitter and prolonged battle of words, pitching Socratic philosophy directly against a doctrine of power, force, egoism, conquest, and domination. This encounter shows in practice the political meaning of Gorgias's rhetorical art, for he taught it merely as a technique of winning through words, with no accompanying philosophy, reflection upon justice, or insight into the Good. Callicles is the same type of person as the brutal and cynical Athenian ambassadors to Melos, known to us from the chilling sketch offered in Thucydides' *History of the Peloponnesian Wars,* V, 85–111.

Lysias and the *Erōtikos*

The burden of my chapter is that it is not Lysias in particular who is Plato's target in the *Phaedrus,* but the whole culture of rhetoric that gained influence in Athens during the 420s and continued in the years that followed, right up through the period of Plato's own teaching activity and writing. There is specifically the figure of Isocrates, a great rival of Plato with a rival school centered on rhetoric. (On the historical Lysias, see the appendix to chapter 2.) Lysias, as portrayed in the *Phaedrus,* was of a new generation, and his style and his claims were different from those of Gorgias. It had fallen to the lot of Lysias to create a leaner and less ornamental style than that of Gorgias, which the later theorists of rhetoric called the plain style in contrast to the grand style of Gorgias.[7] Nevertheless, the eager response of Phaedrus to the speech of Lysias tells us about the continuing glamour of the whole rhetorical movement over a period of decades.

In the first place, there is still the factor of paradox. The actual substance of our dialogue begins (227c) with the delighted Phaedrus telling Socrates that Lysias made the *extraordinary* argument that it is better to accept the erotic attentions of somebody who does not love you rather than someone of who does. Without a second's delay, Socrates registers the improbable character of the claim (227c–d): "Oh, really! And I suppose it's better to be loved by a poor man instead of a rich man, an old man rather than a young man?" Who is not impressed and dazzled by a paradox? The eager youth of Athens certainly were: to escape from intellectual boredom is always a powerful urge. It was an accepted element of the upper-class culture of Athens in those times that a youth might be pursued by an older man who was smitten with him. The youth might allow himself to become a sex object for this man, and in return for that he would be introduced into circles where this man had influence and receive various other benefits from him. We shall go into the social context of this practice in chapter 5. Athenian intellectuals found various ways of praising this kind of liaison—they talked about the wonders of love, the beauty of love, the benefits of love, and so on. The reader can find several such tributes to love in the pages of Plato's *Symposium,* and the speech of Phaedrus himself, *Symposium* 178a–180b, is the very first one and sets the tone for all the rest—the perfect statement of the prevailing ideology of love. In the present dialogue, Lysias is breaking that code explicitly. Why, actually, should you yield to the lover if you would be likely to do better with somebody else? The startling thing is that we are to suppose this speech being addressed to the youth himself, a youth who may have heard himself praised by other suitors and lovers, thus: "You are so *beautiful,* my boy! Those eyes! I would give my life to know what you are thinking right this minute!" Instead of that, Lysias's character is saying, "Look, you aren't anything special to me, and I'm not going to fake it. But I want you to yield to me just the same."

---

7. This distinction seems to go back to Aristotle's pupil Theophrastos. We find it later in a critic such as Dionysius of Halicarnassos in his essays on Lysias and Demosthenes. See Kennedy, *The Art of Persuasion in Greece,* 280–82.

This speech of the *Phaedrus* does not fit immediately into the traditional three divisions of rhetoric—the legal, the deliberative, and the epideictic[8]—for it is expressly dramatic in character.[9] Lysias presents a man speaking to a boy, but it is obviously in private, not in a public court or assembly. It is as if we were seeing them on stage. He is pressing his case on the boy, and we can infer a broader dramatic situation. The boy seems to have shown already a bit of resistance toward our speaker's advances, and there seem to be rivals too, more than one perhaps, self-declared lovers pressing their cases to win the boy's favor. There is a further sense in which this speech is private. When Phaedrus heard the speech read aloud by Lysias, it was not in a public place, theater or assembly, but in the house of Epicrates, read to a smaller group, as a dramatist might read work in progress to a seminar or to a few potential investors. We have no reason to think that Lysias had a real client for this, someone who was trying to win over a real boy. It was a demonstration piece, an *epideixis,* yet at this stage it had not become a public oration. It was a sort of literary morsel.

The argumentation of the speech is simple in the extreme. It circles around a single concept that is stated early on: advantage, *sympherein,* 230e7. The speaker shows in this way and in that way why it will be to the boy's advantage to consort with him rather than with a lover. The opening lines assure the boy that the liaison will be to the advantage of them both, and then the body of the speech offers an itemized list of benefits. Each of the items is tied, logically, to the opening assertion; there is no logical progression, a sense of one point building upon another, but only repeated recurrence to the opening. This shows up in the connectives used in the speech: "And moreover . . . and moreover . . . [*eti . . . eti . . .*]." Later on in the dialogue, 264d, Socrates will call attention to the monotony of the composition, comparing it to an epitaph for Midas that consisted of four lines, but in which the four lines had so little internal arrangement that they could have been shuffled into any order at all. Perhaps we could attribute this internal formlessness of the

---

8. This division was codified for the first time in Aristotle's *Rhetoric,* Book I, chap. 3.

9. Later, at 268c–d, Plato is ready to treat dramatic speeches written by Sophocles and Euripides in the context of an analysis of rhetoric. Socrates says inter alia that speeches in drama must be rightly fitted into their situation in the story. A complete study of ancient rhetoric would have to include dramas, then, and also the great speeches in the historians, especially Thucydides.

speech to its being the work, supposedly, of a legal consultant. Arguments offered in court often pile one piece of evidence upon another, each one pointing to the same conclusion. We shall make a more detailed analysis of the argument when we turn to its actual subject matter in chapter 5. Here we can note the bond between the points he is making and the way in which he makes his points—content and style are very much at one. Lysias's style is certainly different from Gorgias's. His rhetoric is sharp, bare, and analytical. Everything is spare, intellectual, and hard-edged. There are no figures of speech in this address, and if there is rhythm it is close to what we hear when people are doing business. Nothing is vague. This rhetoric has excluded everything that might be uncertain or cloudy. This is the mode of discourse that has shut out mythology from the start. Whereas mythology persevered into lyric and drama, there can be no trace of it in Lysian rhetoric. All the vaguer entities associated with the dialogue's opening myth, the Wind-god, the Maiden-princess, are long since gone from the mind of Lysias. No gods are present. Nothing is left that remains uncertain as to date or place. In mythic discourse, some say Oreithuia was carried off from the Ilissos by Boreas—others say it happened at the Areopagus. Not so in the discourse of Lysias. Rhetoric is a form of discourse that is clear on what entities it can recognize—including abstractions such as "advantage"—and what entities it excludes—gorgons and centaurs, for sure. It is a conscious successor-discourse, consciously displacing the preceding form of discourse and culture.

Lysian rhetoric excludes the cloudy mythology with its familiar emotions and its colorful figures, partly because of how the speech is created. The myth has no text and it has no author, but rhetoric is the work of a definite orator and it has a fixed text, the material scroll, or *biblion,* that Phaedrus can carry away. The author who gave it its form is very much present to us in the rhetorical mode of address. It is not that "Some say she was carried off. . . . " Now it is "Lysias says . . . ," "Thrasymachus says. . . . " Rhetoric is not only the assertion of a thesis ("Helen was not to blame . . . "); it is even more the instrument of the speaker's self-assertion. Rhetorical persuasion is in practice a form of personal power; it is ultimately a political category. As the vehicle for a self-assertion, a rhetorical address has as its key word *I.* When the issue at hand is that of persuasion, the question, Of what have they been persuaded? is not as important as the question Who did the persuading? *Sympherein,* the main concept of Lysias's speech, is central to rhetorical culture. Where I persuade you of what is to your advantage, I am also advancing my own advantage as a leader. The sharper appearance of this is in *Republic* I, where Thrasymachus offers the rhetorical definition of justice, "the advantage of the stronger"—in his own practice as eristic orator, and teacher of the art to others, he is essentially presenting his claim to be the strongest of all. It is also in Callicles that we see the power character of rhetorical speech.

In ascribing the present view of love and lovers to Lysias, then, Plato makes it clear that such would be the profile of love to a forensic and rhetorical culture. The rhetoric of Lysias not only excludes the discourse of myth—in doing so, it also shows its narrowness from a human point of view. Lysias's speaker is seeking a *victory* in the oratory of love, trying to win over a boy by the force of a series of legal-style *arguments.* Plato's intention in this respect is to expose the blind spots that inhabit the rhetorical discourse and culture, by exposing how they would treat the matter of love. As soon as Lysias's address is over, and Phaedrus asks Socrates about it, Socrates' first reaction (235c) is to think of two lyric poets, Sappho and Anacreon, who had much more adequate things to say about love.

The question of Plato's motive in this confrontation with rhetoric must not slip out of focus. Who is it that he is really treating when we offers us a speech supposedly made by Lysias and then submits it to critical scrutiny? As I have said, it is not actually Lysias who concerns Plato, but the whole of the rhetorical movement and the moral effect it had on the city. This is evident from the way the present dialogue begins. Phaedrus needs some exercise after his long morning session, but he is still intellectually supercharged and eager to tell Socrates all about it. "So Lysias is in town!"—for Socrates, too, this is a major event. "And of course Lysias had been speaking"—Socrates has got to hear about it right away. Another dialogue that opens with a similar current of intellectual excitement is the *Protagoras;* the young man Hippocrates races to Socrates' house before dawn with the news that Protagoras, the famous sophist, has arrived in Athens; they absolutely must go to the house of Callias, where the great man is staying. These opening scenes convey the glamour that surrounded the figures of Lysias and Protagoras for the Athenian intellectuals and youth. In that other dialogue, Socrates did go to Callias's house to meet Protagoras, listen to his oration, and ask some questions. But in the present dialogue, we never meet the famous Lysias in the flesh. What is present here is only the *biblion* bearing his speech, a precious token that Phaedrus has obtained. Given the uncertainty of the dramatic date of the *Phaedrus,* we do not know exactly why Lysias is staying at the house of Epicrates. Is he still resident in Italy and just visiting Athens? Or has he moved back from Italy to Piraeus, only spending a day or two with Epicrates? Or has he already been expropriated in Piraeus? At all events, he is now a man sought out eagerly by the Athenian avant-garde. In all ages, we know of this kind of glamour. We read in Friedrich Hölderlin's letter of November 1794 from the town of Jena to his friend Neuffer how word had circulated through Jena that "Goethe had just spent the day in town staying at Schiller's house!" In later times we hear, "Marcuse is on campus!" "Derrida is on campus!"

During the 420s and the 410s, the upper classes of Athens had experienced the impact of intellectuals visiting from abroad, some of them known as sophists and some as rhetoricians, though they overlapped so much that no really clear line can be drawn between the two groups. The great prototypes of that generation were Protagoras the sophist and Gorgias the rhetorician, whose careers overlapped in Athens during the 420s. A much younger Phaedrus appears in the middle of a gathering of sophists in Plato's dialogue *Protagoras*—he sits at the feet of the sophist Hippias, though Plato did not give him any lines to utter. Here, by leaving Lysias offstage and focusing on Phaedrus (the dialogue bears *his* name), Plato enables us to see not only the ideas associated with a certain name, but also the effect of those ideas. In other dialogues, Socrates enters into discussion with those who are his peers in age and influence: Hippias, Gorgias, Protagoras. But here, it is not the professor that Socrates meets, but the student. By this means, we see the transmission of an idea in history, how it gathers force. Plato shows us how an idea comes to generate a school or a social movement. The particular movement here is rhetoric. Phaedrus has been praising Lysias for his speech and his words, which Phaedrus and Socrates usually call his *logos* (227b6, 227c4, 234c6). At 235a1, where Socrates begins to comment on the speech, he calls it by the name of *rhētorikē*.

The question of Plato's intent becomes particularly acute if the opinion is correct that Plato wrote this speech himself. In the first place, why put this particular approach to love and lovers into the mouth of Lysias? And why select the Lysian style, the plain style, to bear the burden of the stylistic criticism? In fact, as we shall be seeing later on, there is something curious and unfair about the stylistic critique by

Plato. Lysias cultivated a very clear style, which seems to be an inappropriate target of the critique.

The Critique of Rhetoric
in the *Phaedrus*

Although his focus in the *Phaedrus* is on Lysias, Plato is not concerned with just one target—he is examining the entire rhetorical movement. This intent becomes clear and explicit later in the dialogue, at 266c–268a, where he reviews the entire history of rhetorical schools in Greece, from Tisias and Corax, though Gorgias, up to Lysias and Thrasymachus. Moreover, it becomes clear at the end of the dialogue (278e–279a) that he also has his eye upon Isocrates, his great contemporary and rival, the director of a school of rhetoric in Athens.

We see Socrates commenting on Lysias's address just after Phaedrus has completed the reading of it—at 234c–237b—and now we shall treat those remarks together with the critical remarks Socrates offers later on, from 257c through to 274, where he resumes the critical discussion of Lysias's address, linking it to the broad critique of the rhetorical tradition. After we have reviewed these criticisms, we must look again at Plato's *Gorgias,* his first sustained encounter with rhetoric. There is evidence in the *Phaedrus* that Plato has modified his position to some degree. Some scholars have postulated a complete volte-face on Plato's part, an acceptance of rhetoric after all; others have maintained that the change was by no means so radical. I think that rhetoric has now become absorbed into philosophy, not eliminated, but as offering a "voice" in which certain topics important to philosophy can be appropriately treated.

At 234c, his reading over, Phaedrus wants a discussion, that is, he wants Socrates to admire the speech. "Yes, indeed," runs Socrates' urbane reply, "it was amazing, great! Actually, Phaedrus, *you* were amazing! I couldn't stop watching your face." And yet Socrates brings up two points in the form of questions.

His first question is, Did you mean I should admire not only the style of the speech but also the content? As for content, I would be surprised if it were true (234e). Earlier on, when they were talking about Boreas and Oreithuia, Phaedrus was quick to ask Socrates if he thought the old story was true, but now, when they have heard Lysias, it is Socrates, not Phaedrus, who wants to raise the question of the truth of the speech.

The second question he raises is, Was there any order or arrangement in the speech? It just seemed to say the same thing over and over (235a). But Phaedrus does not pick up the question of arrangement and order. Instead, he shows his passion for richness of content: Lysias seems to have included everything possible—nobody could outdo him with a fuller speech (235b). Then, after a lot of entertaining byplay, Phaedrus persuades Socrates to try a speech of his own on the same topic, for until he hears another speech, Phaedrus will not believe there could be points that Lysias forgot. What *Socrates* wants, however, is to show that a speech to the same effect could be delivered with greater attention to order, arrangement, and the logical disposition of argument, and that is what he offers, beginning at 237a. We shall make a study of his speech in chapter 5.

The critical points Socrates has made here are the ones he continues to press later in the synoptic treatment of rhetoric beginning at 257b.

Content of Speech

At 259e, Socrates says the first thing that a speaker needs is knowledge of the truth concerning his subject matter. With that, they are launched on a classic bit of Socratic interrogation. This question—the need for oratory to be based on knowledge—is woven throughout the pages of argument that follow, much of which recalls the *Gorgias* and companion pieces from earlier years.

1. Phaedrus has often heard an alternative theory expounded (260a) that to succeed in judicial oratory, for instance, you do not really need to know what is just—you only need to know what the members of the jury *believe* to be just.

2. Socrates himself refers, at 260d, to an argument that supplements Phaedrus's point, one that recalls precisely what Gorgias himself had maintained at *Gorgias* 456b–c: someone who does possess knowledge on a given subject may still not be persuasive to others and will require the power of oratory to accomplish persuasion. Socrates is careful to note here that this argument never forbids us from studying the truth; it only says that the gift of persuasion lies beyond that, a supplement to scientific knowledge. Yet Socrates does point out a series of things on which a rhetorician ought to seek knowledge, under four headings. Lines 260c–d: through lack of political information, the

rhetorician may urge a foolish course of action upon a city; 263a–e: without exact knowledge of language, the rhetorician will often speak ambiguously and bring about undesired results; 268a–269a: the mere mastery of oratorical techniques needs to be supplemented by the wisdom or good sense to employ a technique only in the appropriate situation; 270b–272a: only someone who understands the human soul, for instance, the different types of persons there are, can be a persuasive speaker.

3. The topic of knowledge and truth returns at the end of the treatment of rhetoric, at 272b–274b, in yet another form. Socrates recalls the founders of rhetoric, Tisias and Corax, and remembers the tradition that they preferred to deal with probabilities *(to eikos)* rather than truth, teaching that judicial practice would be better managed on that principle: see 273b–c.

The force of all these replies is to clip the wings of rhetoric: the business of persuasion must be tethered to dialectical or philosophical study.

There have been controversies about Plato's presentation of the rhetoricians in these pages. One of Plato's key objections to rhetoric is the allegation that Tisias and his followers, including Gorgias, preferred to base a speech upon probability rather than truth. Michael Gagarin has argued,[10] to the contrary, that Tisias and Gorgias—and Isocrates and the tradition as a whole—never elevated probability above truth. Wherever truth could be discovered, the rhetoricians would have always preferred to base the argument upon it. Gagarin argues that Plato was not willing to recognize that in most legal and political cases that call upon the skill of the rhetorician, the objective truth is simply not available. It is because of the imperfect situations in which, largely, human beings must live that, in practice, where we set out to persuade our fellow mortals, we must be content to work with "the probable." Gagarin's article is itself persuasive, and it casts a good corrective light on how the idealistic Plato may have misrepresented some of his more empirical rivals.

---

10. "Probability and Persuasion: Plato and Early Greek Rhetoric," in *Persuasion: Greek Rhetoric in Action,* ed. Ian Worthington, pp. 46–68.

Organization of Speech

The other primary topic of critique concerns the form and organization of addresses, and where this is applied to Lysias's address, Socrates in particularly scornful. Lysias failed to see that *love* is one of the words whose meaning is under continuing dispute (263a–d) and therefore was particularly remiss in not opening his speech with a definition of the term. A speech on such a topic must be rationally organized, beginning with a definition of the central theme and proceeding to dispose all the other material rigorously in sequence from that beginning (263d–e). Socrates, of course, does do exactly that in his own speech beginning at 237a. And more generally, far from being rationally organized, Lysias's speech was utterly haphazard, consisting of different thoughts thrown out at random, and Socrates compares it cruelly to an epitaph to Midas whose lines had no logical order at all (264b–d). Indeed, the Lysias speech actually began at the wrong end, saying at the start what would properly come only after the speech itself was over (264a). At this point Socrates makes an organic simile: a speech should be like an animal, with head, feet, and a body in the middle (264c). This discussion of order and logic serves as an introduction to the theme of a *philosophical* method, a study running from 265a to 266b and resuming again at about 269d (interrupted by some thoughts on the history of rhetoric), in which logical order is given a more thorough treatment. To fulfill its own need for order, rhetoric needs the guidance that only philosophy can supply.

Socrates' presentation of rhetoric itself here, however, does seem curiously unfair precisely on the matter of order and arrangement, particularly if we are right to assume that the speech of "Lysias" in our text is actually a parody composed by Plato. The monotony that Socrates complains about here, and that betrays the lack of structure in the speech, is not at all characteristic of the surviving speeches of Lysias. (See the appendix at the end of this chapter.)

Rhetoric and Philosophy

We may now address the question of Plato's overall intent in the *Phaedrus* insofar as it deals with rhetoric. Has he changed his mind since the *Gorgias?* Has he become converted to a program of rhetorical education? The principal reason people thought so is certainly not the rough treatment he gives Lysias. It is because he does seem to offer, beginning at 269a and running to about 272b, an outline of a true rhetoric (*tō onti rhētorikou,* 269c9). Gilbert Ryle,[11] on this basis, was prepared to read the *Phaedrus* as Plato's announcement that he was hanging out his shingle as a teacher of rhetoric in competition with the school of Isocrates—or, rather, that he was sponsoring the young Aristotle, now a graduate student in the Academy, as teacher of the subject. The courses on rhetoric sponsored by Plato's Academy, were, according to Ryle, the soil out of which Aristotle's own treatise on *The Art of Rhetoric* was to grow. Ryle is not alone in this general line of interpretation. Martha Nussbaum, for instance, reads the *Phaedrus* as being reasonably friendly toward Lysias.[12] And the wide difference between the *Phaedrus* and the *Gorgias* is apparent when Socrates makes a running comparison between rhetoric and medicine, 270b–271b, the one treating the soul, the other the body, both succeeding insofar as they base themselves on scientific knowledge. In the *Gorgias,* on the other hand, 464b–465e, Socrates presents the pastry cook as the absurd imitation of a doctor, for he would induce the mere semblance of well-being, not the reality, and it is this pastry cook who stands as the bodily counterpart of the rhetorician. A true judge is the psychic counterpart of a doctor, but the rhetorician is only a flatterer, pandering to low desires.

Despite his increased acceptance of rhetoric, the philosopher is still uneasy with the claims of the rhetoricians. There is according to Socrates in the *Phaedrus,* a "true rhetoric," but Guthrie has argued that this true rhetoric is in fact philosophy itself.[13] Among Guthrie's strongest arguments is the psychological one. Socrates argues that the speaker can only convince an audience if he has understood that audience's soul (270b–272b). But could one have a collective psychoanalysis of the entire people, the *dēmos,* before whom one stood as an orator? Would not that demos harbor individuals different from one another in their psychic constitution? From this, it follows that the true address, and therefore the true form of rhetoric, would be aimed at the individual, or conceivably a small group of like-minded persons, such as we see in Socratic dialogue. The great rhetorical address of the *Phaedrus* 244a–

---

11. Plato's *Progress* (Cambridge: Cambridge University Press, 1966), pp. 259ff.

12. Martha Nussbaum, "This Story Isn't True: Poetry, Goodness and Understanding in Plato's *Phaedrus,*" in *The Fragility of Goodness* (Cambridge: Cambridge University Press, 1986).

13. Guthrie, *A History of Greek Philosophy,* vol. 4, pp. 412–17.

257b is spoken to just one person: Phaedrus himself. Likewise, the best speeches sketched at 276e–277c seem to be those that a teacher offers to a single pupil. Such is Guthrie's pointed answer to Ryle.

On the other hand, it is surely not Plato's intention to denounce all forms of communication, or all uses of language, that do not resemble the philosophical discourse conducted by Socrates or conducted by himself and his pupils within his Academy. He does not deny that there are assemblies and law courts that require some form of rhetorical address. Guthrie's hypothesis seems to imply that Plato, and the *Phaedrus,* simply kept silence on the broader uses of rhetoric in public life. If the *Theaetetus* followed quickly upon the *Phaedrus,* as is generally assumed, it might be apropos to think about the contrast drawn there, 172c–177c, between the life of the philosopher and the life of one who inhabits courts of law, a rhetorician and lawyer. The principal point of the contrast is to demonstrate that a philosopher has a life of freedom, by comparison to a lawyer. But a further point in the contrast is that a philosopher who winds up in the toils of the legal system is often relatively helpless and makes a poor public rhetorician—we can think of Socrates at his own trial. Surely Plato cannot mean that cities can dispense with law, law courts, and lawyers. We have to look more broadly, therefore, at the uses of rhetoric than Guthrie has done.

The figure of Isocrates looms large in the concluding pages of the *Phaedrus,* and, if we keep him in mind, Plato's posture with regard to rhetoric will be understandable. Isocrates was of Plato's own generation and like Plato had been a follower of Socrates, but of Gorgias too. In founding a school of his own in Athens, he too made the claim of imparting "philosophy." In the written orations that he circulated, however, he never ceased to polemicize against Plato and the Academy, with the argument that the Platonic education, requiring detailed study of geometry and astronomy, logic and metaphysics, was illiberal and esoteric. This was not a program for the formation of vigorous and active men who would guide the affairs of Athens and the other Greek cities![14] Isocrates' was a rhetorical *philosophia* that would shape lead-

---

14. Already in his *Against the Sophists,* dated around 390, Isocrates diminished the ideal of pure research in favor of a humane education focused on the art of forceful speech: see chap. 16–18. This is also the burden of his later *Antidosis,* chap. 80–84, and chap. 258–75, which explicitly attack Plato's program of theoretical study and dialectic.

ers and rulers, and Isocrates was especially interested in forming a pan-Hellenic ruling class. To cultivate influential speech, to practice by examples from previous debates and previous law suits, to grasp in the rough practical way the typical situations that recur in public life—this was a training that would only be ruined by the absurdly detailed study of nature or the fine points of logic. We can hear these sentiments expressed by Callicles, the third main interlocutor in the *Gorgias,* beginning at 484c. And what Isocrates and Callicles say is surely true, at least in part. It is certainly true that the persuasion exercised in political rhetoric or forensic rhetoric cannot be reduced to the conviction accomplished through formally valid logical argument. There are many reasons for that, and one of them is that the speaker can exercise persuasion by way of his or her apparent character while speaking, and by the appearance of being deeply convinced of the argument. Moreover, there is often an urgent need to act, and to urge action, before all the facts are known. And surely there are many kinds of human excellence best promoted by other means than rigorous, theoretical education of the Platonic sort. Isocrates had a good case to make.

But at the time he wrote the *Gorgias,* Plato was not prepared to cede one inch of ground to those, like Isocrates, who advocated education in rhetoric. His posture was one of total combat, and the reason is surely that he saw his kind of philosophy in an embattled position, his teacher condemned to death, the partisans of rhetoric claiming to represent culture as such, *paideia,* the whole of it comprehended under rhetoric—precisely the claim of Gorgias and his followers in that dialogue. The rhetoricians, as was mentioned earlier, excluded myth rigorously from their discourse. Unfortunately, they did not grant the validity of philosophy either: philosophy, that is, as Plato understood it, stemming not only from Socrates, but also from Parmenides, the Pythagoreans, and the students of nature. Plato was absolutely right to puncture the inflated claims made on behalf of a rhetorical education. In this, he realized with great depth of insight that rhetoric was more than a few tricks of persuasion—it was a form of life. It sought to disseminate a culture based on the love of glory and repute, and in the long run that could only weaken and destroy the love for truth, the modesty, rigor, and religious tone of Socrates' inquiries and his life. The discourse of rhetoric excluded not only myth but philosophy. In return, therefore, arguing on behalf of philosophy, Plato wanted to defeat rhetoric completely.

But with the *Gorgias* behind him, and after he had founded his school devoted to rigorous philosophy and science, he still had to confront the world of public affairs: laws courts, assemblies, and the arts of government. His first hypothesis, it seems, was that public affairs might be run best, after all, by those who had received precisely his kind of rigorous education in mathematics, science, and philosophy—the hypothesis of the *Republic*. We shall comment on that political program in the concluding chapter, where we shall see that he had to abandon it by the time he wrote the *Phaedrus*.

The *Phaedrus* never suggests that rhetoric could be excluded or defeated, for it recognizes that rhetoric is the instrument of law and government and more clearly so in a democracy than in any other regime. The subtle task Plato has taken on, then, is to rebuke rhetoricians like Isocrates who, by puffing up their own art, aim to undermine rigorous philosophy and science, while also recognizing that there is a legal, political territory in which rhetorical art is necessary. He has to propose a reformed rhetoric. That is because it must not have an entirely free hand even in the territory of law and government, where it functions. The philosopher insists that law and government are still regulated by norms and have something of the *idea* in them—they are subject to the criterion of justice, and justice remains a permanent topic for philosophical thinking. But as Plato continues his critique of the pretension of rhetoric to stand free of philosophy, he must abandon his own high-handed way with rhetoric. Rhetoric must be granted a philosophical vocation, a role to play even outside politics, a role within philosophy itself. The philosopher cannot abandon the will to communicate. The philosophy that admits rhetoric into itself accepts a pluralism in its own constitution in place of its earlier search for discursive purity. And this is one of Plato's greatest moments. It has permitted him to offer the content of his philosophy to a whole world of readers and listeners who would never dream of listening in to purely dialectical discussions as Socrates conducted them or as they were conducted within the walls of the Academy. It is the rhetorical address in the middle of the *Phaedrus* that has won him his readers—indeed, Plato's concessions to rhetoric in the present dialogue are only the recognition of what he had done in practice already, for instance, in the great speeches of Aristophanes, Socrates, and Alcibiades in the *Symposium*. The *Apology of Socrates,* for that matter, standing at the head of Plato's corpus, was already a work of rhetoric, with only a few dialectical passages entered as interruptions. The philosophy that has recognized its own rhetorical voice will now be the effective corrective to the historical rhetoric that was the enemy of philosophy. We shall document this more fully in chapter 5, showing how a rhetorical component is necessary to the philosophy of love.

Appendix: The Historical Lysias

Lysias is a major classical author in his own right. The son of Cephalus and the brother of Polemarchus, he is represented as being present at Cephalus's home in the Piraeus during the discussion in the *Republic*. He was on friendly terms with Socrates and with Plato's brothers. A convenient edition of Lysias's works edited by W. R. M. Lamb recounts the traditional view of his life:[15] born circa 457 in Piraeus, he went around 440 to Italy where he studied rhetoric with Tisias, returned 412 to Piraeus, and maintained a rhetorical school from that time until 404, when he was arrested and expropriated (and Polemarchus murdered) by the oligarchic Thirty, after which he made his living primarily as a speechwriter, and died circa 378. (Modern scholars date his birth a decade or so later.)[16] Up until his disaster in the year 404, Lysias was a very wealthy man; like his father, he was not a full-fledged Athenian citizen but notably partisan nevertheless, supporting the democratic side in Athenian politics. He was one of those democrats, it seems, who admired Socrates despite Socrates' criticisms of democracy, and there is reason to believe that he wrote a speech offering a posthumous vindication of Socrates.[17] If he did, it has not been preserved; of his many written speeches, only about thirty-five still exist.

It used to be widely believed in ancient times[18] and in the nineteenth century[19] that the speech Phaedrus reads to Socrates in our

---

15. *Lysias,* ed. and trans. W. R. M. Lamb in the Loeb Classical Library (Cambridge, Mass. and London: Harvard University Press and Heinemann: 1930), "Introduction."

16. See Kennedy, *The Art of Persuasion in Greece,* p. 133.

17. R. C. Jebb, *The Attic Orators* (London: Macmillan, 1876), vol. 1, pp. 153–54.

18. For instance, by Dionysius of Halicarnassus, who studied critically the works ascribed to the various orators, and by Diogenes Laertius, *Lives of Eminent Philosophers* III, 25.

19. See Jebb, *The Attic Orators,* vol. 1, pp. 305–9.

dialogue was an authentic work by Lysias. (Lysias died about ten years before Plato wrote the *Phaedrus,* but would have been in his prime at the time of the fictional date of the *Phaedrus.*) In style it is as elegant and urbane as the writings we know to be genuine works of Lysias.[20] Moreover, it would seem odd for Plato's characters to be devoting such minute attention to work from a well-published author if it was not a genuine work of his. Yet it is the majority opinion of scholars today that when Plato wrote the *Phaedrus* he himself composed this piece as a parody or imitation of Lysias.[21] Everyone knows that he could write convincing imitations—look at his renderings of Agathon and Aristophanes in the *Symposium,* and nobody ever attributed those speeches to the authors themselves. Here I shall be assuming that contemporary scholarship is correct on this point. If I have a further reason to add, it would be that we know of Plato's own interest in the topic of *erōs,* but there is no evidence, from Lysias's other works, of an interest in a topic like this; it would stand quite isolated in Lysias's corpus.

Historically, the specialty of the real Lysias in rhetoric was to assist clients who had to go to court to speak in their own law cases and who hired him to write their speeches. He was, therefore, a legal consultant as well as a speechwriter. These written speeches also circulated in ancient times and were much admired for their clear and elegant style. Lysias was particularly famous for being able to suit the address to the client's own personality; he was something like a dramatist who fits the words of speeches to the particular characters and to the situations in which they find themselves. Widely disseminated during the 380s, these speeches were certainly known to Plato.

Thirty-four of the speeches of Lysias remain, in Lamb's edition, and all of them manifest very clear structure indeed. His typical speech begins with a preamble *(prooimion)* to capture the interest and sympathy of the audience; this is followed by the narrative *(diēgēsis),* which, in the case of a law suit, lays out the history of the case; then there is the proof *(pistōsis),* in which innocence or guilt is established by argument; and he finishes with the epilogue *(epilogos),* a closure that would

---

20. See, for example, in *Lysias,* ed. and trans. Lamb, "On Aristophanes' Property" or "Eratosthenes."
21. See, for example, Kennedy, *The Art of Persuasion in Greece,* pp. 76, 134; *Plato's Phaedrus,* ed. Hackforth, pp. 16–18; de Vries, *Commentary on the Phaedrus,* pp. 13–14.

prompt the desired decision.[22] He certainly knew what he was doing. Socrates refers in the *Phaedrus* 266d–267d to many of the existing manuals of rhetoric, but with a malicious intent, I think, making them look haphazard in their accumulation of trope upon trope, figure upon figure. His exposé of rhetoric is undertaken to prove how much it needs philosophy.

---

22. The four parts of an oration were given these names later by Aristotle in his *Rhetoric* III, chap. 13, but later critics such as Dionysius of Halicarnassus showed clearly that Lysias's orations themselves already possessed such an articulation. See Kennedy, *The Art of Persuasion in Greece,* p. 11; Jebb, *The Attic Orators,* vol. 1, pp. 179–83.

| Dialectic

In the course of his critical treatment of rhetoric, Socrates makes repeated reference to the alternative that he sometimes calls dialectic
(269b, 276e) and sometimes philosophy (278d, 279a). Dialectic is *dis-
tinctive* of Socrates, what differentiates his thinking from that of Phaedrus and Lysias and those who continued to circulate the old myths. It
is the instrument peculiar to philosophy, and when this voice is heard,
it is different not only from myth and rhetoric but from other modes of
communication such as epic and drama, history and sophistic. In this
and later dialogues, Plato did not pursue any inquiry that lacked dialectic. But does that mean that where dialectic is pursued there can be no
myth or rhetoric? The answer is no. In this chapter, we shall see from
the *Phaedrus* 269–72 one way in which rhetoric and dialectic are integrated. The end of chapter 5 will return to that point. And toward the
end of the present chapter, we shall see that even where its dialectical instrument is fully developed, philosophy still needs myth, a point
that will reappear in chapters 6 to 8. Our main concern in this chapter,
however, is with the description of dialectic itself and the question of
whether it has a unitary character throughout the works of Plato's different periods.

Plato's Earlier Dialectic

Dialectic is not only a Greek word, but a particularly Platonic one: according to Diogenes Laertius (*Plato,* 24), it was Plato who coined the

term *dialektikē*. But the root for this word, *dialegesthai*, is an old verb, occurring in Homer and other writers of verse and prose, that means to discuss something or hold a conversation about it. It is also the root for the word *dialogue*—in Plato's *Protagoras* 335d we read that those who engage in *dialegesthai* are having dialogues, *dialogoi*. We can begin an explanation of dialectic by looking at the character of the Socratic dialogues or discussions that Plato shows us.

In an early work, *Plato's Dialectical Ethics*,[1] Gadamer points out the structural convention of Socratic dialogue: the clear differentiation of roles between questioner and respondent. The former is limited to the function of asking questions.[2] The latter likewise works under constraint, which Gadamer calls accountability (*Rechenschaftsgabe;* see pp. 27, 51), the social and ethical constraint that in giving one's answer one must hold to it from that point on because one has expressed a genuine agreement or a genuine disagreement. The respondent has taken responsibility for the truth of his statement. Dialogue is contrasted with rhetoric in that one party must *wait* for the answer of the other. It is guided by the expectation of coming to agreement on the merits of the case (*sachliche Verstaendigung;* p. 17), but utterly in the absence of any charisma or bewitchment, or any sign of force from the side of the discussion leader. The early dialogues of Plato present us with many such encounters, and in the *Phaedrus* too there remain many traces of the early dialogue practice, for instance at *Phaedrus* 260a–262c, an excellent example of the Socratic method of refutation (elenchus), which could be inserted seamlessly into the *Gorgias* or the *Lysis.*

An organized exercise of discussion can be given the name *dialektikē:* this word is an adjective that came to stand alone, though the ancients understood it as *dialektikē technē,* the dialectical art. Whether or not the historical Socrates used the term *dialektikē,* there are points at which Plato represents him as engaged in his particular kind of questioning and calls it by this name. The earliest clear-cut case of such labeling is probably in the *Cratylus* 390c: "And him who knows how to ask and answer you call a dialectician?" "Yes." Despite this explicit reference to dialectic, there is no reason to differentiate dialectic in that instance from what we discern all over the pages of Plato's early work:

---

1. Hans-Georg Gadamer, *Plato's Dialectical Ethics,* trans. R. M. Wallace (New Haven and London: Yale University Press, 1991; first published 1931).

2. Gadamer, *Plato's Dialectical Ethics,* pp. 51–58.

the Socratic practice of interrogation. Robinson's book, *Plato's Early Dialectic,* offers a good account of the fundamental structure of Socratic arguments and an overview of their development through the early works of Plato;[3] the early account offered by Vlastos is likewise illuminating,[4] as are his last reflections on the subject.[5] For our present purpose, we need only note five salient points: Socrates claims never to hold a thesis but only to investigate what others have claimed; he isolates a single assertion, *p,* of the interlocutor to bear the brunt of scrutiny; he asks whether the interlocutor will also accept some further statement, *q,* usually something widely agreed upon; inferences, *r, s,* and so on, are then drawn from the thesis first asserted and prove to contradict certain inferences, *r1, s1,* and so forth, that were drawn from the further statement *q;* thus if the interlocutor wants to hold on to *q,* he must reject his thesis *p.* And so he stands refuted.

Of the many possible illustrations, we may cite the argument of Socrates against Thrasymachus in the *Republic,* I, 341c–342e. Thrasymachus's thesis, *p,* is that "justice is the interest of the stronger party." The implication, *r,* is that the ruler of the state, who is strongest in the state, makes laws to promote his own interest. Socrates asks whether this ruler possesses a craft, like the sea captain or the physician. In assenting to this, Thrasymachus is asserting another proposition, *q.* But from *q* Socrates derives the implication *r1* that, as with a physician or any craftsman, the exercise of the craft is for the benefit of those who are made subject to it, for instance, the patient. If so, the art of ruling must benefit, not the stronger, the ruler, but the weaker, the subject. So will Thrasymachus abandon *p* or will he abandon *q?* Throughout the texts up to the *Republic,* we can trace some dozens of arguments that have this general form.

When we turn to the treatments of dialectic in the *Phaedrus* and later works, we shall have to ask what resemblance they bear to these earlier inquiries.

---

3. Richard Robinson, *Plato's Early Dialectic* (Oxford: Oxford University Press, 1953).

4. Gregory Vlastos, "Introduction" to *Plato's Protagoras* (New York: Liberal Arts Press, 1956), pp. xxiv–xlv.

5. His views were revised in "The Socratic Elenchus: Method Is All," in G. Vlastos, *Socratic Studies,* ed. M. Burnyeat (Cambridge: Cambridge University Press, 1994), pp. 1–37. Note as well the critique made there of R. Robinson.

Dialectic in Republic VI and VII

Later in the *Republic* itself, the term *dialectic* comes to have a narrower employment. In undertaking to set up the constitution of an ideal state, Plato is also erecting a systematic edifice of scientific knowledge to train his leaders. He is then led to differentiate not only different bodies of scientific knowledge, but different faculties in ourselves and different methods by which these faculties work, with a hierarchy of cognitive powers. In the simile of the Divided Line, 509d–511e, he discriminates knowledge from mere opinion or belief, comprehending illusion and imagination, on the one hand, and mere empirical perception, on the other hand, under the heading of opinion. But as he then moves to the level properly called knowledge, he gives, first of all, an account of sciences that operate at the level of "reasoning," *dianoia,* comprehending in this group the mathematical studies such as geometry, which he uses as his principal instance. Having first asserted the cognitive status of geometry (it is *epistēmē*), the thrust of this passage is to call attention to the limitations it suffers in common with every other body of knowledge achieved by reasoning. First, geometry (and other sciences expressing the faculty of *dianoia*) cannot free itself completely from the domain of perception and the "opinion" that necessarily inhabits that domain. Although it goes beyond perception, it still relies on sensuous images, for example, its schematic drawings of triangles and the like. It treats its drawing as mere "images" of the true mathematical structures, yet the science cannot dispense with the images. Second, geometry and its kin depend on certain axioms and definitions taken as given. Geometry itself cannot generate them. Plato calls them hypotheses (510b) and argues that if it needs them the science itself is hypothetical (we too use this term for reasonings that hold only if something is "given"). The reasoning of *dianoia* proceeds only "downward" from the hypotheses (e.g., axioms) and has no means of mounting "upward," that is, of establishing the axioms themselves.

At this point Socrates introduces another science that expresses another cognitive faculty, an inquiry that surmounts the limitations of *dianoia* illustrated with the geometry example. First, it is able to dispense utterly with sensuous instances, needing no images, *eikones,* for the structures it studies. It does not need to draw circles, triangles, or anything else. It is, he says, able to work entirely with ideas or forms, *eidē* (508b8, 511c1–2), to move around from one *eidos* to another.

Second, this science is able to move not only downward, like the *dianoia* of mathematics, but upward as well. It is the science that establishes the first principles, which are to be taken for granted by the other sciences. And this is *dialektikē*. The cognitive power in us that it expresses is *noēsis*.

Fuller discussions of this important passage can be found in the leading commentaries on the *Republic*[6] and in specialized books and articles.[7] In the present context, what concerns us is especially Plato's reason for using the name *dialectic* for this remarkable science. In the absence of such words as *metaphysics* and *ontology*, he reached for a word that expressed, not the "what" of this highest inquiry, but the "how," and he drew upon the Socratic practice of interpersonal discussion because dialogical practice possessed the freedom to focus its attention upon anything, no matter how sanctified by tradition and custom. One was free to question everything (hence was not even subordinated to sense perception and images), and one wanted to move "upward," away from cases of virtue and courage to the formative *idea*. It is true that this *Republic* passage does not call special attention to the interpersonal, dialogical character of the dialectical science—it is almost as if the dialectical ascent to the highest principles could be accomplished monologically, by a pure meditation. The *Republic* tends on the whole to downplay the interpersonal, dialogical conduct of dialectic, but that is likely a consequence of Plato's style of writing rather than a resolute change of his opinion. After all, the earlier dialogues had depicted Socrates' encounters with his interlocutors in very lively and dramatic style; by the time we come to the theme of dialectic in

---

6. J. Adam, *The Republic of Plato,* rev. ed. (Cambridge: Cambridge University Press, 1963); R. L. Nettleship, *Lectures on the Republic of Plato* (New York: St. Martin's Press, 1962); R. C. Cross and A.D. Woozley, *Plato's Republic: A Philosophical Commentary* (London: Macmillan, 1964); Julia Annas, *An Introduction to Plato's Republic* (Oxford, England: Clarendon, 1981).

7. Nicholas P. White, *Plato on Knowledge and Reality* (Indianapolis: Hackett, 1976); R. E. Allen, ed., *Studies in Plato's Metaphysics* (London: Routledge and Kegan Paul, 1965), especially chap. 2, "Logos and Forms in Plato" by R. C. Cross, chap. 3, "Logos and Forms in Plato: A Reply to Professor Cross" by R. S. Bluck, chap. 4, "Participation and Predication in Plato's Middle Dialogues," by R. E. Allen, and chap. 5, "Mathematics and Dialectic in the *Republic,*" by F. M. Cornford; Robinson, *Plato's Early Dialectics;* Ian Mueller, "Mathematical Method and Philosophical Truth," in *The Cambridge Companion to Plato,* ed. R. Kraut (New York: Cambridge University Press, 1992).

the *Republic* VI and VII, however, the dramatic confrontation of personalities is much diminished, and the interlocutors, Glaucon and Adeimantus, very shadowy figures. The text itself, then, refers only obliquely to the interplay of speakers in dialogue, the consequence of Plato's urgent intention to communicate his own doctrine in writing. It is a didactic text. But that does not imply that the conduct of dialectic itself is monological. One passage, 531d–534e, outlines dialectic and its accomplishments and contains exchanges that suggest more clearly the interpersonal conduct of all dialectic, for example, 534b. More important, the consequence of the discussions in the *Republic* is that the term *dialectic* tends now to refer, not to the process of live philosophizing, but to the subject domain (which we would call metaphysics) for which the only suitable method was the interrogative one, the one that had been called "dialectic" since the *Cratylus*.

Dialectic in the *Republic*, then, means that territory of the highest things, or the ultimate issues, that *philosophia* in the proper sense had always studied. There was no line drawn between philosophy and dialectic.

A hotly debated question in Plato scholarship is whether there is a fundamental shift, from the period of the *Republic* and earlier to the period of the *Phaedrus* and later, over the meaning of *dialectic*. This question leads to the deeper one of whether there is a fundamental shift in Plato's philosophy as a whole. The differences between the versions in the *Republic* and earlier and the version stated in the *Phaedrus* will become still clearer when we look, first, at the *Phaedrus* itself and then at the group of dialogues that seem to have followed it fairly directly: the *Sophist* and the *Statesman*.

Dialectic in the *Phaedrus*

After his negative appraisal of Lysias's rhetoric, 262c–264e, Socrates wants to review his own two speeches—at 263d–e and again at 265a. He exhibits no false modesty. He praises his own speeches, in the first place, for having given a *definition* of their theme, love (263d), and then, in the second place, for having given an ordered, organized, articulated *treatment* of the theme (265a–266c). In both these ways, and especially in the second, he finds *within* his own rhetorical address a core of true philosophy. It is by this means that the topic of dialectic is introduced into the *Phaedrus*. It is a bit of retrospective self-analysis that we have at 265a and following. Socrates looks back at his first address, and then his second address, the Great Speech, examining the most fundamental structure and direction of the two of them. And he brings them into an interconnection. Whereas the first speech argued that it was better to favor the non-lover, and the second one argued that it was better to favor the lover, all this—he now says—only illustrates the ambiguity of the term *love*. The first speech assumed a bad sense of love, the second a good sense, but the truth is that love has both a good form and a bad form. Moreover, both speeches presented love as a type of madness, and Socrates notes that madness, too, may be merely noxious or it may be heaven-sent, so that the speeches are ultimately consistent with one another. Both speeches, he says, seemed to be true, and now he can account for the apparent truth of them both. We have come to a fundamental structure in reality: love is always a kind of madness, but madness itself always divides into a proper form and a sinister form, and this will show up in the twofold nature and character of love. Socrates praises his speeches, then, for having offered, cumulatively, the whole truth about love.

To be sure, puzzles arise when we try to connect this self-interpretation with the earlier text of the two speeches.[8] At 265a-d, Socrates is acting as if his own speeches have been consistent, outlining the two divisions of madness and therefore of love. But we did not detect any overarching unity in the earlier speeches, that is, a generic madness and a generic love that then had the two divisions; these speeches seemed at the time we read them to be utterly in conflict (see 242a-243d). Another surprise introduced at 265b is the suggestion that there were four gods presiding over the four forms of divine madness; in the actual text there was no suggestion that Apollo presides over prophecy or Dionysius over the mysteries, though we did hear of the inspiration of poetry by the Muses and of love by Eros; and Aphrodite was surely understood likewise as begetter of love. Although Hackforth calls these "serious difficulties,"[9] Ferrari seems to me to be on a better course in stressing that the dialogue has made progress and that it is not out of place for Socrates at this later stage to offer a greater clarity than he had achieved before, even at the cost of a retrospective simplification.[10] I would say that this is the way a dialectician speaks, seeing in the pro-

---

8. All commentators have noticed this problem; different aspects of it are well summarized by Hackforth, *Plato's Phaedrus,* notes on pp. 125–26 and 131–34, and by Ferrari, *Listening to the Cicadas,* pp. 59–61.

9. *Plato's Phaedrus,* p. 133.

10. *Listening to the Cicadas,* pp. 61–62

ductions of rhetoric a generic unity, and clarity of distinctions, that may escape the rhetorician himself.

Now Socrates exploits the occasion. By a "stroke of luck" (262c10), he says ironically, we just happen to have in the contrast of the two speeches the perfect illustration for a method of inquiry he wanted to talk about. This method, dialectic, is described with some care at three different points in our text: (1) at 265a–266c it is introduced as a method of research composed of collection and division, (2) at 269b–272b it is shown to afford the foundation for a reformed rhetoric, and (3) at 276e–277c it is presented as the true method for teaching.

Collection and Division

Socrates invokes an art, first, of assembling a group of things together into one *idea* (265d3): it is thus that we comprehended love, prophecy, mysteries, and music under the *idea* of madness. Next, this art proceeds to divide this *idea:* in our case we take paranoia, craziness, as a common form, or *eidos* (*paranoia* is just another word for what he calls *mania* earlier), and divide it initially into two (266a)—on the right hand a divine madness, including love (i.e., the praiseworthy love of the great speech) and the other divisions like prophecy and music; on the left side a merely earthbound madness that would incorporate the kind of love that the first speech attacked and other kinds of degenerate passion. The great emphasis of this passage is the need to make the divisions with skill, and the principle of the skill is that natural divisions be followed. To find the *idea* that really is an *idea,* not a haphazard accumulation of unrelated things, and to divide the *idea,* or *eidos,* where its own natural divisions lie is the skill that Socrates will revere as divine, and it is the skill of the dialectician. Here, for the first time in the *Phaedrus,* 266c, Plato uses the term *dialectician.* This is to be the name of what he has just described, though Socrates offers no reason why this might be the right name for such an expert.

The majority of interpreters, perhaps, see a great novelty in this description, and for many of them this passage signifies a fundamental shift, a substantive and doctrinal shift, in Plato's philosophy.[11] Part of their case is to point to works of Plato written after the *Phaedrus* that

---

11. *Plato's Phaedrus,* Hackforth ed., pp. 134–35, 136–37; W. D. Ross, *Plato's Theory of Ideas* (Oxford, England: Clarendon, 1951), pp. 80–82; Julius Stenzel, *Plato's Method of Dialectic,* trans. D. J. Allan (Oxford, England: Clarendon, 1940), pp. 150 ff.; Nicholas P. White, *Plato on Knowledge and Reality,* pp. 117–20, 123–24.

seem to carry out at length the program announced here, especially the *Sophist* and the *Statesman,* and we shall come to this point shortly. Other interpreters, however, point to cases in the early dialogues that anticipate precisely the present collection and division, admittedly without as much self-consciousness about method as we see here.[12] Consider the *Meno.* At the opening of the dialogue, when Socrates has asked Meno for a definition of virtue and Meno replies by listing a whole series of virtues, Socrates asks him to lift his eyes to that "one virtue," *mian aretēn* (72a, 72c), that is shown in many forms and cases; then there will be the division of the one into the many specific virtues (73a–74b); comparable passages can be found in many of the early dialogues. The continuity in philosophy, and particularly in the concept of dialectic, is a major controversy of Plato interpretation, and we shall continue to explore the details that bear upon it.

The Foundation of Rhetoric

We attend now to the passage 269a–272b, where Socrates proposes to rebuild rhetoric on this foundation. We see, first of all, that in its true and complete character, dialectic is not only a technical operation; it has a moral and personal meaning, an existential meaning, for Plato. Dialectic is introduced as the corrective to the practice of politics and law that was driven by the rhetorical ideals of glory and influence. Rhetoric, after all, was not only a technique of speech but a whole form of culture, and when Plato wanted to reconstitute rhetoric by way of dialectic, he sought to instill virtues such as truthfulness and honest inquiry, which are not merely habits of speaking but virtues of the soul. They inform the character that Socrates exhibits in his encounters with Callicles and Thrasymachus. Dialectic, in this text, then, has inherited all the aura that Plato generally accords to philosophy itself. Dialectic is specific to philosophy itself: it is the form of discourse used by philosophy alone.

Now in its character as the foundation of rhetoric, dialectic remains fully consistent with its character as a mode of research focused on collection and division. Socrates argues at 270b that rhetoric must receive from dialectic *the knowledge of the soul.* No mere formalistic division, this is a full-scale moral and metaphysical psychology. And Soc-

---

12. Guthrie, *A History of Greek Philosophy,* vol. 4, pp. 430–31; Wilamowitz-Moellendorff, *Platon,* cited later in this chapter.

rates presents this knowledge at 270b–272b as being dialectical in the sense of a collection and division. The knowledge will first focus upon the soul as a whole, that is, as one, carrying out the movement of collection (270c1–2, 271a5–8). Then it will proceed to a division, discriminating the different types, *genē,* or *eidē,* of soul (271b1–2, 271d–272a). And this is repeated at 273e1–8. This knowledge concerning the soul is no mere empirical classification, but an application of the complete philosophical psychology of Plato, the divisions of the soul into the types that have been presented already in the Great Speech. We should not suppose that what rhetoric needs is an empirical psychology that represents human types as different classes that could be approached or manipulated in different ways, in the way that an advertiser today might prepare different versions of his copy, one tailored to women and the other to men, one for whites and one for blacks, one for the youth audience and one for the elderly, and so on. The psychology that Plato means is precisely the self-knowledge that Socrates has been seeking throughout his life and mentioned near the beginning of the present dialogue, the self-knowledge that Lysias lacked, and that has now been offered to us. This philosophical knowledge to which Socrates has already brought Phaedrus will be our theme throughout part 3 and includes the knowledge of the origins and destiny of the soul, its different parts, and its two states: winged and wingless. That is what justifies Socrates' reference to the grandeur of this science at 270a1 and to the greatness of the topic at 274a2–3. The different types of soul are those that proceeded to Earth according to their different destinies as recorded in the great mythical speech (248d–e), for Socrates ridicules the rhetorician's appeals to merely empirical differences between people: one who is weak but brave, another who is strong but cowardly (273b–c). What the dialectician practices, then, is the full Socratic art of thinking and living, and only that gives an adequate buttress to rhetoric.

The undergirding that rhetoric receives from dialectic is the study or knowledge of the soul, but this is then fused together with an account of the types of speech, carried out at 271b and 271d. This repays careful study, for it shows a genuine unification of rhetoric with dialectic.

Teaching

It is dialectic alone that constitutes genuine teaching (276e–277c). At this point, near the end of the dialogue, Socrates has turned from the topic of rhetoric in general to the topic of speech-writing, and he is now engaged in contrasting live speech with writing, a topic we shall take up in chapter 4. He presents the dialectician here as one who engages in live discussion with a pupil—he does not write on paper, but writes directly on the living soul. The words can germinate and grow in this living soul: they do not remain inert like inscriptions on paper, but bring forth greater abundance, for the pupil understands what is said, and as a living soul he can come to the defense of the words, and the teacher, with further words. Socrates acknowledges in his speech at 276e–277a that the dialectician must select a suitable type of soul to receive this teaching. This dialectician, who plants and sows the seed of truth in the pupil's soul, is the same figure as the lover who studied and guided the soul of the beloved at the conclusion of the Great Speech. The living soul of the pupil, the beloved, will bring forth the harvest of truth that is infinite and never ending.

Thus, pulling together the discussions of dialectic, we see that as Plato builds a positive philosophy, he sets out dialectic as a method for *study and research,* that is, collection and division, as a foundation for the *communication* of truth rhetorically and as a method for the kind of *instruction* he undertook in his own Academy. There is far less emphasis here than in the early works on the practice of Socratic interrogation and refutation. This change certainly yields some difference in the conduct, the visible practice, of the philosopher, and it is likely the difference between Socrates, with his refutations, and Plato, the systematic philosopher. But do the differences in procedure amount to a revolution in the metaphysics and epistemology of Plato? I have already offered one piece of evidence to the contrary—that the dialectical collection and division, when it finds application to the soul, will draw upon the metaphysics of the Great Speech in the *Phaedrus*. That is one indication of a broader point, the dependence of the later pages of the *Phaedrus,* from 257 on, upon the earlier ones, 244–57, and therefore a first indication of the genuine unity of the *Phaedrus*. Next, after a look at the *Sophist* and the *Statesman,* and at Plato's Academy, I shall present further evidence for this unity, evidence that will have an even broader bearing, tending to show a broader unity in Plato's work as a whole. Those who divide the late works from the middle ones always have to cut the *Phaedrus* in two.

Plato's Later Dialectic

The *Sophist* is perhaps the most profound metaphysical study ever written by Plato. It cannot be my purpose here to probe it as a whole—my interest is just to mention it as an exemplar of dialectic. The discussion between the Eleatic Visitor and Theaetetus does turn to an explicit treatment of dialectic at 253c, in which the interlocuters describe dialectic as the art of dividing forms—and they explicitly agree that this is the art of the philosopher who is differentiated in that respect from his parasital imitator, the sophist, who sows confusion. The description is perfectly in accord with the account of collection and division in the *Phaedrus*. Moreover, this dialogue is in practice a series of exercises in division: there is a practice division accomplished right at the start (218e–221c), where the figure of the angler is defined by a method of division that starts from the genus, Art, which is then divided into the productive and acquisitive, and then by the introduction of other differentiae in a descending series, eventually terminates in "that form of fishing that hooks with an upward motion" (221b–c).[13] Following this pattern, the speakers next attempt to define the sophist (221c–231b), yet the task is complex enough that they try six or seven different approaches that have the feature of attempting downward divisions beginning from different generic starting points. The Eleatic Visitor summarizes their bewildering attempts in the passage from 231c to 231e. These preliminary efforts certainly focus our attention on the difficult problem of making the preliminary collection: to what family of things shall we raise our sights when we wish to descend upon the sophist with an accurate defining division? The solution of this particular problem is accomplished partly at 231b–235a—the correct genus for our sophist will be image making—and partly at the end of the dialogue, 264e–268d, where a full and apparently satisfactory definition is stated, by a series of divisions of this family: "The art of contradiction-making, descended from an insincere kind of conceited mimicry, of the semblance-making breed, derived from image-making, distinguished as a portion, not divine but human, of production, that presents a shadow-play of words—such is the blood and lineage which can, with perfect truth, be assigned to the authentic Sophist" (268c–d).

As for the *Statesman,* I shall just point to a few of the formal, methodological similarities it shares with the *Sophist* that mark it, too, as a primary document of Plato's later dialectic. Seeking to define the statesman, *politikos,* the Eleatic Visitor also makes a preliminary exercise in division near the start (258b–268d), but it too has an unsatisfac-

---

13. F. M. Cornford, trans., *Plato's Theory of Knowledge* (*the Theaetatus and the Sophist*) (New York: Liberal Arts Press, 1957).

tory result—beginning this time from the genus Science, *epistēmē,* we approach the *politikos* in the division of applied rather than pure science and eventually track him down as a kind of herdsman of hornless, featherless bipeds. The comic misadventure of this definition brings about a number of methodological reflections and another model exercise in collection and division that yields the definition of the weaver (279a–283b), which will play a paradigmatic role in the *Statesman,* parallel to the *Sophist*'s definition of the angler. The dialogue concludes with a definition of the *politikos* by way of a division (287b–311c) that displays the king or the politician as the one who weaves together the different powers that constitute the state.

Those who stress the difference between the early and the late dialectic of Plato rely in part upon the technical aspects of these descriptions, especially the collection-and-division procedure. But in part they see further differences, of a more general and metaphysical nature, that supposedly mark off the later work. And if we look at Plato's later philosophy more broadly, we see another whole aspect of our question: Plato was not only a writer. He was a teacher too, and director of the Academy, which, especially during the 370s through the 350s, attracted scholars from around the Greek world, including Aristotle, who came as a young man shortly after 370 and stayed until 347.

This Academy was, undoubtedly, a unique thing: was it a club, school, college, religious society? And Plato himself—should we call him a teacher, founder, leader, president, college president? I introduce the present topic in the form of questions because, even in the present state of scholarly research, the nature of the early Academy and Plato's activity in it still seems a riddle, as it was called by Harold Cherniss.[14] But the present topic cannot be avoided: it has to come up in a study of the *Phaedrus* because the topic of dialectic has come up. Socrates, sitting under the plane tree, has told Phaedrus (266b) that he is a lover of dialectical collections and divisions. There is no doubt that it is the author Plato of the year 370 B.C.E. who has projected backward onto his Socrates a commitment of his own, a commitment of *Plato* to dialectical collections and divisions. And all Plato's readers, I believe, are prepared to read the later dialogues, *Theaetetus, Sophist,* and so on, as

---

14. Harold F. Cherniss, *The Riddle of the Early Academy* (Berkeley and Los Angeles: University of California Press, 1945).

springing from and expressing some of the philosophical life going on between Plato and the members of his Academy during the 360s.

We have external evidence that in the Academy a method of teaching and research prevailed that drew especially on dialectical collection and division. The fourth century comic poet Epicrates wrote a play from which the following fragment has been preserved:

> What about Plato, Speusippus, and Menedemus? What subjects are they dealing with now? What thought, what argument are they investigating? If you've come knowing anything please tell these things to me with discretion.
>
> I can talk about these things clearly. At the Panathenaic festival I saw a band of gay youths in the gymnasium of the Academy and heard them say unutterably weird things. They were making distinctions concerning nature, the life of animals, the nature of trees, and the genera of vegetables. Among other things they were studying the genus of the pumpkin.
>
> How did they define it? What is the genus of the plant? Reveal this to me if you know.
>
> Well, first they all stood silently, bent over, and they thought for a considerable time. Suddenly, while the young men were still bending over and reflecting, one of them pronounced it a round vegetable, another a grass, a third a tree. A Sicilian doctor who heard these things blew a fart at the fools.
>
> That must have made the students very angry. I suppose they shouted out against the man's derision. For it is out of place to do such things during a discussion.
>
> It didn't bother them. Plato was there, and he enjoined them, very gently and without agitation, to try again from the beginning to distinguish the genus of the pumpkin. They proceeded to do so.[15]

We can be convinced by this fragment that the program of collection and division proclaimed in the *Phaedrus* was the backbone of the research and instruction undertaken in the Academy. The more we can learn about the Academy, then, the better background we have for reading Plato's later works. Further external evidence about the activities of the Academy, which loom large in the interpretation of the later

---

15. Epicrates, in *Comicorum atticorum fragmenta*, ed. Theodor Kock, 3 vols. (Leipzig: 1880–88), vol. 2, pp. 287–88. I quote the translation offered by Ian Mueller in *The Cambridge Companion to Plato*, pp. 171–72.

works of Plato, derives from Aristotle, who for twenty years was en-
rolled as a member of the Academy and whose own philosophy was
substantially created there—the finest flower the institution yielded, no
doubt, though by no means the only one. Aristotle in his writings re-
lates many insights about the Academy, its prevailing intellectual temper, and the person of Plato, its president. We find a great deal of this
material in the *Metaphysics,* M and N (XIII and XIV), and other scattered remarks throughout the *Metaphysics, the Nicomachean Ethics,* and
the physical writings.[16]

In chapter 4, devoted to writing, I shall return to the discussion
of the scholarly work on Plato's Academy and Aristotle's evidence.
Apart from those issues, however, many recent scholars have seen profound differences between the early and the late *writings* of Plato.
Often, these scholars interweave technical, methodological divergences
over the conduct of dialectic with broader metaphysical issues. The
translators Nehamas and Woodruff, for instance, maintain that Plato's
dialectical philosophy in the *Sophist* and other later works "is obviously
not the same as the theory of Forms we find in Plato's middle works,
especially the *Phaedo* and the *Republic.*"[17] The later works knit the
ideas together, but, they say, the middle dialogues, including the Great
Speech of the *Phaedrus,* isolate them from each other (p. xliii). The divisions practiced in the later works are at odds with the indivisibility
central to the ideas of the middle works and the Great Speech (p. xliii).
In the middle period, including the Great Speech, the ideas are para-
digms, or supreme exemplifications of themselves; in the later dialectic, this is not so (pp. xlii–xliii). So "we can now read Socrates' Great
Speech as Plato's farewell to the theory of forms it describes" (p. xlv).

The work of Julius Stenzel, a German scholar of the 1910s and
1920s, I think, pioneered this interpretation. Though it has not always
received due attention outside Germany, inside Germany Stenzel remains a formidable force. *Plato's Method of Dialectic* was assembled in
English by D. J. Allan to give a representative selection from Stenzel's
German-language studies.

In Stenzel's interpretation, the doctrine of ideas led Plato into a

---

16. These references are collected and explained in Ross, *Plato's Theory
of Ideas,* chap. 11, "Plato's 'Unwritten Doctrines'," pp. 142–53, and, in far
greater detail, in J. N. Findlay, *Plato: The Written and Unwritten Doctrines*
(London: Routledge and Kegan Paul, 1974). See especially Findlay's appendix 1.

17. *Phaedrus,* trans. Nehamas and Woodruff, introduction, p. xlii.

number of intellectual conundrums. Do these ideas exist separately, by themselves? How are the particular instances of a virtue related to the idea of the virtue? Stenzel's view was that these conundrums that could not be solved within the framework of the early theory of ideas were solved in the dialectic of collection and division.[18] And as Socrates, too, was associated in Plato's mind with those transcendent ideals of virtue he had once explored, the figure of Socrates tends to disappear when Plato undertakes to offer a new, non-Socratic philosophy. The method of collection and division does *not* operate upon transcendent ideals like Justice, but takes its start always from the pragmatic domain, and seeks to formulate concepts that encompass individual entities, objects of study that are evident phenomena, things like love, madness, anglers, statesmen, and so on. These concepts are not, like the old *ideai,* recollected from a previous life, that is, in Stenzel's neo-Kantian formulation, they are not a priori as the Socratic ideals had been. This reading of the text enables Stenzel to see the late Platonic dialectic as paving the way for a more empirical method of science, with far more place granted to observation, which will show up in the later Academy and in Aristotle's biological works. This is the view, I think, that also appears in most of the work done by G. E. L. Owen, though his own philosophical approach was not neo-Kantian, but influenced by English logical researches of the 1940s and 1950s. He sharply separates the middle dialogues (including, for him, the *Timaeus*) from the "sophisticated metaphysic of the . . . profoundly important late dialogues."[19]

But Stenzel's reading led to a curious interpretation of the *Phaedrus.*[20] In the new dialectic, there can be no place for recollection and so it disappears after the *Phaedrus,* just as the figure of Socrates tends to be eclipsed after the *Phaedrus,* even though the Great Speech of the *Phaedrus* contains the most exuberant statement of the recollection theme in all of Plato. Socrates is made here to introduce a new doctrine, the late dialectic, just after his Great Speech that proclaims everything the new doctrine will avoid. Thus the question of the unity of the *Phaedrus,* its internal consistency or inconsistency, is directly connected to the overall relationship of Plato's late philosophy to the early philosophy. If there are an early and a late philosophy, they are both

---

18. Stenzel, *Plato's Method of Dialectic,* p. 44.
19. "The Place of the *Timaeus* in Plato's Dialogues," in R. E. Allen, ed. *Studies in Plato's Metaphysics,* p. 338.
20. Ibid., p. 150.

contained in the *Phaedrus*. Stenzel returns repeatedly to the *Phaedrus*, granting the terrific strain, or even contradiction, imposed on the work by his interpretation, but he is not willing to abandon the interpretation. He reads the *Phaedrus* as an imperfect transitional dialogue.

Standing in opposition to Stenzel, and to earlier neo-Kantian scholars who had anticipated Stenzel's position in certain ways, was Wilamowitz. On the most important overall relation of Plato's early and middle work to his late works, he made some remarkable observations. He granted that there were differences between the early and the later works, but did not construe them as signifying a conversion in philosophy.

> In the writings that show us Plato the academic teacher, Plato the poet appears but rarely, and where this does happen there is the effect of a clash with the context. He is preoccupied now with problems in logic and epistemology, and his way of treating them—more so, actually, than the content—differs so sharply from the *Phaedo* and the *Republic* that anyone would be taken aback. Scholars who could not make head or tail of this some decades ago would declare the *Sophist* spurious, or else say that it was actually inspired by the young Aristotle who was guiding his old teacher. Nowadays people are busying themselves trying to make a system of philosophy out of the writings of the older Plato, and treating his greatest works as mere preliminaries—or, rather, as containing just a few bits and pieces that can be taken seriously. Either they become squeezed into the logical theory of the *Sophist,* or else his work is divided into periods and the later Plato is supposed to have denied the theory of ideas. Philosophers are suspicious of his ethical and religious thought: they call it mysticism (and that can't be good!)
>
> Admittedly it is rare for Plato in his later years to speak about the eternal ideas, the Good, the Beautiful and the True, and when he does it is hardly with his old warmth and enthusiasm. But that he should have rejected any of it, that he was conscious of having given something up, is only a misunderstanding. It is true that he does not repeat himself. And why should he? He had new things to study and to say, not because he rejected what came before, but rather because he was confident of what he had accomplished, and now looked about to the surrounding vistas. His school and his own development both prompted him in this direction. If, first of all, he had concentrated upon his own soul and its well-being, and then upon the rescue of others (in their terrestrial life, as

well!), he had now gained a secure faith. He had reached his goal—
now he looks around, and he looks back upon the pathway he had
gone. He had gone through pure thinking, and so now he focuses
his attention upon that. He wants to teach his pupils to think. He
had not studied nature because he had not wanted to be confused
by its currents of coming to be and passing away. But in pure being
he had found the wellspring of becoming. And now he begins to
examine not only how the lawfulness of all becoming is secured by
being—and this leads him to the laws of nature, for nature is indeed a "kosmos"—but also how human thoughts and sensations
arise, which leads him to the body, its senses, its organs, its whole
constitution. There are indications of his interest in these questions long before he sets out his system of nature [in the *Timaeus*]:
the *Phaedrus* already refers to Hippocrates.[21]

Wilamowitz's view seems right to me and highly relevant to a study of
the *Phaedrus*. The account the *Phaedrus* offers, in the Great Speech, of
our supernal vision is not contradicted at any point in the later pages
on rhetoric and dialectic. Indeed, I indicated earlier that the dialectician's study of the soul (270b–272b) actually invoked the psychology of
the Great Speech. The three main passages of the *Phaedrus* that treat
dialectic (265a–266c, 269b–272b, 276e–277c) are, according to this interpretation, descriptions of the philosopher's daily encounter with various interlocutors and various themes and situations. But there is a secret, hidden, and higher condition for this practice of dialectic—the
soul's primordial vision.

There are, after all, in the later pages of the dialogue from 257 on,
copious references to justice, truth, beauty, and temperance, the same
ideas that had been the focus of the soul's supernal vision as narrated
in the Great Speech.[22] The most dramatic reference, probably, is the
one found in Socrates' concluding prayer to the god Pan, which invokes
beauty and temperance together, the very conjunction that had once
been seen by the soul: "Dear Pan and all the other gods of this place,
grant that I may be beautiful within . . . and as for gold, let me have just
as much as a temperate person might carry with him" (279b–c). Those
who would divide the *Phaedrus* in the middle might not be ready to
hear echoing in these references to truth, beauty, temperance, and

---

21. Wilamowitz-Moellendorff, *Platon,* pp. 508–9.
22. On knowledge of good and bad: 260c; on truth: 260d, 262a, 262c,
273d, 277b, 278c; on the just and unjust: 261c, 263a.

knowledge the doctrine of the eternal ideas. But that would be to beg the question! Why would we *not* suppose that these things the dialectician needs to know in his daily practice are the ideas once seen by the soul? *Anamnēsis* remains the condition for dialectic, and a prayer is precisely that act of the mind that recalls in the midst of daily practice the things it once learned on high.

The Great Speech, then, far from being undermined by the later treatment of dialectic, is precisely the exploration of the grounds for the practice of dialectic, and, for that matter, of rhetoric too. One question that arises from this reading of the *Phaedrus* is whether an account of the primordial vision could be conducted in dialectical fashion—after all, it is exploring the very ground of the possibility of dialectic. Perhaps the primordial vision would be appropriately treated, instead, by myth. That is by no means an ironclad inference, however, and we shall return to this question in chapter 8 after we have made a study of the Great Speech itself.

CHAPTER FOUR | Writing

Throughout part 1 we have been studying the different "voices" of philosophy—forms of discourse and communication that it may employ—with the aim of seeing how Plato brings them into a harmony. Part 1 as a whole is introductory to the study of the Great Speech, translated in part 2, and the analysis to be made of it in part 3. If philosophy can speak, now in myth, now in rhetoric, and now in dialectic, we shall see, I hope, that the Great Speech brings the voices together in treating the theme of love. But it is just figuratively, of course, that I refer to voices and to speaking. There are only two actual speakers in the present dialogue; our three "voices" are abstractions used for a literary analysis. Moreover, Socrates and Phaedrus are only "speaking" in a literary sense: we do not hear them or see them, but we read the words on the page. Our author was very much concerned with that fact, for, just as he wrote here about myth, rhetoric, and dialectic, he also treated writing and its relation to speech. We cannot doubt that Plato believed that the spoken word was a more appropriate vehicle for philosophy than the written word: that idea is the conclusion of the *Phaedrus.* And yet even this, I think, is not a position Plato held with doctrinaire assurance. I hope to show in this chapter how Plato the philosopher came to terms with Plato the writer, how even writing, in spite of all its limitations, can also express the voices of philosophy.

Socrates and Phaedrus have agreed, back at 258c–d and 259e, to discuss two topics: what constitutes good speech making as opposed to bad, and whether writing is a worthy activity. They have completed the first topic—now, at 274b, on to the second. Socrates approaches it by offering Phaedrus a little fable (evidently Plato's invention, to judge from

Phaedrus's remark at 275b) telling how the Egyptian god Theuth was the inventor of writing, but that when he brought his invention to the king, the latter prophesied that it would bring evils upon human kind, above all the weakening of our power of memory. As Socrates interprets the story, 275c–e, the mistake of Theuth was to suppose that writing represents that which is stable and durable. What is durable can only be the soul itself and what is in the soul—words written on paper at one time may serve at a later time to call up in the soul a memory, but the memory must be actually lodged there already, in the soul. All three of them, Theuth, the king, and Socrates in his recounting of the story, are treating writing merely as the art of recording messages for oneself, not for communication to others. Socrates adds two more significant weaknesses of the written word—and now he clearly goes beyond this hypothesis of a private writing. At 275d, he reproaches the written word for lack of life—it cannot hear what you say or what you ask; it cannot respond to you. Frozen and unmoving, it is to the spoken word as a painted animal is to the living animal. Not only does it fail to explain itself—if you challenge it, it cannot defend itself. Writings need somebody to come to their aid. Moreover, at 275e, Socrates reproaches writing for its publicity or promiscuity—it can come into the hands of anyone including the most unsuited, and it cannot speak differently to different persons or different types, as can a living speaker. He uses the metaphor of the vulnerable girl who needs her father as defender and champion.

The conclusions Socrates draws from these reflections are that one does not put anything serious (*spoudē,* 276c) into written form (later, 278d, he says one does not put valuable things, *timiōtera,* into writing), but uses writing only as a form of play or pastime (*paidia,* 276d) and that one does not write in the expectation of circulating the work and having it come into many hands. One writes fundamentally for oneself, memoranda to give one pleasure in one's old age (276d).[1]

The alternative to writing is the practice of dialectic, described at 276a–e with a brilliant fusion of metaphors—sowing seeds in gardens

---

1. There is at least one commentator who took this conclusion seriously. Lutoslawski, in his *Origins and Growth of Plato's Logic* (cited by Robin in his edition of the *Phèdre,* p. lviv), made the claim that the dialogues were not intended to circulate outside the Academy, but were set pieces to be used within the Academy only for logical and philosophical instruction, like finger exercises for piano students.

and sowing them in souls, forcing short-lived plants or waiting for a true harvest, writing in water and sowing with the pen—and in a moment we shall examine them. First, though, there is the huge question, on which much ink has been "sown" over the decades, of whether Plato himself can possibly have been serious in the denigration of writing. Plato? the master of Greek prose? The likelihood that he was serious is increased if we adduce a parallel passage from the *Seventh Letter* in which Plato (if he is, as I believe, the author) complains of a written summary of Platonic philosophy that had been put into circulation by Dionysius II, the tyrant of Syracuse.

> There is no writing of mine about [the problems with which I am concerned], nor will there ever be one. For this knowledge is not something that can be put into words like other sciences; but after long-continued intercourse between teacher and pupil, in joint pursuit of the subject, suddenly, like light flashing forth when a fire is kindled, it is born in the soul and straightway nourishes itself. And this too I know: if these matters are to be expounded at all in books or lectures, they would best come from me. Certainly I am harmed not least if they are misrepresented. If I thought they could be put into written words, adequate for the multitude, what nobler work could I do in my life than to compose something of such great benefit to mankind and bring to light the nature of things for all to see? But I do not think that the examination, as it is called, of those questions would be of any benefit to men, except to a few, i. e., to those who with a little guidance could discover the truth by themselves. Of the rest, some would be filled with an ill-founded and quite unbecoming disdain, and some with an exaggerated and foolish elation, as if they had learned something grand. (341c–e, trans. G. R. Morrow.)

Oral and Literate Culture

Plato's intent will become clearer to us if we bear in mind that he did not write the *Phaedrus* in isolation—he was responding to many of his contemporaries and to the experience of a cultural transformation of which they were all more or less aware. Among the rhetoricians, in particular, debate ensued about the relative status of speaking and writing, reflecting the entire shift of civilization itself, which reached from the middle of the fifth century to the middle of the fourth, from a culture based on oral communication to one based on writing and reading. The earliest epic poetry had been composed orally, and although poetry was composed in writing after Homer, it remained true until the end of the fifth century that the written poem was destined for oral recitation. Choral odes and lyric poems were like dramas in this way: the rhapsodes might acquire a text, as actors did, but the audience at large would *hear* the work. When Thucydides spoke consciously of his research and how he aimed to preserve in writing a record of the Peloponnesian war for ages to come (*History of the Peloponnesian Wars* I, 22), this was a novelty in writing. And, as I said, it was among the rhetoricians in particular that this became a burning issue. Lysias was reproached for having offered speeches for sale in the market, treating an oration as a commodity instead of as the direct utterance of the soul. The issue came to a head with Isocrates in the fourth century, for, though he was not a legal *logographos* like Lysias, he did treat rhetoric as an essentially literary practice, putting speeches into circulation in written form without ever delivering them from a podium. Isocrates was criticized for this by some of his fellow rhetoricians, Alcidamas in particular, who upheld the tradition of a nonliterary form of oratory.[2]

In the present passage, Plato is striding into the center of this debate, taking sides deliberately against a literary rhetoric such as that of Isocrates, against a literary history such as Thucydides's, and, presumably, against a literary philosophy. But whose literary philosophy would that be? It must be his own. How are we to understand this? Let us look at the way the critique of writing is stated. When Plato intervenes in the debate about writing, he raises the debate from a pragmatic to a philosophical level, for the indictment of writing is stated here by way of the central ontological categories of his philosophy. The written word is nothing more than the image, the *eidōlon,* of the spoken word (276a). This contrast of original and image implies the contrast between the living and the dead (275d, 276a), between the internal and the external (276e), and between knowledge and ignorance (277d).[3] That gave Plato a means for solving the debate about writing versus speech by formulating a philosophical criterion for writing. Writing is legitimate if it is based upon *knowledge,* if the writer himself can defend it *in speech,* and if that writer can *demonstrate the inferiority* of the written product to what he says in living speech (278c). Such a person will then be called,

---

2. On this issue, consult Guthrie, *A History of Greek Philosophy,* vol. 4, 56ff.

3. The broad philosophical import of Plato's point is aptly put by Friedlaender, *Plato: An Introduction,* vol. 1, pp. 110–13 and footnotes.

not a writer but a philosopher (278d). The discussion of writing comes to a conclusion that is closely parallel to the conclusion of the discussion of rhetoric as a whole: where rhetoric (or writing) is deliberately harnessed to research and knowledge, and subordinated to dialectic, it may claim respect. Where writing (or rhetoric) refuses to be yoked to philosophy, it must be condemned. The criterion stated at the end is certainly applicable to the *Phaedrus* itself, particularly the curious third proviso, that the writer, in order to earn the name of a philosopher, must not only be able to come to the aid of the writing but must even be able to show the inferiority of that writing to the living word that defends it: the *Phaedrus* itself makes the case for the inferiority of writing.

But it does so *as a written text.* Is this paradoxical, contradictory? Commentators have sought at times to soften the critique of writing in the *Phaedrus* just because the critique appears in a written text. Ronna Burger has argued that the critique is applicable to a number of literary genres including rhetoric and treatises in theory, but not to written dialogues such as Plato's own.[4]

> The very structure of the dialogue would point to the distance between the Platonic art of writing and that condemned by Socrates in alliance with the Egyptian god-king. . . . Socrates' critique of the silent written word is thus shown to be a condemnation of a part, and not the whole, of the art of writing. . . . Precisely that written work which betrays an awareness of its own lack of clarity and firmness, and thereby demonstrates its knowledge of when to speak and when to remain silent, would reveal the possibility of overcoming the reproach against the shamefulness of writing alienated from Socrates' erotic dialectics. (p. 91)

Griswold, although critical of some details in Burger's account, takes an essentially similar approach, showing how Plato's writing of dialogue in particular solved the problem he thought plagued other kinds of writing.[5] Viewed from this perspective, writing dialogues, with their manifold characters, their possibilities for irony, and their avoidance of heavy-handed statements of conclusion, is not subject to the criticisms stated in the *Phaedrus.* Yet it may be said in reply that although

---

4. Ronna Burger, *Plato's Phaedrus: A Defense of a Philosophic Art of Writing* (Birmingham: University of Alabama Press, 1980).
5. Griswold, *Self-Knowledge in Plato's Phaedrus,* pp. 219–26.

the treatment of writing certainly takes its start in the present dialogue within the context of rhetoric, the critique becomes broadened with the introduction of the fable of Theuth. That story and Socrates' interpretation of it do not seem to be restricted to rhetoric or any other specific modes—they encompass writing as such.

A more extreme thesis than the foregoing ones is Derrida's. His essay "Plato's Pharmacy"[6] grants that Plato's critique of writing was a universal one, not restricted to a few genres. For Derrida, the paradox of a literary critique of literacy expresses a dilemma in Platonic philosophy, indeed in the entire tradition that stems from it, the tradition of Western metaphysics as a whole. Plato's discomfort with writing does give utterance to the deepest ontological categories of his system—original and image, internal and external, and so on—just as we noted earlier and found clearly expressed by Friedlaender among others. At the core of this philosophy is the belief that knowledge and salvation are to be found in the encounter of the soul with true being, above the heavens, in an intuition that is to some degree inexpressible and which if it can be communicated in any way requires the living presence of speaker and hearer, where the spark can leap immediately from soul to soul, the experience of living speech as distinct from the outer medium of writing. The Platonic concept of knowledge, where the soul is present at the scene of true being, is what Derrida has baptized logocentrism, and the favoring of live speech over writing is what he has called phonocentrism. But, guided by the maxim that writing and written language can never be the docile servant of an intellectual's program, Derrida wants to show that writing will play tricks on anyone who takes it for granted, and this generates the dilemma or predicament of Plato and logocentric philosophy generally. There is a prank played by language in the *Phaedrus,* subverting Plato's logocentric, phonocentric intention even as he writes. Take the story of Theuth; according to that god, writing would be for humankind a *remedy* for forgetfulness, that is, a *recipe* for good memory, a *pharmakon* (274e6), a drug. But, said the king, this would be only a *pharmakon* for reminding us of things, not for real memory. As Derrida interprets it, Plato is being led unconsciously by the copresence in the word *pharmakon* of op-

---

6. Jacques Derrida, "Plato's Pharmacy," in *Dissemination,* trans. B. Johnson (Chicago: University of Chicago Press, 1980). The article originally appeared in French in the journal *Tel Quel* in 1968.

posed positive and negative meanings (they are also in the English word *drug*)—both remedy and poison. And this leads Derrida to explore various occurrences in the *Phaedrus* and other Platonic and non-Platonic texts of this word and cognate words like *pharmakeus,* covering a vast semantic field. This "deconstruction" of the text lays bare motifs vitally present in writing itself, that is, in the written language, which work against the conscious intention of the author. This deconstruction of the *Phaedrus* does not stand alone, but is accompanied by Derrida's parallel studies of many literary texts of the tradition, exhibiting on the one hand their determined subordination of writing to speech, and on the other hand, the tricks played on them by written language in return. Jean-Jacques Rousseau, for instance, followed Plato in calling writing a mere "supplement" to speech, yet Derrida shows how the word *supplement,* in relation to its entire semantic field, played tricks on the earnest Rousseau, invoking all sorts of curious political and sexual reverberations.[7]

All the laborious pages of "Plato's Pharmacy" do not shed much light on the *Phaedrus,* for they take us far afield in Greek lexicons and Egyptian history, directing the reader away from the dialogue itself. Nevertheless, Derrida's starting point is surely right, that anyone who communicates a logocentric, phonocentric philosophy in writing is caught in an ambivalent posture. There are, however, more positive approaches to this dilemma than the deconstructive one.

Unwritten Philosophy 1—Dialectic in the Academy

Plato's written philosophy does not stand alone—it is accompanied by unwritten philosophy. But I should like to indicate two different meanings of that controversial phrase.

First of all, unwritten philosophy can refer to a set of doctrines Plato may have held without writing them down or making them evident in his dialogues or which he may have taught to pupils in the Academy without writing them down or making them evident in his dialogues. The most ancient tradition, from Aristotle on, refers to unwritten doctrines of Plato, *agrapha dogmata* (*Physics* 209b15; see also

---

7. This is the argument of pt. 2 of his work *Of Grammatology,* trans. G. C. Spivak (Baltimore, Md.: Johns Hopkins University Press, 1976). French text first published in 1967.

De Anima 404b16–21), and there is some transmission of them not only through Aristotle but through the Academic and Neoplatonic traditions. This point is not at all a novelty of recent research.

But there are contemporary scholars who not only reconstruct the life and teaching of the Academy, but who also postulate a special "unwritten doctrine" of Plato that was confined to oral presentation in the Academy, a doctrine that Plato consciously refrained from publishing. After all, Plato employed the greatest literary skill in all his works. At the opening of the *Phaedrus,* for instance, we can follow Socrates and Phaedrus in their walk up the Ilissos, and in the pages that follow hear their discourses as they sat in a summer's day under the plane tree. Other works evoked the city scenes of Athens and Piraeus in the closing years of the fifth century with equal skill. Yet the brilliant author who laid these scenes always concealed himself—and he was writing decades after these supposedly took place. We do not readily discover this author. Most of Plato's own time was taken up, in the years of his authorship, with the work of his Academy: he was anything but a full-time writer. But the dialogues do not refer to this at all directly.

The modern research on Plato's unwritten doctrine goes back to the French scholar Robin,[8] but it has been made into a major research program by a group of recent German scholars, sometimes called the Tübingen school.[9] There is considerable evidence from ancient times that Plato offered a lecture, or course of lectures, "On the Good,"[10] and, though Plato referred obliquely to the Form of the Good in the *Republic* 504e–509c, he did not in his writings advance beyond the obscurity and mystery conveyed in that passage. But Kraemer and his colleagues believe they can reconstruct this Academy lecture on the basis of indirect evidence of various kinds. It cannot be my purpose here to sift through all their research; but, to summarize their work, they have sought out these doctrines systematically from all the available sources and thereby have given substance to their claims that this is a uni-

---

8. Leon Robin, *La théorie platonicienne des idées et des nombres d'après Aristote* (Paris: F. Alcan, 1908).

9. Hans-Joachim Kraemer, *Aretē bei Platon und Aristoteles* (Heidelberg: Winter Universitaetsverlag, 1959), and his *Plato and the Foundations of Metaphysics* (Albany: SUNY Press, 1990); Konrad Gaiser, *Platons Ungeschriebene Lehre* (Stuttgart: E. Klett, 1963), and his "Plato's Enigmatic Lecture *On the Good,*" *Phronesis* 25 (1980): 5–37. See also Findlay, *Plato: The Written and Unwritten Doctrines,* and Giovanni Reale, *Towards a New Interpretation of Plato* (Washington, D.C.: Catholic University of America Press, 1996).

10. See Ross, *Plato's Theory of Ideas,* pp. 147–49, for the evidence.

tary first philosophy, that many passages in the dialogues can be clarified through reference to it, and that it was not confined to the late period of Plato's teaching in the Academy but accompanied him from the early phases on. One of their techniques is to examine aporetic passages such as the account of the Idea of the Good in *Republic* 509, showing that where the discussion breaks off, Plato was not in a void of uncertainty himself, but rather believed that he could not communicate any more of his doctrine in that literary context. The hypothesis of the Tübingen school has led to some significant reinterpretations of many works, early and late, but particularly of the *Philebus*.

The unwritten Platonic doctrine that Kraemer and Gaiser have reconstructed is a dialectic. It brings together a dialectic of the One and the Many (or the Dyad) with the dialectic of collection and division. Hence, *if* their reconstruction is correct, it will enable us to understand the place of the *Phaedrus* dialectic within a larger whole, and this has the promise of exhibiting unexpected connections among the written works as well—for instance, in Kraemer's view, the *Phaedrus* has close affiliations with the *Parmenides* and the *Philebus*, connections that open up the fullest scope for a dialectic of collection and division.

What is, perhaps, the most controversial and difficult problem in the scholarship devoted to Greek philosophy of the classical period is the question of how to evaluate Aristotle's evidence on the philosophical work of the Academy. On this problem, there seem to be two extreme positions, with a spectrum of positions in between. At one extreme was Cherniss, who maintained that the evidence of Aristotle was almost entirely worthless. In two influential books,[11] he maintains that Aristotle misunderstood Plato's philosophy root and branch and that any correct thing he says can be documented from Plato's written dialogues. So there was no special teaching offered to members of the Academy. Plato's philosophy is found in the written dialogues and only there. Although this is, today, an extreme position, it coincides in practice with a long tradition of Plato scholarship that disregards everything except the text themselves—F. D. E. Schleiermacher's Plato interpretation,[12] for instance, extremely influential during the

---

11. Harold Cherniss, *Aristotle's Criticism of Plato and the Early Academy* (Baltimore: Johns Hopkins University Press, 1944), and *The Riddle of the Early Academy*.

12. Schleiermacher published his German translations of Plato's dialogues, with introductions, between 1804 and 1810.

nineteenth century, made a point of ignoring everything outside the texts.

The other extreme is the Tübingen school, whose members seek not only to excavate the unwritten philosophy from the fragmentary evidence, but to read the written works of Plato in the light of this system that they have reconstructed. It seems there may be truth on both sides and some grounds for a critique of both. Since Cherniss at least does not deny that Plato had an Academy, one must surely reply to him that an active philosopher such as Plato would have said much, or "taught" much, to members of the Academy that did not find its way into his writing. Whether or not Aristotle is a reliable witness, it is extremely unlikely that in oral discussion, Plato never moved outside or beyond his own written texts. On the other side, in reply to Kraemer, the fact that Plato engaged in live discussions, or "teaching," does not in itself imply that there was a different philosophy that he withheld from his writings. Gadamer has warned against the tendency of the Tübingen school to speak of an unwritten philosophy as an *esoteric* philosophy, even, perhaps, at odds with the published work and withheld in secrecy from the public. And in the essay I cite, Gadamer has some shrewd critiques of the manner in which Kraemer and his colleagues have drafted their versions of the "unwritten dialectic."[13] It is one thing to concede an oral practice of teaching to Plato, but quite another to sit down and draw up, *in written form,* a resume of what Plato left unwritten. The difficulty lies not only in gaining access to this so-called teaching, but in bringing it to expression ourselves. It is a hermeneutical problem, similar in some ways to the effort to reread a literary work in the light of what we have divined the author's intention to be.[14] We need to see that the "unwritten dialectic" of Plato is in part unwritable.

Unwritten Philosophy 2—The Critique of Writing

One of the central pillars supporting the thesis of an unwritten doctrine derives from the concluding pages of the *Phaedrus,* 274b–279c,

---

13. Hans-Georg Gadamer, "Plato's Unwritten Dialectic," in *Dialogue and Dialectic: Eight Hermeneutical Studies on Plato,* trans. P. Christopher Smith (New Haven, Conn.: Yale University Press, 1980), p. 125.

14. See Graeme Nicholson, *Seeing and Reading* (Atlantic Highlands, N.J.: Humanities Press, 1989), pp. 219–27.

on the merits and the defects of written speeches, and in fact of writing as a whole. In the course of that discussion, Socrates seems to speak very slightingly of the written word, regarding it as dangerous in some ways, and trivial in others, and in any case far inferior to communication through living speech. Kraemer and his colleagues are convinced that this is a cardinal belief of Plato's, reflecting a deep-seated philosophical conviction. The implication they draw from it is that, given his own views, Plato would hardly have entrusted his most serious teachings to the fallible medium of writing. He would adopt the practice of the dialectician as he himself describes it at *Phaedrus* 276e–277a—plant and sow his words in the living souls of his pupils. Why else have an Academy at all?[15]

Now there is, I think, a second sense of "unwritten philosophy" that is relevant here, and it has shown up in some recent work on Plato—I think particularly of Thomas Szlezak.[16] His argument is in fact deeply interwoven with the earlier arguments of the Tübingen school, and at one level his work is coming to their aid in replying to attacks that have been mounted upon them. Much of his grounding for the case is the same as theirs—he too is dissatisfied with the aporetic passages as they stand; he too is prepared to formulate a system for Plato. Like them, he rests a heavy part of his case on the critique of writing in the *Phaedrus* and in the closely parallel text in the *Seventh Letter.* Yet Szlezak's interest does not lie so much with sketches of an unwritten dialectic as with the claim that in principle philosophy is never complete in its written form. His case differs from theirs not so much in its groundings as in its consequences for the reading of Plato. For Szlezak, Platonic philosophizing is continuous through and through with Socratic philosophizing. No writing can truly institute understanding, as the Egyptian king and Socrates both said, and will always require the living spoken word to come to its aid. Even in the opening passages of the *Phaedrus,* we are shown how the written speech of Lysias stood in need of the aid that Socrates furnished, first in his improvements in its form in his first speech and then in his correction of its content in his second speech. But of course that is only a kind of literary icon repre-

---

15. Kraemer, *Aretē bei Platon und Aristoteles,* pp. 393ff.
16. *Platon und die Schriftlichkeit der Philosophie* (Berlin and New York: De Gruyter, 1985). A shorter version of his argument is "Was heisst 'dem Logos zu Hilfe kommen'?" in *Understanding the Phaedrus,* ed. L. Rossetti (Sankt Augustin: Akademia Verlag, 1992), pp. 93–107.

senting the true relation of living speech to writing, and we realize
from the end of the *Phaedrus* that Plato's true practice was not literary
but to sow the seed of truth into the living souls of his pupils. The same
aim, by implication, is true of ourselves. Plato does not invite us to absorb the doctrines of his dialogues, but to seek out other living philosophers. Szlezak is critical of Burger and other proponents of ironic reading, for they have not admitted the depth and scope of the critique of
writing, still believing that somehow the truth lurks between the lines
of the text. In the spirit of Socrates, says Szlezak, the truth must be
living—and lived.

The alternative to writing that Plato has in mind is teaching,
or what might be better called philosophical friendship, referred to as
synousia, or *koinōnia.* The references here to sowing in souls do not so
much indicate a different, esoteric content, as a certain kind of social
life and practice. If today we look back on the life of the Academy it
should not only be to recover secret teachings but a kind of life. And
the primary issue for Plato is not whether a doctrine reaches the soul
through reading or through hearing, but how philosophy as a whole can
take root in the soul at all. If philosophy is a kind of existence, nobody
can put philosophy on paper.

Yet there is some doubt about whether Szlezak has dealt with a
question that arises here in all its simplicity: why then did Plato write
at all? He was under no institutional pressure to do so, in contrast with
Athenian playwrights and modern academics. If Szlezak is right in
linking Plato so intimately to his master, Socrates, why did Plato depart
from his master on this score? Szlezak is aware that Plato's own answer
to that question would be "My writing is play, *paidia.*"[17] Yet we do not
find in his book an adequate treatment of play, or, what in this context
is the same thing, art. Szlezak's treatment of the Socratic sense of philosophy, and the philosophical life, is excellent, but what we are in need
of now is a further step, an account of the way in which *Platonic writing,* understood as art and as play, arises as a further perfection of the
philosophical life. A few quotations from Wilamowitz may bring us to
a deeper understanding of that matter.

> Socrates needed only the spoken word, and he had made an im-
> pression that could never fade. A book was dead, but speech could
> not stand still—how often Plato said that! This was confirmed

---

17. *Platon und die Schriftlichkeit,* pp. 331–36.

daily in his experience with students, whom he taught by way of
question and answer, and when he sharpened their intellect so that
they could follow him in thought, he won their hearts as well. Writing seemed dead, an unfruitful business, just as mere rote-learning
remained dead. A seed would sprout only when the living word
was sown into a living soul. Neither a bare treatise nor one that
was decked out rhetorically could replace that, and Plato could not
write either of those.

Yet he had to write; he could do no other. He knew it was mere
play, but that point was no hindrance—one just had to avoid over-
estimating it. That we were always in need of play was in fact one
of the truths that he never forgot, though people often overlook it
when they think of his yearning for a higher, purer world. . . . And
writing was the form of play by which Plato refreshed himself. It
might not have more value, or be longer-lasting, than those fast-
growing flowers that the girls prepared at the time of the feast
of Adonis to adorn their garments, and that withered away just as
Adonis himself had to die. Plato sowed fruitful seed in the souls of
his followers, but for his own enjoyment he grew lovely flowers in
the form of these compositions. He could do no other: he conceded
that when he condemned the business of writing even while being
a writer himself.

What drove him to write? This too he asked himself. Self-ex-
amination taught him that he was overcome by something that he
could not resist, and it became clear to him that he really was
a poet. In his haughty youth, the philosophical aspirations awakened by Socrates brought him to the point of throwing his dramas
into the fire, and in his *Ion* he would make fun of poets who did
not keep a sober mind and did not really understand what they
had produced, being overcome by the Muse. Now he could see that
he was no different. . . . Now he had to grant that he had made a
one-sided judgment [concerning poetry in the *Republic*], and now
he took account of his own experience. For what, after all, were his
myths? It was not his intellect that forged his pictures of Hades,
yet they expressed one part of his convictions, just as he was aware
that it was through such offspring of his imagination, gifts of the
heavenly Muse, that he exercised the greatest influence on his
readers. It was in the speech of Diotima that he dared to give utterance to his deepest motivations, but that was not the product of
his intellect. The condemnation of poetry at the end of the *Republic* was followed by a tremendous myth about the soul's primordial
choice in Heaven of an earthly life. Plato had to concede that it
was not at all a contemptible thing, but something genuinely di-

vine, when the poet was overcome by an inner force. And so Socrates' pupil came to recognize that the unconscious was a power that had its own right, a divine right. He had already granted that in principle in the *Meno* when he granted that a statesman could attain his goal under the guidance of right opinion: he had already abandoned his simplistic insistence on pure knowledge. Socrates would not have gone this route. The verses that he wrote in prison were certainly nothing more than imitations of existing models. The compulsion that he felt to write them merely expressed his awareness that the domain of creative imagination had been closed to him. Once, Plato had surrendered to the intellectualism of Socrates, but he came in time to acknowledge, unconsciously, what he had lost—for he always was a poet and not only in his myths. What the more scholastic types criticize as his "mysticism," and what the "mystics" praise as his revelation, is actually his poetic art and poetic power. Even the Idea of the Good was not disclosed to his intellect, for the intellect had to labor to follow the way, and this Idea is truly the God of Plato, to whom he leads those who follow him, and in whom he found peace. It was no logician calculating with concepts, but a poet, who was able to see the eternal ideas. A contradiction may lurk therein, and Plato may have asked himself in great anxiety whether he had a right to take the way of the poet. But now he had the answer, through his recognition of the power of the unconscious, which he tied together—in a poetic way, to be sure—with his doctrine of the soul. . . .

Why then does he write, and why does he write this very dialogue? As he tells us himself, it is play. And why does he play? Anyone who grasps this dialogue as a whole has no difficulty in seeing the answer. He has to write; he is driven by something unconscious, an inner force. This too is a divine madness. The poet within drives him to write, and no matter how low he may set the value of poetry, he lets poetry flourish just as, now, he has let rhetoric flourish. On one condition: one must have recognized the truth and be prepared to defend it (278c), one must have that goal before one's eyes and seek with all one's might to accomplish in words that which will please the gods (273e). Wisdom belongs to God alone, but we can all become lovers of wisdom.[18]

---

18. Wilamowitz-Moellendorff, *Platon,* pp. 453–55, 486.

Socrates' Great Speech
Phaedrus 241d–257b

SOCRATES: . . . There, Phaedrus, that will do. Not another word shall you hear from me. You'll have to let that be the end of the speech.

PHAEDRUS: But I thought you were just halfway through and that you'd have as much to say about the nonlover, and why it was better to bestow favors on him! You were going to pick out all his good points! Why would you stop now, Socrates?

SOC.: My excellent man, couldn't you tell that I'm already **e** speaking in epic style, even more elevated than my dithyrambs earlier, and this when I'm still speaking critically? How do you think I'll end up if I begin to speak in praise of the other man? I will become inspired by the nymphs here—you can see that. In fact, you've purposely thrown me into their clutches! I say, then, in a word, that for all the faults we found with the one, we can ascribe the corresponding virtues to the other. What need is there for a long speech? Enough has been said about the two of them. The tale no doubt will meet with whatever fate it will, and, as for me, I'm going to take my leave now and cross over this river before you force me into anything more. **242**

PHAE.: Oh but not yet, Socrates, not before the heat of the day has gone! Don't you see it's almost noon, the time of day when the sun stands still, as they say? No, stay, and let us discuss all the things that have been said, and then when it's cooled down we can go.

SOC.: You are a prodigy when it comes to speeches,

Phaedrus, really amazing. When I think of all the speeches that
have been produced during your lifetime, I'm sure that nobody
b has been responsible for as many as you—either you composed them yourself or else you forced them out of others in
one way or another. I leave Simmias the Theban out of account, but you prevail over all the others. And even now it
seems that again you are causing me to bring forth a speech.

PHAE.: That's certainly good news. But how does that
come about?

SOC.: Just as I was going to cross the river, Phaedrus, I
had an experience of that divine sign that often comes to me—
c it comes to stop me when I'm just about to do something—and
then immediately it was as if I heard a voice that forbade me to
go away until I had purified myself. For I have sinned against
the divinity. I am a kind of prophet, you see, not very great,
to be sure—I'm like someone who is hardly schooled at all—
but I am at least sufficient for myself, because I do understand
quite clearly wherein I have sinned. Indeed, my friend, the soul
itself is a kind of prophet, for I was shuddering even as I uttered that earlier speech. I feared that I was sinning in the way
d Ibycus meant when he spoke of "doing wrong to the gods so as
to gain the honor of men." And now I know what my transgression is.

PHAE.: What are you talking about?

SOC.: That was dreadful, Phaedrus, a dreadful speech that
you brought along, and so was the one you forced me to give.

PHAE.: Why?

SOC.: It was stupid, and besides that it was virtually sac-
religious. What could be more dreadful than that?

PHAE.: Nothing, if you're right in what you say.

SOC.: Well, don't you believe that Love is a god, the child
of Aphrodite?

PHAE.: So they say.

SOC.: But that's not what Lysias said, nor that speech
e you made me utter, by casting a spell over my mouth. If Love
is a god or in some way divine, and surely he is, then he can't
be bad, and yet that is the way he was treated in those two
speeches. That's why they were a transgression against Love—
they were just a bit of elegant foolishness, and what they said

was neither wholesome nor true, even though uttered with the appearance of a grave truth, enough perhaps to deceive a few **243** little men and earn their esteem. But now I must be purified, my friend. There is an old purification for those who err in speaking about divine things—it was not known to Homer, but we have it in Stesichorus. When his eyesight failed him because he had defamed Helen, he wasn't at a loss the way Homer was. He was skilled, and he was able to understand the reason, and so without delay he wrote

> That was no true word,
> You never went in the well-decked ships,
> Never voyaged to the citadel of Troy. **b**

And so he composed the whole of his so-called Palinode, and straight-away he received his sight. Now on this point I am going to be cleverer than either of those two: I shall try to make my palinode as an offering to Love before I suffer any consequences from having defamed him, and I shall speak with uncovered head, not like before when I covered it up for shame.

PHAE.: Nothing you could say, Socrates, would please me more.

SOC.: All right, my dear Phaedrus, you understand then **c** that to utter both those speeches was shameless, both this one and the one you recited from the scroll. What if someone should have happened to hear us, perhaps a gentleman of fine character who loved someone akin to himself, or who had done so at an earlier time? He'd have heard us saying that lovers are always starting quarrels over the most trivial things, and that they are jealous and abusive in their treatment of those whom they love. Don't you suppose he'd think he was listening to the coarsest kind of people, very badly brought up, people who had never seen anything of a better kind of love? Wouldn't he be far from agreeing with our indictment of Love? **d**

PHAE.: Yes, by Zeus, he would, Socrates.

SOC.: The thought of him makes me ashamed, and now I am frightened of Love, so I want to wash away those bitter words with a sweeter discourse. My advice to Lysias too, for the very same reason, is that he should lose no time in writing a speech on why it is better to bestow favors of the same kind on a lover rather than a non-lover.

PHAE.: Be assured that he will learn of this. If you speak in praise of the lover, I shall make it absolutely imperative for him to do a speech to the same effect.

SOC.: That I certainly believe, you being the person that you are.

PHAE.: So speak away.

SOC.: But where is that young fellow I was speaking to? For he must hear this before he acts on the advice that he ought to indulge the non-lover.

PHAE.: Here he is nearby, and he'll stay as long as you wish.

SOC.: So then, my fine young fellow, you shall bear in mind that the first speech must be attributed to Phaedrus, the son of Pythocles, citizen of Myrrinus. But the one I am about to deliver belongs to Stesichorus, the son of Euphemus, citizen of Himeraius. And this is what we must say:

That was no true speech that said it is right to give your favor to a non-lover rather than a lover who is with you, on the grounds that the lover is mad and the non-lover of sound mind. If being mad were simply and solely a bad thing, that might have been well said. But in fact the very greatest of good things come to us through madness, for madness can be given us by a divine bequest.

It is in the state of madness that the prophetess of Delphi and the priestesses of Dodone exercise their great leadership on behalf of the Greeks, both in private concerns and in public matters, but when they are sensible and of sound mind they accomplish little or nothing. And if we were to speak further about Sibyl and those others who by divine possession give prophecies foretelling with truth many of the things that happen, we would only be prolonging our account with what is obvious to all. Here, though, is something worth mentioning as evidence. The ancients who established the names of things did not consider madness to be shameful or in any way a disgrace—to the most wonderful art, that of telling the future, they attached this very name, *manic,* "madness." They held it to be a fine thing when it came about by a divine dispensation, and thus they settled on the name, though the people of today, in a rather vulgar fashion, have inserted a *t* and call it *mantic.* Now as for the efforts of sane people to tell the future through watching birds and other kinds of signs, originally, this was a craft of guiding human beings through a mixture of Conviction, Insight and Knowledge (all that went to make up the old word *oionoistic*). Since then, the word was changed to *oiōnistic* and people think of it as reading the flight of a bird, *oiōnos*. Now name stands to name as function does to function, and so, to the degree that real prophecy is something higher and more honored than bird-reading, this was confirmed when the ancients recognized the madness that comes upon us from a god as a higher thing than good sense.

d

Second, there have been terrible illnesses and sufferings that afflicted some families owing to ancient crimes and curses, but through a form of madness they find relief: through prophecies, through prayers and service to the gods, and through purifications and rites, that lead them out of danger— both those who perform the rites and their posterity through the following ages. The right kind of madness, then, is the remedy for those in affliction.

e

The third madness comes when the Muses lay hold of a chaste and tender soul, bringing arousal and excitement with odes and other kinds of poetry, and such a one can educate the coming generations by recounting the great deeds of old. But anyone who would approach the door of poetry without the madness of the Muses, believing that technique alone will suffice to make a poet, will be ineffectual himself, and his poems, by comparison with those that were composed in a state of madness, will vanish.

245

Such wonderful things as these, and even more that I can mention, are the result of the madness that comes to us from the gods. So there is nothing here to fear, and we should not be troubled by the argument that we have heard, saying that it is better to be the friend of a sensible person rather than one who is passionate. Anyone who wanted to prove that would have to show the key point, that love is not sent down from the gods to benefit the lover and the one who is loved. Our case will be the opposite, that this sort of madness is the highest happiness given by the gods. The proof may not convince those who are merely clever, but it will carry conviction with those who are wise. What is necessary now, in the first place, is to see the truth about the nature of the soul—that must be about

b

c

gods and mortals alike, both in their affections and their actions. The proof has its beginning here.

Every soul is immortal—for anything that is in motion forever has to be immortal.

Anything that transmits motion to something else, and that receives the impetus for its own motion from something else again, will cease at some point to be in motion. And anything that ceases to move ceases to be alive. But consider that which moves itself. It is not, after all, going to become separated from itself, and for that reason, it will continue in an uninterrupted motion. Moreover, only that which moves itself can serve for others as the spring or origin of their movement.

d   Anything that is an origin is ungenerated. That is because anything that happens can be traced back to its origin, and because this origin cannot have a still earlier origin itself. If it had come to be out of an origin itself, then it would not really be an origin.

And an origin, because it is ungenerated, must necessarily be indestructible as well. For given the destruction of the origin, then neither could it be regenerated itself, nor could that which proceeds from it ever be generated either, not if everything that happens proceeds out of an origin. Thus the origin of movement must lie with that which moves itself.

It is not possible for an origin to be either destroyed or created, for let us suppose the contrary, that such were possible.

e   If that were actually to occur, the entire universe and everything that happens here would come to a standstill, and there would not exist any point from which motion could once again be originated.

What we may properly call immortal, then, is that which has the power of moving itself. Nobody need now shrink from saying that the essence and the definition of the soul consists in this power. Every body whose motion is derived from outside is soulless, but a body whose motion derives from itself has a soul, for that is the very nature of a soul.

246   This being the case, then—that the soul is nothing other than that which moves itself—the soul is necessarily ungenerated and immortal.

That will suffice on the immortality of the soul; something must be said now about its nature. To say precisely what sort of thing the soul is would be altogether too long a tale, something for a god to relate, but a mere mortal may try something smaller: offer a likeness. So let us discuss it that way. Let the soul be likened to the united power of winged horses yoked together, and their charioteer. The steeds of the gods are all noble and of noble breeding, and so are their charioteers. In others, however, it is mixed. In our own case, first of all, the leader drives the pair of horses, and one of the horses is beautiful and good and of the best breeding, but the other is the opposite. Within ourselves, then, it is no easy task to guide the chariot, but necessarily onerous and painful.

b

Now we must try to say how it is that we speak of mortal beings and immortal beings. Every soul has in its care that which is soulless, and it penetrates through to all parts of the heavens, taking on different forms at different times. When it is intact and fully winged, it will fly through the air and supervise the whole universe. But a soul that has shed its wings will be borne downward until it seizes hold of something solid, where it will settle down and take on a body of earth. This body might look as though it were moving itself under its own power, but a living being is the whole thing, soul and body joined together, and that is what we mean by "mortal." As for the immortal, we do not usually discuss it in any consistent way, but, never having seen such a thing or given it sufficient thought, we visualize a god as a kind of immortal creature endowed with a soul, but a body too, the two of them joined together for all time. On matters such as these, however, let it stand in whatever way would be pleasing to the god.

c

d

Now we must look into the reason for the loss of wings and their falling from the soul. It happens this way. It is in the power of wings to raise on high that which is heavy, lifting it up to where the race of the gods dwells, and, most of all bodily parts, they have a share in the divine. That which is beautiful and wise and good, and everything of such a nature, is divine, and from all this the plumage of the soul will be nourished and made to grow. And it is corrupted by all that which is vile and base, and opposed to goodness, until it is utterly destroyed.

e

The mighty ruler in heaven, Zeus, driving his flying chariot, leads the way, mustering all and caring for all. The ranks of gods and spirits follow after him, arrayed in their eleven

247

divisions. For Hestia remains alone in the house of the gods. The others, then, as many of them as are numbered among the twelve ruler gods, they too lead the way according to the order in which each of them has been appointed. Many are the majestic sights within the heavens, and the pathways on which the race of blessed gods go coursing, each doing what is his to do. And any who so wishes, and who has the power, may follow in their train, for no envy is to be found within the company of the gods. When the gods go up for their banquet and their feast, soaring to the uppermost heights of heaven's vault, their chariots move with ease, for they are balanced well and obedient. But the others ride with difficulty. For the horse whose nature is base weighs heavily, and sinks downward toward the earth, unless the charioteer has trained him well. And it is now that the soul confronts its uttermost struggle and pain within.

Whenever those that we call immortal go up to the summit of heaven, they go outside and take their stand right on heaven's rim, and as they stand there they are carried along by the rotation and see the things that are outside the heavens. No poet here on earth has ever sung of that place above the heavens, and none will ever do so fittingly. Yet now we ourselves must dare to speak about it truly, because our very theme is truth.

It is thus. Far beyond all that is colored and all that has shape and all that you can touch, there is being that truly is. It is glimpsed only by the charioteer of the soul. And that is the place for the things that become known by the only kind of knowledge that is worthy of the name. For as the mind of a god is nourished by unmixed reason and knowledge, so it is for every soul so far as it takes pains to receive what is fitting for it. If it is gazing out upon that which is, at length it will be content, and seeing truth it will be nourished and made well. And then the revolution of the heavens will bring it back again.

As it soars through its cycle, it looks out upon justice itself, and it looks out upon temperance, and it looks out upon knowledge, but not the kind of knowledge that comes to be, that which, always varying in some way, stands within the domain of the variable, the domain that people today call the real. No, this is the knowledge that belongs together with that which has true being. And it looks out upon all the rest of them; it sees everything that enjoys such true being, and it feeds upon it, and then, coming back again inside the heavens, it returns to its home. When it has returned, the charioteer takes the horses to the manger and feeds them with ambrosia and gives them nectar to drink. Such is the life of the gods.

As for the other souls, the best of them, having followed a **248** god and become like him, would have raised up the head of its charioteer into the place above, and been carried along with the rotation. But with the struggling of the horses, it has had difficulty in seeing the things that are. Another one would be now rising and now sinking, and driven by the power of the horses, it would see some things, but not others. And others are striving upward and straining to follow though they cannot; carried along below the summit, they trample on each other and jostle, each one trying to get in front of the others. In this **b** uproar and struggle and sweat, many are injured because the charioteers have failed, and many suffer broken wings. For all their great pains, they have not been initiated into the true vision, and they depart, and turn to feed upon food of semblance. And their great zeal to see the truth on its own plain arose be- **c** cause out there, on that meadow, is the pasturage that is the best of all and most fitting for the soul, for it nourishes the virtue of the wings by which the soul is borne aloft.

Here now is the decree of Necessity. Any soul that has been able to follow along with a god and to see something of truth will remain safe until the next cycle, and, if it is always able to do this, it will remain unharmed forever. But whenever it cannot follow and does not see, and through suffering some mischance it is struck with forgetfulness and evil, it will de- scend. Heavy-laden and without wings, it falls down to earth. And the law is that, this time, in its first birth, it will not be **d** planted into a beast. Rather, the one who has seen the most will enter into human seed, for a man who is to be a philoso- pher or a lover of beauty or a music maker and lover; the sec- ond will enter a seed for a lawful king or a warrior and ruler; the third into a politician or businessman or merchant; the fourth into a trainer or gymnast or someone who cares for the physique; the fifth into the life of a prophet or a priest of **e** the rituals; the sixth into one who makes imitative poetry or other compositions; the seventh into a craftsman or farmer; the eighth into a sophist or demagogue; the ninth into a tyrant.

In all these lives, anyone who conducts his life with justice may expect a better fate, and one who lives unjustly a worse. For a soul does not return to the place from which it was sent **249** out for ten thousand years—the wings cannot grow before then—except for someone who engages fully in philosophy or who loves and raises the young in a philosophical way. Such a person may complete three periods of one thousand years, and if that soul should choose that same life three times in succession, it can gain back its wings after three thousand years and fly away. But the others, when they have completed their first life, must be brought to trial. Some of them will be condemned to go beneath the earth to a place of punishment to make full payment of what they owe. Others will be borne aloft by Justice to a place in the heavens where they will lead a life worthy of what they merited when they lived in human form. Both of **b** these, then, in the one thousandth year, will come to make the choice of a second life according to their wishes. Now a soul could go into the life of an animal, or one who earlier had been human can come again out of the animal into a human frame. But a soul that has never seen truth will not enter into this frame. For it is by way of a form that human beings comprehend something that is said, something that comes out of many **c** perceptions and is gathered into one through reasoning. This is their recollection of those things that at one time our soul saw as it journeyed with a god. Then it ignored the things that people now call real, while mounting up to that which truly is. Hence it is right that the mind of the philosopher alone should regain its wings, for it remains eternally close in memory to those things the proximity to which gives to a god his very divinity. The man who keeps the right memory of these things has the initiation into the greatest mysteries and he alone will **d** become truly perfect. Standing apart from all the affairs of men, he moves toward the presence of the divine. Though the world at large thinks he is out of his senses, it is a divine inspiration that he has within, hidden from the many.

Everything we have said up to this point has concerned the fourth kind of madness, the kind in which, when somebody sees beauty here, he is reminded of true beauty and he becomes winged. With new-grown wings he would eagerly fly again and yet he cannot. Like a bird he looks upward, taking no thought for things here below, because he has been visited with a madness. It is the highest kind of divine possession, it **e** comes from the highest source, and it is the best, both for the one who has it and those who keep company with him. It is because of sharing in this madness that the lover of beauty is given the name of lover.

According to what we have said, every human soul, by nature, has seen the things that are, or else it would not have en- **250** tered into this creature. But it is not easy for every soul to be reminded of them by the things that are here—not for those who then saw what was there only briefly, or those who by some misfortune were cast down here and through keeping bad company have committed unjust deeds, quite forgetting the holy things that once they saw. Just a few remain who still retain a sufficient memory, those who, whenever they see here a likeness of what is above, are amazed and lose control of themselves, in a passion they cannot understand because their **b** discernment is not sufficiently clear.

Now justice and temperance and other things prized by the soul do not really gleam with splendor, nor do their likenesses here below, and owing to the dimness of our organs, when we come upon their copies here, we are barely able to discern the things of which they are the copies. But beauty at that time was bright to see when that joyful throng—we ourselves following along with Zeus, the others with the other gods—saw the blessed and divine vision and celebrated the rites that have been ordained most blessed. And we ourselves were whole then as we made our celebration, not afflicted by **c** the evils that were in store for us in the time to come; whole and simple and serene, we were initiated into the most joyful mysteries, witnessing them in the pure light, for we ourselves were pure, not entombed as we are now in what is called a body, fettered like an oyster in the shell.

Let that be the homage to a memory that led me to speak at greater length of the former things for which I yearn. As for beauty, as I have said, it stood among the others, and it was radiant. And here, we apprehend it through that sense of ours **d** which is the clearest, for beauty glitters most brilliantly. Sight is the sharpest of our bodily senses. Wisdom is not seen by us: how powerful our love for it would be if it had ever appeared to us through an image we could see! All the others too we would surely love. But this is ordained for beauty alone, as being the most radiant and the most to be loved.

e Now when one who has not been newly initiated or who has been corrupted sees a namesake here of beauty itself, he cannot quickly make the step from what is here to the beauty that dwells beyond. So he looks at it without reverence and he yields to pleasure. Mounting up in the manner of a four-footed beast, he sets out to beget children. He is driven by a wanton urge to have sex and, fearing nothing and ashamed of nothing,

251 he even pursues pleasures that are against nature. On the other hand, with one who has been newly initiated or one who saw the former things extensively, whenever he should see a god-like face or bodily form, he is easily reminded of beauty. And first he shivers and there comes over him a kind of ancient fear and, as if he were seeing a god, he is filled with reverence, and if he were not afraid of appearing to be utterly mad he would offer a sacrifice to his beloved youth as if he were the statue of a god. With the sight of him, he is moved by a shiver and seized

b with sweating and an unaccustomed warmth. Beauty streams in upon him through his eyes, bringing warmth and moisture where the wing grows. With the warming the outer parts begin to melt, for earlier a stiff shell had closed it off and shut in any power of growth. But with the flow of nourishment, the wing swells and begins to grow from the root and the stem, and it spreads over the entire form of the soul. For earlier the whole soul had been winged.

c And now the whole soul is seething and throbbing, and, just as with the pain when a tooth has grown in, and the gums are ticklish and irritated at once, so the soul is affected when the wings begin to sprout. It seethes and throbs and is tickled as the wings grow. Whenever it looks upon the beauty of the youth, all its parts are overtaken with this gushing—and this is

d what we call desire—as the warmth and moisture bring it relief from pain. But when it is separated from him, the soul becomes dry and the openings where the wings grew become parched and choke off the buds of the wings. Inside, where the desire has been blocked, there is a throbbing as the roots of the wings push against the block, stinging it all around. The whole soul is goaded, surging back and forth between its anguish and the memory of the beauty of the beloved. The soul is troubled by the mixture of its unexpected passion and the frenzy of its release, and so it remains. It cannot sleep by night nor can it remain still by day—off it runs, yearning to know where it might see its beautiful one, and when it does see him, the flood of desire overwhelms everything that had been blocked off before. It recovers its breath, and feels the ceasing of all its spurs and pains, and it tastes the sweetness of pleasure in the presence of the beloved. And from there it will not readily take its leave, and it finds nothing worthwhile except its beautiful one. It forgets mother, brothers, and friends, caring not at all if it should lose all its possessions, and indifferent now to everything customary and everything lovely that had once been its pride. It is ready to sleep where a slave would sleep if only nothing prevents it from being near to its beloved. It worships him and his beauty, and he alone can be the physician for the soul's great pains.

Now, my fair young man, to whom I am speaking, this passion is what human beings call love, but the gods call it something else that may amuse you as a young man. It was some of Homer's followers, I think, who had some lines that are not widely known, and two of them were about Eros—rather rude lines, I must say, and not very metrical:

Mortals call him Eros in his flight,
But the immortals know he makes the wings [Pteros] to sprout.

Perhaps you will believe this, perhaps not, but it will do for the moment on the cause of the passion of love.

A follower of Zeus who becomes seized by love will show his weighty nature, and will be well able to carry the burden of the winged god. But when one who followed in the company of Ares in the circuit of the heavens is captured by love, he may often think that his beloved has done him some wrong—and then he is ready to kill, ready to sacrifice both himself and his beloved boy. Thus depending on the god in whose throng each person belonged, he will still honor and imitate that god as far as he can while he is uncorrupted and living in his first incar-

e

252

b

c

d

nation, and this is how he will act both toward his beloved and toward everyone else. Each one has love for the kind of beauty that is in his own fashion, and, as if he were erecting a monument to the god and adorning it, he honors and celebrates his

e beloved. Those who were followers of Zeus seek a beloved of the very same nature, and when they see someone with a philosophical nature and the gift of leadership, they love him, and they do everything that promotes such a nature. If they have not entered upon this pursuit before, they endeavor to learn the way to the best of their ability and to continue practicing

253 it. They look within themselves to track down the nature of their own god, because they have the need to gaze upon their god. Grasping him in memory, celebrating him, taking from him their code and their whole conduct of life, they come to share as far as is possible for human beings in the divine. But all this they owe to their beloved, and so they love him even more. If they have been led by Zeus, then they pour out their wine like the Bacchants, pouring it into the soul of their beloved so that he too will come to share in the likeness of their

b god. Those who were following after Hera seek out a royal nature, and when they have found him they do the same things for him. And so it is with those who followed Apollo and each of the other gods: according to which god it was, they go about seeking a boy of a suitable nature, and when they have found him, they themselves imitate their god, and then persuade and educate the boy to adopt those ways, following the pattern as

c far as possible. They show no jealousy, no hardness or cruelty toward him, but rather they do what they can to lead him to be like themselves and like the gods that they honor. This is the wish of all those who love truly and perfectly. If they can accomplish what they wish in the way that I have said, and if the lover can capture his friend, they may live a beautiful and happy life, bound together by love and persevering in friendship. Here now is the way the friend may be captured.

At the beginning of the story, we divided each soul into three parts, two in the form of horses, and the third part in the form of a charioteer. Let us return to that now. Of the two

d horses, one was good, we said, and one was not, but we did not say what constituted the excellence of the good one or the vice of the bad one—so let us now look into that. The one that stands on the right is of an upright form and figure, with a high neck and a noble nose, white in color but with black eyes. A lover of honor, temperate and modest, he pursues genuine glory and he needs no whip, but responds to commands guided by the word alone. The other horse is big and crooked, with a **e** formless body and a thick, short neck, snub-nosed with black skin and bloodshot white eyes. He is lustful and boastful, shaggy around the ears, and deaf—he needs to be goaded by a spur and even so he hardly submits. When the charioteer looks into the eyes of the beloved, the whole soul is warmed by all the senses, it is tickled and stricken with the pangs of long- **254** ing. The obedient horse, still governed by its habitual modesty, stops himself from leaping at the beloved, but the other horse is not even restrained by the spurs and whip of the charioteer. He springs forth, pulling the whole chariot along with him, his companion horse and the charioteer, forcing them to approach the boy to remind him to offer them the favors of sex. The other two are vexed and resist his force, lawless and dreadful **b** as it is, but finally, when they are at the limit of their pains, they give way and follow along with his prompting. But as they approach the beloved boy, they are dazzled by the beauty of his face. Then there comes upon the charioteer again the memory of the nature of beauty itself, and now he sees it, raised up alongside temperance on a pedestal of purity. Seeing the idea, he is awestruck, he falls back before it, drawing the reins backward at that moment, hard enough to force the two horses **c** back on their haunches. One of them obeys without resistance, but the lustful one does so most unwillingly. By the time they have backed farther away, the first horse has soaked the soul through and through with sweat, partly on account of his shame and partly because of his amazement. The second horse, recovering from the pain of the bit and his fall, can only breathe with difficulty, but then he takes to complaining in anger, reproaching the charioteer and the other horse for being timid and unmanly, and departing from what they had agreed on. Still they will not consent to approach the boy; with diffi- **d** culty they make the unruly horse acquiesce by begging him to delay it to another time. When that time has come, though they pretend to have forgotten, he reminds them—pushing, neighing and pulling—and he forces them to approach the boy once

e again with the same proposition. When they get near, he
pushes his head down and stretches out his tail and bites on
the bit, pulling on it shamelessly. Yet the charioteer still has the
same feelings, even stronger by now, and, just as with a racing
team that falls down at the starting gate, he pulls back the bit
with the greatest force on the teeth of the lustful horse,
bloodying his foul-speaking tongue and his jaws, and forces his
legs and hips down onto the ground, causing him the greatest
pain. Now when the lustful horse has suffered such pain many
times over he is finally humbled, and he will obey the wishes
of the charioteer. From this point on, whenever he sees the
beautiful boy, he will practically die of fright. So the soul of
the lover has come to be in harmony with itself, and it reveres
the boy and follows him in an attitude of awe.

255 And so the beloved enjoys every possible favor, waited on
as if he were a god, and not by one who makes himself act like
a non-lover but by someone who really is a lover through and
through. Moreover, this boy is likely to be a natural friend, in
any case, for the one who is attending him. It may be that the
people he went to school with, or perhaps others, tried to poison his mind, saying that it is a disgrace to associate with a
lover, and made him send any lover away. But time goes by, and
as he matures and comes to see the necessity in things, he is
b ready to admit the lover into an association. It is not the way
of things that the bad should be friends with the bad—nor that
the good should not be the friends of the good. He awaits the
lover's attentions both in words and friendship, and as he
grows nearer to the goodness of the lover's own nature, he is
astonished, realizing that all his other friends and family do
not offer him a friendship that can compare with the one that
has been inspired by a god.

As the lover continues to do all these things, and seeks out
the boy, perhaps embracing him in the gymnasium or in the
course of other pursuits, this is the source of that stream that
c Zeus called "desire" when he was in love with Ganymede. It
breaks in upon the lover, and as it sinks into him he is filled
up to the brim, so that it overflows and runs off outside him.
And like a wind or an echo that bounces back from the
smooth rocks and returns to its source, so the stream of beauty
is borne back again into the beautiful one through his own

eyes. It reaches right into his soul, and when it arrives there, it makes the wings grow: the mouth of the wings is watered and **d** they start to grow, and now the soul of the beloved too is filled with love. He loves, but he knows not what—he does not know what it is, nor has he anything to say. It is as if he had caught an infection of blindness from the eye of the other. The lover is to him like a mirror: he can see himself there, but without any recognition. And so whenever the lover is with him, his pain is relieved, just like the lover's, but when the lover is far away, he yearns for him just as the other yearns for him in return. He has the copy of the love, a counterlove, although he **e** thinks of it and calls it a friendship rather than love. But he too has a desire that is just about the same as the lover's, though it is weaker; he wants to see him, touch him, kiss him, and lie down with him, and very likely he soon does what he desires. As they lie together, the unruly horse of the lover starts to urge the charioteer that, after all the pains he's been through, it's time to give him a bit of release. The boy's horse, however, has **256** nothing like that to say—he is swollen, to be sure, but he doesn't understand. He embraces the lover and kisses him and shows himself most well disposed to him, and, when the two of them lie together, he would not refuse to do his part for the gratification of the lover if that's what he really wants. But the boy's companion horse and charioteer stand opposed to that with modesty and reason. Now if it comes about that the two of them enter into an orderly life and practice philosophy, so that the better part of their minds has prevailed, henceforth **b** they will lead a blessed life in harmony of mind. Strengthening themselves, well ordered within, they will enslave that by which evil enters the soul, and liberate that by which virtue enters. At the end of their life, they will have become winged and light, having won a victory in one of the three rounds of this, the true Olympiad. No greater good that this can come to any human being, neither through human temperance nor through divine madness.

But it could be that they embark on a more coarse and **c** unphilosophical way of life, perhaps devoted to the pursuit of honor, and then, sure enough, under the influence of drink or through some other kind of negligence, the undisciplined horse can seize command of the unwary soul. The two will be led together into that act so many people call a blessing, and when they've made that choice they will do it again. So they would

d continue for the rest of their lives, but with restraint, for that is not the wish of the entire soul. Such a pair will be friends with one another, though less so than the other pair, both at the time of their love and in the years that follow. They believe that they have given and received the greatest things from one another, so that it would never be right for them to be estranged. At the end, they will depart from the body wingless, to be sure, yet their wings have begun to grow, and it is no small prize that has come to them by way of the madness of the lover. For the law releases all those who have embarked on the journey up toward the heavens from the fate of having to go down into the darkness under the earth. As they journey in the light, happy

e with one another, the grace of love will furnish them both with wings at the appointed time.

So great and so divine, then, is that which the friendship of a lover gives to you, my young man, whereas that of a non-lover is mixed with a kind of worldly prudence, and results in a calculative form of life. It will breed in the soul of the be-loved a vulgar hardness; though many may speak in praise of

257 such a thing, it leads to a fate of wandering around for nine thousand years upon the earth, and then, as a dead soul, down under the earth.

And now, dear god of Love, this has been the Palinode to pay what is owing unto you, the best and the loveliest that was in our power. If some of our words have had to be poetical, that was for the sake of Phaedrus. Will you now forgive our earlier words because of these ones, and be merciful to me because of the art of love which you gave to me. Do not in your anger take it from me or make it weak, but grant that ever more I may be honored by those who have beauty. If, in the words we spoke

b before, Phaedrus and I have given you offense, it was because of Lysias, the begetter of the speech. Will you put an end to these his speeches, and turn him to philosophy like Polemar-chus his brother. And may his lover here cease from double-mindedness, and devote himself in all simplicity to love and philosophical thought.

The Philosophy
of Love

This is a dialogue that celebrates Eros as a god, no mere demon or spirit intermediary between gods and mortals as in Diotima's speech in the *Symposium*. That is the cumulative point of the three speeches in the *Phaedrus*. The first two speeches constitute an abuse of the god and create a need thereby for Socrates to make the third speech in vindication of the god. In the *Bacchae* of Euripides, Pentheus, the young ruler of Thebes, wants to stamp out the worship of Dionysius that has enlisted even his own mother Agave. In lofty contempt, he dismisses the claims of this god, and, not recognizing Dionysius himself when he appears in Thebes, throws him in prison. But prison cannot contain the god, and, when Pentheus creeps out to spy upon the Dionysian revelers by night, he is torn limb from limb by a pack of revelers led by his own mother. At the end we hear:

> Agave: Terribly has Dionysius brought disaster down upon this house.
> Dionysius: I was terribly blasphemed, my name dishonored in Thebes.[1]

The *Phaedrus*, by contrast, is a peaceable work, and the vindication of Eros undertaken by Socrates is a speech that replies to the previous speeches, a dialectical triumph as well as a rhetorical one. The speech itself is a work of love, inspired by the god Eros (243d3–4), offered to him at the end in a prayer (257a–b), and throughout spoken as if to a young man in a kind of love speech (243e4–8).

---

1. *The Bacchae,* trans. William Arrowsmith (Chicago: University of Chicago Press, 1959), lines 1375–78.

Love's divinity is a theme for philosophy once it is no longer wedded to the purity of an abstract dialectic and can recognize its own kinship with myth and rhetoric. When Socrates is compelled to break off his antierotic discourse, he is reminded of ancient truth in the ancient myths, and he introduces Phaedrus to the place of Eros among the whole panoply of gods—our theme in chapter 6. Pondering the gods leads Socrates into new and unaccustomed depths in the study of the human soul—our theme in chapter 7. Before Socrates can give his definitive reply to Lysias, he must chart the eternal homeland of the soul, its own kinship with truth and true being—our theme in chapter 8. Then he is able to offer the true and adequate account of love and beauty—our theme in chapter 9.

I hope to show that the ancient debate, whether love or rhetoric is Plato's principal theme, postulates an unnecessary Either/Or, a choice between examining a discourse and examining the topics of the discourse, a choice philosophy cannot make. This debate has been revived recently, guided now by studies of the dialogue's literary structure.[2] Rowe (and in this he is followed by the translators Nehamas and Woodruff in their introduction to the *Phaedrus*) subordinates the theme of *erōs* to that of rhetoric in order to rescue the last half of the dialogue from the status of a mere appendix or afterthought. Heath's reply casts doubt, correctly, in my view, on the need for "one primary theme." At the end of chapter 5, I'll return to the connection between the theme of love and the theme of rhetoric.

---

2. C. J. Rowe, "The Argument and Structure of Plato's *Phaedrus,*" *Proceedings of the Cambridge Philological Society* 32 (1986): 106–25; M. Heath, "The Unity of Plato's *Phaedrus,*" *Oxford Studies in Ancient Philosophy* 7 (1987): 150–73; Rowe, "The Unity of the *Phaedrus:* A Reply to Heath," *Oxford Studies in Ancient Philosophy* 7 (1987): 175–88; Heath, "The Unity of the *Phaedrus,*" *Oxford Studies in Ancient Philosophy* 7 (1987): 189–91.

Two Speeches against Love
Phaedrus 230e–234c, 237b–241d

Dialectic is certainly the ruling method of philosophy in the *Phaedrus,* and it forms the substructure of the work. The dialogue takes its start from a thesis against love by Lysias, which is then supported by a speech of Socrates, both of them in preparation for the counterthesis, the defense of love stated in the palinode. Accordingly our study of the palinode is prefaced by an examination of the first two speeches, looking this time at their content rather than their form, appraising them as philosophical treatments of the theme of love. Before that, a word on the social and ideological setting of the debate is in order.

Social Setting: Greek Homosexuality

The speech of Lysias, with which Plato introduces the topic of love in the *Phaedrus,* is given in a completely down-to-earth tone, and although it does concern love, its actual focus, we might say, is sex. That is, the speaker is concerned especially with sexual desire and with love triangles, which are really triangles of possession and desire. We are to imagine, first of all, somebody smitten with love, an *erōn* or *erastēs,* lover. Then we are to imagine the person who is the object of his love, the *erōmenos,* beloved. And then there is the third party, the rival, who wants to make love with that same person, the *erōmenos,* but without being in love, the *mē erōn,* non-lover. He wants sex without love, we could say, and he makes this speech to persuade the *erōmenos* to yield to him and to dismiss the lover. It is indeed a clever speech, and we are not surprised that Phaedrus would admire it. But readers today must sense a social and sexual background behind this speech, which Phaedrus and Socrates, but not ourselves, can take for granted. We shall bring some of that into the foreground, so as to be able to grasp the particular angle of Lysias that stood in contrast with common opinions and thereby captivated Phaedrus.

There was a segment of Greek society at that time that particularly celebrated the powers and the gifts of love. Plato himself placed a statue of Eros in front of the Academy. Phaedrus is portrayed in Plato's *Symposium* as a devotee of the cult of love, as are the other speakers in the *Symposium:* Pausanias, Eryximachus, Aristophanes, Agathon, and Socrates himself. One element particularly stressed by Phaedrus's friend Eryximachus is the universal power of love: it moves not only humans but all the animals and even plants; it drives the fluids through the bodies and guides the seasons of the year (*Symposium* 186a–b, 188a). In expressing the cosmic power of love, Eryximachus is drawing upon the earlier philosophy of Empedocles, for whom the ultimate powers in the universe are Love and Strife, *Erōs* and *Eris.* Phaedrus himself, in the *Symposium* 178b refers to the even more ancient teachings of the poet Hesiod, for whom Eros was one of the first gods to be born and ancestor of many others. But it was in the human scene, of course, that the devotees of Eros saw its great power, though they often differentiated between a creative heavenly form of love (heavenly Aphrodite and Eros) and carnal sexual urges. Not only philosophers—the tragedians too represented the raging power implanted in men and women by the earthly Aphrodite. Euripides' play *Hippolytus,* first performed in 428, showed the wildness that came upon Phaedra, wife of the king Theseus, because of her uncontrollable desire for Hippolytus, the king's son by his first wife. Shame and rage drove her to her death.

But in the background of the Platonic text, there is this further variant of love—a homosexual world. It was a culture that existed from about the sixth century onward, up to a time much later than Plato's death. This setting is assumed in the *Symposium* and the *Phaedrus:* the homosexual triangle that constitutes the setting for Lysias's speech is still assumed in the background of the two speeches Socrates offers and in the analytical discussion in the dialogue.

Kenneth Dover has sketched the main features of this particular culture by studying not only the literary texts of Plato and other authors, but also historical evidence bearing on the behavior of different classes and the record of the visual arts, especially pottery.[1] His studies have confirmed the old view that sexual relations among men were particularly common, beginning in the armed forces of Sparta, and that during the fifth century the custom grew increasingly among Thebans, Athenians, and others, initially in the army and then outside it. Even in civilian life in the fifth and fourth centuries, women remained isolated from the social, financial, and intellectual life of men, at times living virtually in harems. Older citizens and priests frequently condemned the practice of homosexual love, but despite that it did gain hold in the upper classes, and there is some evidence for it in lower classes and also among women. It was not often openly defended, and it never entirely lost its stigma. Plato is the first literary author to discuss it at all fully, and he himself is ambiguous and ambivalent about it.

The custom as it existed at the time of Lysias brought together a man in his mature years with someone in late adolescence, a *meirakōn* or *meirakiskos*, around eighteen or twenty years of age, no longer a child, not quite a man, a liaison that might last two or three years at most. The man was usually married, with children of his own, and the boy (as we may call him) fully expected to take up sexual relations with women and in a few years to get married. At 237b2, Socrates begins his speech, "There was once a boy [*pais*]," but immediately corrects himself, "or rather a young man [*meirakiskos*]." The first term was too loose, since it can mean "child," and children were not involved in these liaisons. Yet later, once the clarification has been made, Socrates reverts (e.g., 237b4) to a looser idiom and calls this fellow a *pais* after all—others would use the word with that meaning, and Socrates does not want to be fussy and technical. What the man derived from this liaison was a *charis*, favor, a sexual favor that usually took the form of intercrural sex (*crus*, meaning thigh, leg) in which the man, embracing the boy from the front, thrust his penis between the boy's thighs and came thus to climax. The usual idea was that the boy experienced no sexual pleasure from this encounter: it was a favor bestowed. In return, the man would undertake to become a patron to the boy, introduce him into his social world, and watch over his education.

Dover has shown from the visual evidence of the vases that the idealized boy in these relationships looked a lot like a woman and that

---

1. Kenneth Dover, *Greek Homosexuality* (London: Duckworth, 1978).

intercrural sex looked a lot like heterosexual relations in the missionary position. Since, moreover, these were temporary relations between a man, usually married, and a boy who expected to be, this is evidently something quite different from the modern experience of homosexuality. To speak of these ancient Greeks as being gay is faulty optics, and to introduce the modern concept of sexual orientation is confusing. Taking this term in the contemporary sense, we must say that these ancient Greeks had no sexual orientation. Men had sex with women and with men (i.e., "boys"), and there is more evidence today that women too could have varying sexual partners. All this, of course, varied by region and by social class and was changing with the decades. But, for us, the point is that all these sexual relations were expressions of *erōs*.

Considerable light has been thrown on this by the modern philosopher-historian Michel Foucault. His analysis of this world, and, briefly, Plato's treatment of it, is one part of a study of the historical differences that separate ancient *aphrodisia* from the divine institution of Christian marriage and all the other variants of love and sex throughout Western history, up to our modern discourse about "sexuality."[2] Foucault has made us aware of the provincialism and "presentism" of a good deal of modern thinking about ancient and medieval and early modern life.[3] For Foucault, it was the framing of that word *sexuality* in the nineteenth-century that actually gave birth to the thing itself, along with its variant subforms such as homosexuality. This was the consequence of the "medicalizing" of erotica in nineteenth century discourse.[4] In other words, these Greeks did not divide persons into classes or types according to sexual behavior, or according to their inner "orientations" that would yield such differences of behavior. The "homosexual" as a type of character was constituted in the nineteenth century along with other types that were seen in the nineteenth century according to the optics of medical pathology. Among the ancient Greeks, there were different kind of sexual acts, but anyone could perform them; persons were not differentiated by orientation. The Greeks we are looking at saw *ta aphrodisia* alongside the other pleasures offered

---

2. Michel Foucault, *The Use of Pleasure,* vol. 2 of *The History of Sexuality,* trans. Robert Hurley (New York: Vintage, 1985).

3. Ibid., pp. 187–225.

4. See Foucault, *The History of Sexuality,* vol. 1, trans. Robert Hurley (New York: Vintage, 1978).

by life, such as food and drink,[5] the use of which was to be regulated for the achievement of excellence.[6] To achieve excellence was the goal of the serious man. Enslavement to sex or to any such pleasure would debase a person in character or in body. Foucault's point is well illustrated by the speech of Lysias in our text, for it paints a dark picture of the obsessed lover, so besotted with sexual desire that he is ruined as a man.

As in all his historical studies, Foucault puts at the center of his treatment the "code" that guided the Greeks in their experience of *ta aphrodisia*—the regulation and the discourse by which the individual brought his or her behavior into line with the governing structures. This aspect of Foucault's analysis is in accord with the "structuralist" milieu in which he first worked out his thought. Foucault does not specialize in the subjective experiences of love or in the poems or Platonic dialogues that gave expression to the experiences. He is interested in how people discern the code by which to live, not in exploring the inner terrain of feelings. If by love, or *erōs,* we mean a passion of the soul, Foucault, we could say, avoids it in favor of the reconstruction of a whole "economy." Foucault even attempts to justify his avoidance of the deeper issues by accusing Plato of "displacing the very object of discourse,"[7] away from social codes onto ontology or metaphysics.

I have highlighted one or two aspects of the social setting of Lysias's speech, for the purpose of showing what made that social background different from modern-day practices. The modern reader should keep it in the back of his or her mind in pondering Lysias's argument, but avoid the error of thinking that homosexual sex is the *topic* of the speech. The fact that the *erastēs,* the *erōmenos,* and the *mē erōn* are all male is not the aspect that Lysias, or Plato as the author of the dialogue, wanted to put before us for our judgment. Much closer to the moral content of the speech is the factor of inequality between the man and the "boy." Unequal in age, the two of them are therefore unequal in social status, and they have opposite goals, though symmetrical and compatible, in entering into their sexual relationship. This is true equally whether the "boy" yields to the non-lover or to the lover. A little later in the chapter, I will offer some modern parallels to prove that

---

5. Foucault, *The Use of Pleasure,* pp. 46–51.
6. Ibid., pp. 53–62.
7. Ibid., p. 236.

the moral issue posed by Lysias's speech—inequality—is as vital to modern societies as it is to ancient ones.

The *Erōtikos* of Lysias, 230e–234c

Lysias is seeking to subvert the ideology of love. This was the common hypothesis of all the speeches in the *Symposium,* of course, but in addition to that the speech of Lysias is also sweeping aside the vast array of human experience—Eastern or Western, classic or romantic, religious or secular—that shows a reverence for love. Along with all these heritages, the *Symposium* speeches mean by the word *love,* or by *erōs,* both our sexual experience, *ta aphrodisia,* and a passion deep within the soul. But Lysias detaches the one from the other, *ta aphrodisia* from the passion, and instead of venerating that great passion of the soul, he finds nothing good in it, neither for the lover nor for the beloved.

To analyze the speech now in more detail than we did in part 1, we can say that it ties everything to the concept of advantage, *sympherein,* mentioned at the opening of the speech (230e7), or benefit, *ōphelia,* mentioned at the end (234c3). It is a utilitarian speech. There are, perhaps, twelve distinct considerations that show how the non-lover can be more to your advantage than the lover, stated in order after the opening appeal of the speech starting at 230e6. We can take an overview of them, identifying them with their opening lines:

1. 231a2: The lover is driven by a passion, which will someday come to an end, but the non-lover consorts with you purely out of free choice.
2. 231a6: The lover will always blame you for distracting him from his business affairs, but not the non-lover, who always puts business first in any case.
3. 231b7: A lover is nice to you as long as love lasts, but later on he will prefer someone else—it is a madness he has.
4. 231d6: If you are wondering who can do you the most good, why restrict the field to those who happen to be in love with you?
5. 231e3: Lovers boast of their conquests, which will certainly make you an object of gossip; non-lovers are discreet.
6. 232a6: When you are seen with a lover, everyone knows what for; being seen talking with a non-lover raises no suspicions.
7. 232b5: Lovers' quarrels are the bitterest.

8. 232c4: The lover cuts you off from beneficial contacts; the non-lover is happy to see that you secure advantages.

9. 232e3: It is sexual desire that motivates the lover, not admiration for your character—but the non-lover is a friend first of all.

10. 233a4: Lovers flatter you because of their desires; the non-lover tells you the truth about yourself.

11. 233d5: If we yielded to people just because of the urgency of their desires, would we not end up inviting beggars to our feasts instead of our friends and those who are good?

12. 234b1: A lover often brings friction into your family, but not a non-lover.

In my commentary, I shall highlight three aspects of Lysias philosophy, referring to these considerations by the numbers preceding the line locations.

First, Lysias's speaker (remember that the speech was composed for a sort of client, someone seeking to win a boy over; strictly, Lysias is not speaking for himself) differentiates the parties in a love triangle according to the roles they take on in social life. Thus the speech's style is close to that of social comedy; it does not characterize persons according to any inherent disposition or moral character. Its point of view is external, visible behavior, and what results may be expected from this course of action or that course of action; there is no probing into an inner life. The triangle contains three "types": lover, beloved, non-lover. Each of them is positioned in a broader network of family, city, and business acquaintances. What the "beloved" might hope to gain from the lover is patronage, education, and introductions, and the non-lover is trying to convince the boy that he can expect more in that line from him. One difference between Lysian utilitarianism and the Benthamite version of the nineteenth-century is that the former sets a greater value on reputation, being thought well of. This is an "outdoors" ethic, a Mediterranean ethic of *la bella figura*. Modern utilitarianism attributes value, no doubt, to reputation, but more as an instrumental value, for to be thought honest and clever will bring you further advantages that are more substantive. In Lysias, one of the greatest advantages you might expect from the non-lover is a positive influence on how you may appear to others, get along with them, and incur their admiration. Thus in argument 5, the lover will go around boasting of his conquest of you— to your shame—whereas a non-lover will be discreet. In argument 6, everyone will immediately think the worst when you are seen with a lover, but will not jump to this conclusion when you are seen with a non-lover. The sanction of social shame remains very operative for Lysias, and indeed for the tradition of Greek rhetoric as a whole; in this way, it has not changed from the shame culture of earlier decades.[8]

Second, in many passages of the speech, the emotional involvement of the lover is always spoiling whatever benefits you may have derived from him—but not so the non-lover. In argument 1, the non-lover acts freely and voluntarily, whereas the lover does not, being driven by a passion. Argument 3 states that the lover has no control over himself, and argument 5 says that the non-lover has complete self-control. According to argument 2, the non-lover's coolness gives him the lucidity to identify his own interest, and we see in argument 10 that the same coolness makes him able to calculate what will be in the interest of the beloved as well. It is the clear mind and self-possession of the non-lover that are needed to identify what is advantageous and to pursue it with an effective course of action. The lover, driven by passion, is also volatile and unreliable (arguments 1, 3, and 9). Not only may he desert you—he is not in a position to improve your mind (arguments 9 and 10). Moreover, his jealousy separates you from friends, family, and teachers (argument 8).

Last, the man who brings you benefits will make you excellent; he does not just flatter you, but gives you the guidance you need (argument 10). His guidance will therefore produce solid and justified self-esteem in you, not the mere pleasure of being sought out and praised. Here, especially, we note that the speech is being delivered to a younger person. The moral is that the connection to a powerful person is in your best interests. But the lover, by contrast, is like a beggar, a leech, a parasite (argument 11). Moreover, non-lovers offer a broader field to choose from if you are in search of good connections or improvements of any kind (argument 4).

A Modern Application

The social, sexual context in which Lysias composed his speech is remote indeed from what most modern readers know. And yet this speech and the others of the dialogue bring before us the psychological

---

8. See E. R. Dodds, *The Greeks and the Irrational* (Berkeley and Los Angeles: University of California Press, 1963), chap. 2, "From Shame-Culture to Guilt-Culture."

reality of love, and the reactions it provokes in those who feel it, those who do not feel it, and in those who interact with both groups, in such a way that a reader living in a vastly different world can still recognize love. Love itself, in its highest and its lowest forms, is a permanent reality of human life, not identical to a particular social setting in which it may appear, and Plato's thought is more universal than the homosexual setting he assumed, a matter we shall take up in chapter 9.

Consider a different social structure. Literary narratives, for instance, from the eighteenth-century up to our own time, and modern lyrics, dramas, and movies, give a profile of love in which, at times, the things we hear in Lysias and Socrates leap out at us again. Suppose it is not a boy of nineteen but a girl of nineteen. Suppose the issue is not whether she should yield sexually, but whom she should marry. Suppose the story is told, not from the viewpoint of the older suitor, as it was by Lysias, but from the subjective viewpoint of the young person herself. It may be a novel rather than Plato's device of an oratorical competition, that presents the crisis

Jane Austen's novel *Persuasion,* published in 1818, signifies even in its title the moral territory Plato has explored. The heroine is Anne Elliot, who, at nineteen, has fallen in love with Captain Frederick Wentworth of the Royal Navy, as he surely has with her. Yet her family, in particular Lady Russell, exercise their persuasion upon her to break off the match, which they deem "a very degrading alliance . . . a most unfortunate one." Lady Russell laments: "Anne Elliot, with all her claims of birth, beauty, and mind, to throw herself away at nineteen, involve herself at nineteen in an engagement with a young man who had nothing but himself to recommend him, and no hopes of attaining affluence, but in the chances of a most uncertain profession, and no connexions."[9] Anne is constrained by formidable and coercive persuasion to refuse Captain Wentworth's offer of his hand. Lady Russell has a different candidate in mind, the future lord of the manor of Kellynch. In the English novel, it is the family, not the seducer, who try to tie up the girl. "I own that to regard you as the future mistress of Kellynch, the future Lady Elliot, . . . my dearest Anne, would give me more delight than is often felt at my time of life,"[10] proclaims Lady Russell. Indeed, Anne is moved and excited by the prospect offered by the future lord. And yet

---

9. Jane Austen, *Persuasion* (Harmondsworth, England: Penguin, 1965), p. 55.

10. Ibid., pp. 171–72.

> That he was a sensible man, an agreeable man,—that he talked well, professed good opinions, seemed to judge properly and as a man of principle,—this was all clear enough . . . but he was not open. There was never any burst of feeling, any warmth of indignation or delight, at the evil or good of others. This, to Anne, was a decided imperfection. . . . She prized the frank, the open-hearted, the eager character above all others. Warmth and enthusiasm did captivate her still. She felt that she could so much more depend upon the sincerity of those who sometimes looked or said a careless or a hasty thing.[11]

Like so many modern novels, *Persuasion* focuses mainly on the feelings of a young person, in Anne Elliot's case love for one man and absence of love for another. That differentiates it to a degree from the speech of Lysias, in which the boy's own feelings were treated with indifference. Modern literature as a whole manifests a greater subjectivity than Plato's work: the emotional response of the woman is a matter of the greatest importance to it. But the difference should not be overstated. Her love for Captain Wentworth answers to his love for her, in its warmth, enthusiasm, and sincerity. Her lack of love for Mr. Elliot (the future lord) corresponds to the coldness of this man of calculation, good sense, and lack of openness. We are, then, able to say that the persuasion exercised upon Anne by her family was indeed that she should prefer the non-lover over the lover, in this way replicating in a modern context the morality of Lysias.

Socrates' First Speech, 237b–241d

We saw in our earlier treatment of rhetoric that both at 235a and at 263a Socrates is scornful of the lack of form in Lysias's address and that when he proceeds with his own address, 237b–241c, it had a more adequate backbone.

237b–d. An address should begin by defining the thing under discussion, which in this case is love. Lysias has dealt only with the various parties to a love triangle and has given no attention to the inner nature and power of love itself. This is the first defect to be remedied. See also *Symposium* 194e–195a, where the poet Agathon, influenced by Gorgias,

---

11.   Ibid., pp. 172–73.

begins his speech about love by arguing that the speakers who had preceded him that evening had not really dealt with love itself, but only with its effects. Of course, there is something faintly ludicrous about beginning the present speech with a definition. It is not supposed to be a showy *epideixis* like Agathon's speech but words addressed to a boy to win him over. One might not find that exact definition was the best strategy in a seduction! Still, Socrates does proceed with it, and he offers the variations and types, not of love itself, but of that genus of which love is a member, *hybris,* meaning wantonness or lewdness.

Because my interest is the morality of the speech, rather than historical details of a long-lost social world, I shall take the liberty of introducing feminine pronouns along with masculine pronouns during the following exposition. Socrates' criticism of *erōs* here proves to be strikingly similar to some modern feminist critiques of masculine love-making and the culture of romantic love.

237d–238c. The human soul contains two forces that compete to offer direction: a natural or innate desire, *epithymia,* for pleasure, *hēdonē,* and an acquired judgment or opinion, *doxa,* concerning what is best, *ariston.* The well-ordered soul subordinates *epithymia* to *doxa,* but in the diseased soul (see 238e4) there is maladjustment—*epithymia* has gained the mastery. Such a condition in general is called *hybris,* and it arises in one form where our desire is fixated on food contrary to good judgment (gluttony), in another case on drink (drunkenness), and in another case on physical beauty (love, *erōs*).

238e–239c. Whoever suffers from *erōs* is not only in a pathological state himself—he will bring harm to others and particularly to the object of his love, the *erōmenos.* The unrestrained sexuality of the lover begets the urge for domination, and it begets possessiveness. First of all, the mind and thought of the beloved must be mastered and no independence allowed him (or her). His (or her) information must be controlled and restricted so that the opinions of the dominant lover will prevail. He (or she) will be sealed off in the house, with as little outside contact as possible.

239c–240a. Next, the lover will regard the physique of his beloved as a mere sex-object, affording stimulation for him. He (or she) will be kept cozy and slack, with plenty of make-up, instead of being invigorated with exercise. As the ultimate expression of the urge to dominate, the lover will resent any independent wealth of the beloved as well as resenting his (or her) family and friends.

240c–241c. The sexual gluttony of the aging lover is repulsive. And then, with the passage of time and the cooling of his ardor, he will be revealed as entirely self-serving.

Indeed this is the picture of a foul and repulsive love. But the interpretation of this speech is one of the most controversial topics in the literature on the *Phaedrus*. There are commentators who see in this description a genuine phenomenon, a kind of love that presents us with a moral danger. To quote Hackforth, "The whole attitude of the speaker, unlike that of Lysias's speaker, shows a real concern for the welfare, especially the moral welfare, of the boy, a concern which it would have been unconvincing to attribute to a genuine cold-blooded sensualist. . . . In the substance of all this there is nothing un-Socratic or un-Platonic; indeed we may see in it the popular germ of Platonic psychology which . . . is firm-rooted in common human experience."[12]

Let us add to that the earlier analysis by Grube.[13] According to him, the moral point of view presented by Socrates' first speech is far higher than that of the speaker in Lysias: "[i]t very obviously is a thoroughly sound attack upon immoderate physical passion, mere brute infatuation." The speaker shows himself a true friend in warning the youth that if he yields to such a passionate lover, he will be rendered physically unfit, a mere creature of convenience to the dominant lover, and economically subject to him. Yet this certainly raises some questions: it *is* difficult to take this speech straight-forwardly as a Platonic moral lesson. What does Grube make of the interruption of the speech, when Socrates refuses to continue it, so as to give the equivalent praise to the non-lover? "Here, as is not infrequent," says Grube, "Plato's humor has misled most of his commentators" (p. 108). He seems to mean that Socrates' sense of having transgressed in his criticism of *erōs* was only humorous. Presumably, then, he must find the invocation of the "divine sign" to be humorous as well, for the divine sign intervenes to warn Socrates that he must make recompense for his insult to *erōs*. "Of the substance of his magnificent indictment of mere physical erotic madness he does not need to retract a single word" (p. 108). Although he does not quote Shakespeare here, I am led to think that Grube reads Socrates' speech against love quite solemnly, as in the lines of Shakespeare's Sonnet 129.

---

12. *Plato's Phaedrus,* ed. Hackforth, pp. 40, 42.
13. G. M. A. Grube, *Plato's Thought* (London: Methuen, 1935), pp. 106–8.

Th' expence of Spirit in a waste of shame
Is lust in action, and till action, lust
Is purjurd, murdrous, blouddy, full of blame,
Savage, extreame, rude, cruell, not to trust.[14]

Such is one current in *Phaedrus* scholarship, but we need to see that there are other possible lines of interpretation. In Ferrari's analysis, the imagined speaker impersonated by Socrates is repressing his own *erōs,* and, owing to self-hate, painting *erōs* itself in ugly colors.[15] This subtle analysis takes the speech not at all as expressing an antierotic moralism, but as a kind of character sketch or psychoanalysis of the kind of lover who resorts to concealment. The earlier commentators were certainly less subtle than that!

To attempt further progress in interpretation, let us (1) compare the speech with other Platonic dialogues and (2) scrutinize it in light of later pages of the *Phaedrus.*

1. It is possible to read this speech as harmonizing with the morality of other dialogues, very likely much earlier works, in which a kind of intellectualism was expressed. Though this similarity might be found in the *Gorgias* and elsewhere, the text that comes most readily to mind is the *Protagoras,* in particular 351b–358d. In this famous and profound passage, Socrates is seeking to convince Protagoras that knowledge is all-sufficient for the regulation of life and for the constitution of human virtue. He shows that in many situations in life we appear to be tempted away from virtuous action through the enticements of pleasure, and he introduces the common opinion that although we know what is right to do, we are overcome instead by pleasure. But the deep conviction Socrates expresses in this passage is that it cannot be our *knowledge* that is overcome in situations of temptation; we are overcome because of *absence* of knowledge, *defective* knowledge; we fail to measure the evils that will be brought upon ourselves through intemperate or cowardly action. Though Socrates is advocating a revolutionary moral thesis, he is certainly also working with a dualism of psychic elements that a person of the era would accept as valid: on the one side our appetite for immediate pleasure; on the other side, our knowledge

---

14. I quote from *The Penguin Book of English Verse,* ed. John Hayward (Harmondsworth, England: Penguin, 1956), p. 64, which reproduces the spelling of the first edition.

15. Ferrari, *Listening to the Cicadas,* pp. 97–102.

or lack of knowledge concerning long-term goods and evils. The strong soul, furnished with knowledge, never yields to temptation—in fact, very likely, does not experience temptation—but the weak, ignorant soul is seduced by pleasure into courses of action that produce great evils in the long run.

The *Phaedrus* text is a parallel in being generally dualistic in its view of the soul. Here, however, the power in the soul that stands against appetite is only opinion, opinion formed through experience and training—Socrates cannot call it knowledge. Presumably, he would not, since here he is dealing with a weak soul, self-indulgent with respect to sex. Had he gone on to praise the strong soul, the non-lover, he would probably have shown that he had knowledge, which would be powerful enough to govern his appetites and pleasures. The *Protagoras* defended such an ethics of autonomy and strength, expressing scorn for self-indulgence in all its forms, including the weakness for food, drink, and sex. This *Phaedrus* speech echoes it by reducing *erōs* to one of the vices that had been charted there, self-indulgence in sex. Yet I sense a coldness in the present *Phaedrus* speech that goes beyond anything in the *Protagoras* or other early works, and I think Plato would have realized that, in its attack on *erōs,* it exceeded any speech he had written for Socrates before.

By linking the *Phaedrus* speech to earlier Platonic work, we see that *some part* of its morality had roots in his earlier thought, particularly in the Socratic intellectualism that had some hold over Plato's early years. In the present dialogue, by setting out an extreme anti-erotic position to be refuted, he is cleansing himself of whatever intellectualism he may have had in his younger days. That will be fulfilled in the palinode, which does not remain with a binary opposition in the soul, but reveals its true threefold constitution.

2. We have already noted, in chapter 3, that the speeches of Lysias and Socrates are subjected to analysis in the later pages of the *Phaedrus,* and here we can pursue that discussion, particularly to see whether it casts light on the moral position of Socrates' first speech. We noticed that when the speeches were made subject to a dialectical analysis, 262c–266c, certain differences crept in: the speeches were now arranged in a new kind of order, exemplifying the two parallel divisions of madness and love, demonstrating the dialectical method of collection and division. Dialectic has taken us to a sovereign, elevated standpoint where, looking downward, we comprehend the generic unity of things that at first had not seemed to have this connection. For in our

first reading of the *Phaedrus*, we came upon the first speech of Socrates as a companion piece to Lysias's speech, contrasted with it in point of form but not content, since Socrates was to make the same points, but make them better. The first reading took both of them rhetorically. Here there was no hint that the *erōs* under discussion might not be the whole of *erōs;* that the earlier *erōs* is incomplete is precisely the point that is made later as we proceed into the retrospective analysis. Later in the dialogue, when we learn to interpret the speeches dialectically, we learn that the Lysian speech and Socrates' first speech have dealt only with one-half of love, the bad half, leaving the other, good half to be treated in the palinode. And in our first reading of the palinode we took it rhetorically too; that is, we took it as an outright attack on the two speeches that insulted *erōs* and as the vindication of *erōs.* Socrates does not state at this point that there is a bad kind of love, which Lysias and he have been right to attack, though to be sure the invocation of divine madness at the start of the palinode does leave the door open to the idea that there are other, all-too-human kinds of madness under which we might comprehend one kind of love. The rhetorical effect of the palinode is that it is treating *erōs* as such, *erōs* as a whole, and in this light the atmosphere is one of contending with the earlier speeches, disputing them.

But it is decisive for the interpretation that this rhetorical effect, or the rhetorical reading, cannot be removed by the subsequent dialectical reading. We do not forget that Socrates had to do penance for his blasphemy of Eros. And in the impact of the dialogue as a whole, this rhetorical point remains important. It would be a misunderstanding to suppose that the good kind of love and the bad kind are two neutral species or divisions of love, indifferent to one another. The truth is that the bad kind of love is a corruption of the good kind, a disorder of love, love falsely directed. A dialectical discussion of the two kinds of love that did not see that point would be a faulty dialectic indeed. *Therefore, the rhetorical force of the palinode remains.* The palinode is making war upon the two previous speeches, for they had confused the bad kind of love with love as a whole. Though there may be a bad kind of lover, there is something even worse: a false rhetorician who condemns love as a whole by failing to see that the bad kind is a corruption of the good kind. Lustful and selfish love is bad, but even worse is the blasphemy that rules out the spiritually creative love as well as the possibility that a human being could be led on to the good love even after beginning with the bad.

And love and rhetoric themselves are not utterly unrelated things, a point that helps us to understand the unity of the *Phaedrus*. First of all, if we think of love, can we suppose that it would never be given expression in speech? Can we love without speaking to the one we love, and without speaking about love? Could we even experience love in the absence of language? Or, on the other hand, if we start out from the topic of rhetoric, it should be clear that some speeches can be made in a spirit of love, and other speeches can be made without love or in violation of love, up to the point of being speeches of hatred. Love, then, is certainly connected to the power of speech; one of the manifestations of love is its expression in speech.

The Gods
Phaedrus 241d–244a

At 241d Socrates interrupts himself; his enthusiasm is ended, and he
will say no more. He says (241e) that he has broken out into dithyrambs
and even epic verse, due to the inspiration of the local nymphs; later
(242b), he ascribes it to the inspiration of Phaedrus—in any case, he has
been carried away. Some scholars accept these avowals of possession seriously, and therefore see some degree of possession, demonic or divine,
from local divinities or nymphs, in Socrates' first speech.[1] When Socrates launches on his second speech in a still greater state of possession,
then, they read the dialogue as containing a progress by degrees, going
through the moderate degree of possession in the first speech, mounting up to a more exuberant possession in the second. Against that interpretation, we must note that the first speech is consciously composed
as a rhetorical exercise in competition with Lysias to rectify formal
weaknesses in Lysias's rhetoric, so its inspiration is human, all too human. Socrates' first speech begins with a sort of burlesque (237a–b) that
makes a parody of inspiration; 235c–d also parodies the inspiration of
poets. Moreover, Plato would have had little reason to present an *anti-
erotic* speech as due to divine or demonic inspiration. More fitting, I
think, is to see it as a bit of Socratic irony to characterize a rather pe-
destrian speech as being inspired through his possession by nymphs.
The speech has been thought out with conscious human calculation,
and it is halted now by the outraged conscience of Socrates, who is

---

1. Hackforth, for one; see *Plato's Phaedrus,* pp. 36f., 47. Griswold, *Self-
Knowledge in Plato's Phaedrus,* pp. 51–57, supplies a corrective.

ashamed of having participated in a mockery of the gods. Therefore, I think, the theme of inspiration and the divinities does not enter into the *Phaedrus* when Socrates begins his first speech. It enters first when he ends the speech, at 241d. The present juncture is the point of turning in the dialogue, a conversion from frivolity to what is serious, and from impiety to what is divine. The exchanges after Socrates breaks off his speech are laced with the language of religion, inspiration, and divinity.

Now first of all, 242b–c, there is the "divine sign" of Socrates. This famous phenomenon has no evident connection to any religious tradition and is historically unique to Socrates, a component of his personality. It is a sign (*sēmeion*) that comes to him, usually as a voice (*phōnē*) that gives him a warning. We have encountered it before, in the *Apology* (31c–d, 40a–b, 41d), the *Euthyphro* 3b, the *Euthydemus* 272e, and the *Republic* 496c. (The other Socratic phenomenon, a trance in which he could stand abstracted for hours at a time—see the *Symposium* 174d–175d—should not be confused with the divine sign.) In the *Apology* this sign is called both divine (*theion*) and demonic (*daimonion*), but in all the other texts including the present one the adjective is *daimonion*. As he tells the Athenian jury in the *Apology,* his sign never orders him positively to do something, but only offers warnings—in the context of the trial, the point is that he has received no such warning in making his defiant speech of self-defense. Here in the *Phaedrus,* the sign or voice has warned him that he may not take his leave of the spot by the Ilissos until he has offered a fitting expiation for the offense his first speech had given to the god. His is a private and subjective "spirit" or god, but it shows up here in the milieu of traditional Athenian gods and spirits and intervenes on behalf of the well-known god Eros, celebrated by many Athenians, not only Socrates.

We must observe that the sign does not intrude until *after* Socrates has decided, on his own initiative, to break off the oration, and *after* he has expressed his disgust over his own speech and, by extension, that of Lysias. It is Socrates' own ethical judgment that terminates the speech, and it would have prompted him to leave, but the supernatural sign requires still more of him, an act of recompense to the god. In the other dialogues, too, we must suppose that the purely human virtue and wisdom of Socrates are at work in his deeds and words, and that the sign is granted him as a further gift only because he has already judged well and done well by his own human standards.

If the divine sign is unique to Socrates, its way of appearing in the *Phaedrus* is also unique in Plato's work. In the other texts we mentioned, the divine sign is just referred to by Socrates or one of the other characters. But here it breaks in to interrupt the action. The speech of Socrates ending at 242a2 announces his intention to leave, and then Phaedrus starts (242a3) trying to persuade him to stay: "Oh but not yet, Socrates, not before the heat of the day is gone." But we know from the speech of Socrates about fifteen lines later (242b8–242c3) that, just as he was announcing his intention to leave, the divine sign came to warn him that he must not leave before completing an act of expiation. The reader ought to mark the text with an asterisk right at 242a2, when Socrates finishes his speech of farewell, to signify the moment when the divine sign comes to inhibit him. In the books of the Roman Catholic mass, there is sometimes entered a mark of the cross to signify the moment of the consecration of the bread and of the wine. So here the asterisk would signify the intrusion of the divine sign into the action of the dialogue. Although it acts in silence, and although Plato wrote no stage direction for it, the action of the sign at that moment gives the dramatic action of the *Phaedrus* its most important turn.

Another clarification is called for here concerning the route Socrates and Phaedrus take on their walk. The older accounts offered by Thompson and Robin are fairly detailed but leave one significant point open.[2] When Socrates and Phaedrus settle down under the plane tree, this must be on the eastern bank of the river, the left bank; they have crossed over from the city side.[3] This becomes evident at 242a–c. Socrates has been making his speech to denigrate love and lovers, and he breaks it off. He announces that he is going to leave "and cross over this river before you [Phaedrus] force me into anything more" (242a). At precisely this moment, the inner voice comes to Socrates, to warn him that he must make a correction. So he tells Phaedrus, "just as I was going to cross the river, I had an experience of that divine sign that often comes to me . . . and it forbade me to go away" (242b–c). This is the clue about the location. Partly in shame, partly in disgust, Socrates wants to

---

2. *Phèdre,* "Notice," pp. xix–xx. Robin allowed for either a left-bank or a right-bank location. W. H. Thompson, in his 1868 commentary, *The "Phaedrus" of Plato,* commenting on 229c, located the plane tree much farther upstream than later scholars did—his claim was that he had found the actual spot during a tour of Athens in May 1856.
3. The location is rightly identified by R. E. Wycherley, "The Scene of Plato's *Phaedrus,*" *Phoenix* (1963): 88–92, and by Luc Brisson, *Platon, Phèdre* (Paris: Flammarion, 1989), pp. 29–32.

get away from Phaedrus. But why is Socrates out there beside the river in the first place? He is always in the city (230c–d). What has led him out is only the prospect of hearing Phaedrus and learning from him what Lysias had been expounding (227d, 228b–c, 230d–e). Now that he is eager to escape Phaedrus, would Socrates be proposing to escape deeper into the Attic countryside? Of course not. He would escape back into the city, "crossing the river" back toward Athens. Therefore, the setting for the greater part of the dialogue is on the eastern bank of the river, opposite the city.

At 242b–243e, it is Socrates' own sign that introduces all the talk in the text about gods and goddesses, blasphemy and purification. Socrates has sinned against divinity (*hēmartēkota eis to theiōn,* 242c3). And the lines that follow are suffused with the language of religion: his soul has been a prophet, *mantikos,* 242c7; now he realizes his transgression, *hamartēma,* d2; the speeches have been shameless, *anaidōs,* 243c1 — much of this the language we recall from the *Euthyphro.* That it is the god of Love, Eros, who has been offended in this way becomes clear a little bit later (*hēmartanetēn peri ton Erōta,* 242e4), where Socrates puts to Phaedrus the challenge: does he not acknowledge that Eros is indeed a god or something divine (*theos e ti theion ho Erōs,* e2)? Eros, coeval with Earth itself in Hesiod, was, according to later traditions the child of Aphrodite. On the other hand, Eros had an equivocal status in Greek poetry and myth over the centuries. Homer never speaks of Eros as divine; he has a psychological understanding of *erōs* rather than a theological one: it is the passion of sexual desire (*Iliad* I, 315, XIV, 315; *Odyssey* XVIII, 212). Yet those in later centuries who, following the lead of Hesiod, asserted the divinity of Eros were inclined to attribute this belief to Homer too. In Plato's *Symposium,* Phaedrus and Pausanias, asserting the divinity of Eros, also ascribe that belief to Homer. In the *Symposium* it is Socrates who denies that Eros is a god. But now in the *Phaedrus* he repents of that idea. Having offended Eros by the first speech, he states that "Now I must be purified," 243a2–4. Just as at an earlier time the beautiful Helen was dishonored by verses of the poet Stesichorus, and he was punished by blindness until he purified himself by an ode of recantation, so here the offense done to Eros by Socrates must be expiated by a new speech that tells the truth. The majesty of Eros will be Socrates' theme from 244a to 257b. In that great speech there will be copious references to other gods along with Eros, above all to the Olympian divinities, Zeus, Hera, Apollo, and the rest of them. These gods appear as leaders of the hosts of lesser spirits, demons, and human souls on their flight through the heavens, and, especially in 246 and 247, as the leaders and marshals of philosophy. In addition to the Olympian deities of the Great Speech, we find throughout the *Phaedrus* a wealth of references to Olympian and other deities and besides that a still broader array of subjects that are called divine, *theios.*

Religion: Traditional and Orphic

We shall make a closer approach to the topic of the gods by an examination of Greek religion and Plato's relation to it, and particularly the aspects of religion that are prominent in the *Phaedrus.* For a treatment of Plato's view of traditional religion, one can consult the book by Michael Morgan.[4] We can trace Plato's interest in religion right back to the *Euthyphro,* the critical attitude of which reappears in the *Republic,* in the speech ascribed to Adeimantus, 362d–367e, in his dialogue with Socrates. It is likely that both Adeimantus and Socrates, in their dialogue, express two sides of Plato's own convictions, the one being the brother with whom he had shared his childhood, the other being his guide in philosophy. Adeimantus appeals to Socrates to offer a better rationale for justice than the usual sort. We must ask whether the religious teachers who, as he recounts, offer their contemptible case for conventional morality are intended to represent religion itself in Plato's view, or have they also distorted religion, corrupting it with double-mindedness? It would seem that the speech of Adeimantus can be read either way, as an indictment of religious instruction as such, or as exposing a corrupt form of it. It is only in the dialogue of the succeeding pages that we are able to discern that the latter was Plato's intention. Later in the same book, at 376e, Adeimantus has returned to the discussion after his brother, and he begins to ask Socrates how the instruction of the young can be improved, what stories about the gods the youth should be told, and what stories from the rough Homeric tradition should be kept from the young. Socrates is not at a loss. He proceeds to a critique of Homer's theology (*theologia,* 379a—the only occurrence of that term in Plato), applying to the stories his own philosophical form of reasoning, improving the stories by the criterion of what is fitting for a god to be and to do. In his constructive theological reply to Adeimantus, Socrates is also speaking for the author Plato. The

---

4. *Platonic Piety* (New Haven, Conn.: Yale University Press, 1990).

mythical ending of the *Republic,* with its own doctrine of rewards and punishments after death (and the comparable passages of the *Gorgias, Phaedo,* and *Phaedrus*) do not, in his mind, violate the sensibility, so beautifully expressed, of his brother Adeimentus.

Adeimantus has referred to different tendencies in Athenian religion, and Orphism is one of these, a religion that was to leave a notable mark on some of Plato's dialogues, the *Phaedrus* most of all. The reader often senses in Plato an ancient and complex religious background, for instance, in the passage in the *Meno* 81, where Socrates invokes mysteriously the ancient teachings of the "wise," and "priests and priestesses." The reader wants to gain some understanding of that religion apart from and before Plato so as to grasp what was at work in his mind. And there are many studies of the Orphic tradition. Some of what scholars have discussed concerning myth and ritual, priesthood and mode of life, does not appear in Plato and may not be directly relevant to his writings. Though his writings were shaped perhaps by a religion, the philosopher also mutated it, and from his texts one may not recognize the prephilosophical form that the religion had. Fortunately, however, there have been scholars who have been able to pull together the earlier tradition and its later impact. I must mention in particular, among authors to aid the reader of Plato, W. K. C. Guthrie and Walter Burkert. Guthrie's full-length treatment of Orphism is an excellent work to orient the philosophical reader,[5] but here I shall draw on the more abbreviated treatment he gives in his synoptic book *The Greeks and Their Gods.*[6] A second and more recent treatment is Walter Burkert's in *Greek Religion.*[7] Both these books conclude with chapters devoted to Plato and Aristotle after their treatments of the Orphic materials, and they are extremely valuable chapters.

Orphism was a religious movement that gained adherents from the sixth century onward past the time of Plato. Though it was named after the legendary musician and hero Orpheus, its worship was focused on Dionysius, god of wine and of ecstatic revels. Whereas the official cults of Athens and other cities promoted festivals, "mysteries," and rituals

---

5. W. K. C. Guthrie, *Orpheus and Greek Religion* (London: 1935; 2d. ed. 1952).

6. W. K. C. Guthrie, *The Greeks and Their Gods* (Boston: Beacon, 1950), chap. 11.

7. Walter Burkert, *Greek Religion,* trans. J. Raffan (Cambridge, Mass.: Harvard University Press, 1985), chap. 6, section 2, "Bacchica and Orphica."

that were corporate in character, embracing the whole city, Orphism was a religion of individuals joined in a semisecret society, who learned it out of books and out of a musical tradition of hymns.[8] They learned a doctrine about the preexistence of the soul of each person and a fate that had been ordained for each. Owing to a primordial sin, each of us was fallen out of our true place of being—the starry heavens—ordained to fall into a body and to live there through many trials and pains, with the hope that through the purification of our life we might be saved again and return to our true home. For the soul is a fragment of divinity.[9] By practicing purifications such as ritual bathing and abstention from meat, by quietness and meditation, and by gathering for the singing of hymns, we prepare ourselves for our divine destiny.[10] There was a richly detailed theology, including especially the narrative of the primordial rending of the child Dionysius by the Titans, for which we bore the guilt, for we were descended from them and from the thunderbolt of Zeus that punished them.[11] But purification will purge us of the stain, so upon our death we may hope to be restored to our true state of divinity. Golden plates, found in graves in southern Italy and Crete, contain verses that express the Orphic hopes. The soul arriving in Hades is greeted with the words "Hail, hail to thee journeying the right-hand road, to the holy meadows and groves of Persephone." The soul is then given these instructions:

> Thou shalt find to the left of the house of Hades a spring, and by the side of it standing a white cypress. To this spring approach not near. But thou shalt find another, from the lake of Memory cold water flowing forth, and there are guardians before it. Say, "I am a child of Earth and starry Heaven, but my race is of Heaven alone. This ye know yourselves. But I am parched with thirst and I perish. Give me quickly the cold water flowing forth from the lake of Memory." And of themselves they will give thee to drink of the holy spring, and thereafter among the other heroes thou shalt have lordship.[12]

---

8. Guthrie, *The Greeks and Their Gods,* pp. 313–14, pp. 326–32; Burkert, *Greek Religion,* pp. 296–301.

9. Guthrie, *The Greeks and Their Gods,* pp. 318–21.

10. Ibid., pp. 323–28; Burkert, *Greek Religion,* pp. 297.

11. Guthrie, *The Greeks and Their Gods,* pp. 318–26.

12. Ibid., pp. 322–23. I have included a few words here that for some reason Guthrie left out. See, for example, Jane Harrison, *Prolegomena to the Study of Greek Religion* (New York: Meridian Books, 1955), pp. 659–60.

Guthrie and Burkert have both made it plain that the Orphic movement exercised a great influence upon the Pythagorean communities, and so we have to recognize that the latter constitute a second source of the Orphic influence upon Plato, reinforcing what he had picked up independently from his own exposure to the Orphics.[13]

Scholars of Greek religion are divided over the scope and importance of the Orphic movement; E. R. Dodds can speak for all those who are skeptical about the alleged influence of Orphism on our literary and philosophical sources.[14] Nevertheless, on the striking opposition between the whole Orphic set of ideas and practices and those of the mainstream Homeric tradition, there is no disagreement. Where the Homeric poems can see little in the great "Beyond" that would compensate us for the loss of our bodily strength, martial power and sexual loving, Orphism makes a reevaluation in which the here and now is diminished by comparison to the heavenly destiny of the soul. Likewise, it is not a corporate or civic religion, but one in which individual life and destiny is all-important. This is not to deny some form of community or fellowship in the eternal order, but one's neighbor, one's fellow Athenian or Theban, is not necessarily one's partner in the eternal order—the mate for your soul may have been unknown to you in everyday life. Orphism has therefore been interpreted in modern times as a puritanical and life-denying religion, the very progenitor of such tendencies in Plato, and highly uncongenial to modern thinkers of a materialist bent, or of a Nietzschean, "life-force" persuasion, tendencies that tend to hog the foreground in modern intellectual debate. Now it is time to look for the marks that Orphic religion left upon Plato's philosophy.

The Platonic Mythology

Chapter 1 quoted the first brief passage from the *Meno* 81, which includes the heroic verses of Pindar. Here we review the four longer texts of Orphic-like mythology.

The first extract, *Gorgias* 523a–527e, has a grimmer import than did the *Meno* passage, for its burden is especially the last judgment that

---

13. Guthrie, *The Greeks and Their Gods,* p. 314, Burkert, *Greek Religion,* pp. 296–301.

14. *The Greeks and the Irrational,* pp. 147–50. See also his edition of Plato, *Gorgias* (Oxford: Clarendon, 1959), pp. 372–76.

falls upon those who have done evil in their lives, the worst of whom are sent into everlasting punishment in the underworld—Tartarus. As Socrates narrates it here, there will be another class whose evil deeds have been less extreme and who are then assigned punishments for their purification. This is the first literary text of the West that clearly differentiates a purgatory from an inferno; the distinction could be Orphic, or Pythagorean, or original to Plato, but, as Dodds points out in his commentary on this passage of the *Gorgias,* Plato's Purgatory differs from the later Christian one in that it purifies the soul not for heaven but for a return to Earth, for the eventual reincarnation of those who receive the purification is pretty clearly indicated at 525b–526d. The myth does allow the souls of those who are judged to have lived justly to proceed directly to the Islands of the Blest, where, as in Hesiod's original teaching, they may remain forever. The specific contribution of the *Gorgias* (526c) to this old idea is to single out *philosophers* as subject to that happy fate.

Turning next to the *Phaedo,* 107c–115a, we find no disagreement with the *Gorgias* myth, but more detail added—above all, the eschatological tale is interwoven with a lesson in the geography of Earth and its place within the Heavens resulting in a fascinating tour of Platonic science. The cosmology as such is probably independent of any religious or Orphic inspiration, although the beautiful text conveys its religious and its scientific teachings at once in a style of serenity and calm that, in my view, are the hallmark of Orphic writing at its best. Where a focus on the punishment of the unjust is in keeping with the pugnacious style of the *Gorgias* as a whole, it is fitting, given the *Phaedo*'s setting in the death cell of a just man, Socrates, that more attention is given in the *Phaedo* to the fate of the good:

> For when the soul comes to Hades she brings with her nothing but her education and training; and this is said to do the greatest help or hurt to the dead man at the very beginning of his course thither. What men say is this. At death the guardian spirit of each, to whom each was allotted for life, undertakes to lead each to a certain place; there those gathered must stand their trial, and then pass on to the house of Hades with the guide whose duty it is to conduct them hence to that place. . . . The soul which has passed though life purely and decently finds gods for fellow-travelers and leaders, and each soul dwells in her own proper dwelling place. (*Phaedo* 107d–e, 108c, trans. W. H. D. Rouse.)

The others, however, must go over the river Acheron for purification, or else are thrown into Tartarus for eternal punishment.

The geographical and cosmological character of the *Phaedo* myth is expanded and extended in the myth of Er that concludes the *Republic,* for where the *Phaedo* had described in great detail all of Earth's dim hollows and corners where we live, by contrast with the brilliant shining of the higher regions of the Earth and the upper air and *aithēr,* the *Republic* myth (614b–621d) concentrates on the upper region and the highest heavens. Plato indulges his reader with gorgeous descriptive passages on the spherical composition of the universe, the universe's central axis of shining light, and the concentric circles in which heavenly bodies rotate around the rotating Earth. And the religious focus of the story has altered from its form in the *Phaedo.* It is no longer primarily a moral of rewards and punishments, but a drama of choice and freedom. For what this man Er reported, when he came back from the dead, was that he had seen not the ways a life may have ended, but the ways it had begun. His is a story concerned with those who must return to Earth to live again, not with those whose eternal punishment or eternal blessedness has already been settled. Souls who had once come for judgment after a life on Earth and who had spent a thousand years of purifying labors or heavenly happiness were now required to assemble on a plain to make their choice for a new life, the lots among which they could choose being laid out by Necessity and the Fates. One eager soul chose too quickly, opting to be an absolute tyrant in his next life, not seeing that he would then commit terrible crimes, for which, after his next death, he would pay with terrible punishments. Er saw them all choosing their lots and then departing to begin their new lives, before the Fates ordered him too back to Earth, where he would awaken again and tell of his travel into the eternal kingdom.

It is in accord with Plato's Orphic sources that he would have as much to say about the dramas that *precede* our birth here on Earth as about the fate that awaits us at the *end.* And this is the special focus of the *Phaedrus* myth. Our next three chapters will be devoted to its great central speech (*Phaedrus* 244a–257b). But I think it will help us later if, before that exposition, we connect the details of its theological system to the earlier texts and their Orphic background. Here, too, Plato shows the preexistence in heaven of the souls of those who have been born here on Earth (246c); the souls that descend here to be born may enter into different kinds of lives (248c), and the kind of life entered is determined by the person's prenatal experience in heaven (249b has a reference to souls' *choosing* their lives). At 248c–e Plato differentiates nine kinds of lives in descending order of merit, from the philosopher down to the tyrant, similar to the descriptions in the *Republic* VIII and IX. The practice of philosophy, if it is chosen in three lives, can lead to the soul's final return to fellowship with immortal gods, with no further incarnations (249a, c–d); others may live through ten different lifetimes in the hope of ultimate redemption (248e), with a thousand years separating each lifetime from the next, the intervening time spent in purgatory. This story has no eternal punishments, but nothing seems to rule out the possibility that the whole cycle of rebirths, ten of them over ten thousand years, might be repeated endlessly. We also see, as in the *Phaedo* 81e–82b and the *Republic* 620a–b, that in some cases souls can enter into animals (249b).

Another detail that I believe recalls the Orphic texts is the scene laid at the beginning of the *Phaedrus.* We see that Phaedrus has taken the lead in inviting Socrates to come walking and in setting up the themes of rhetoric and *erōs.* But it is actually Socrates who sets their direction north-east up the Ilissos and Socrates who introduces *Phaedrus* to the winged soul and the true nature and mission of love.[15] The opening scene, therefore, is not only an emblem of Socratic education. Beyond that, it re-creates in a purely literary mode the Orphic story of the soul welcomed by its *psychagōgos,* its tutelary spirit or *daimōn,* and taken over the purifying river to become reunited with the gods.

Disordered Discourse on the Gods

Plato's dialogues exhibit so many references to gods, and different kinds of references, that the modern reader may pass over them with little attention. Here, having said a word about the religious and mythological atmosphere of Plato, we may try to discuss the key *beings* so invoked. The *Phaedrus* is rich in references both to gods, and, more generally, to what is divine.

Both partners of this dialogue are called from time to time divine: Socrates considers that he himself might be (230a5), and he later refers to Phaedrus that way (234d6)—the term, in this locution, is equivalent

---

15. Anne Lebeck's article, "The Central Myth of Plato's *Phaedrus,*" *Greek, Roman and Byzantine Studies* 13 (1972): 267–90, gives an excellent account of the way the prologue to the *Phaedrus* reflects the viewpoint of the Great Speech, 244a–257b.

to "excellent." Socrates' oratory is moved by a divine inspiration (*pathos*—238c6). The atmosphere of the scene beside the river (238c9) has something divine about it, and 279b2 says, retrospectively, that there were gods here who had inspired Socrates. At 242a Phaedrus's love of *logos* is called divine, and at 279a9, likewise, the aspirations of Isocrates. Especially we remember the famous references (244a7, d3; 245b, c; 256b, e) to divine madness in its four forms. There are divine and human souls, of course, but the human soul likewise has something divine about it (246d–e). At 242c3 there is recognition of offense against *to theion* and at c9 offense against gods. After the Great Speech, there are just a few references to divinity (265a10, b2; 266b, c; 274b9, c6; 279a). Besides all these references, there are many references, innumerable, really, to gods: especially to Eros (242d9, 242d–e), to Pan (279b8), and to all the Olympians collectively (especially 246–47 passim) as well as many indefinite references to "the god" (238d6, for example). The lines in 246c–d contain an important reflection on the imagination and representation of the immortal gods. Besides all this, we have so many predications of *makarie* (blessed) and of *daimonion.* What extravagance of the *Phaedrus*—gods innumerable!

In addition, there are more prayers uttered in the *Phaedrus,* I think, than in all the rest of Plato's works put together. There are the formal prayer to Eros with which the Great Speech concludes, 257a–b, and the formal prayer to Pan and other gods with which the dialogue concludes, 279b–c. At 236d–e Phaedrus takes an oath, not by a god, however, but by the plane tree—this has the mark of levity—and a few lines later, 237a, Socrates invokes the Muses, perhaps in a similar spirit of levity. But at 278b5–6, Phaedrus states with seriousness that he will pray to remain true to the advice of Socrates. Other dialogues of Plato refer to prayer (*Euthyphro* 14c; *Laws* 687–88, 801b–e, *Cratylus* 400e; *Republic* 362d–367e, 607a; *Phaedo* 60 c–61b), but actual prayers uttered in the text appear (and even these are not clear-cut cases) only in *Timaeus* 27b–d, *Critias* 106a–b, and *Phaedo* 117c.

Plato's writings recognize a large number of gods. In the *Phaedrus,* we have the gods that lead their squadrons in the sky and crowds of spirits, or *daimones,* of lesser rank. There are, we saw, local spirits and local gods by the Ilissos, and in other places too, of course, and demigods and nymphs, both of which are offspring of the gods. Plato expends little effort in the *Phaedrus* marshaling this great throng. There are, however, later texts of Plato where we can discern principles of ordering among different groups of gods, *degrees of divinity* therefore.

The *Laws* IV, 717a–b, making provisions for public worship, states that there shall be services for Olympian deities, gods of the particular cities, gods of the underworld, local spirits or demons, and heroes. At that point in Plato's writing, he seems to have intended that a different status be accorded to each of these groups.

The *Phaedrus* can be more casual about the whole subject because the gods of the *Phaedrus* are not objects of philosophical thought. True being is what the philosopher is seeking and seeing, and the gods appear as the companions and leaders of the philosophers. The gods too are gazing out beyond the heavens to see Justice itself, and the other ideas; the philosopher's aspiration is to bring in to view, not the gods, but that which the gods themselves are seeing. Plato conceptualized this contemplative or even philosophical life of the gods right from the beginning, in the *Euthyphro* (see 10a–11: the gods love what is holy because they recognize it as holy). But if Plato all along had been truly serious about the existence of these gods, he would have been led to postulate, or at least inquire into, the *idea* of god. This *idea* could have appeared in the *Phaedrus*, lying out beyond the heavens, as the guarantee of that which *is* a god. If there were an *idea* of god, Zeus and the other divinities would have been images of divinity, cases of the *idea*. But Plato never said such a thing, neither in the *Phaedrus*, nor elsewhere. His treatment of the gods leaves them at the level of beings or entities without detailed inquiry into them—hardly a philosophical theology. There is a remarkable passage at *Phaedrus* 246c–d in which Socrates comments critically on the accustomed habits of the Greeks for representing gods, noting that they mixed up real gods with the habits of their defective imagination. Immediately, however, he adds this further doubt or irony: "On matters such as these, however, let it stand in whatever way would be pleasing to the god." The comment of Wilamowitz on this passage is incisive:

> This acknowledges more clearly than does any other passage that Plato recognizes the gods of mythology only because of the place they held in traditional piety. They always recur in Plato's myths, quite in keeping with his reluctance to lay a hand on the customary forms of worship, and with his readiness to find truth in ancient traditions and the works of the great poets (as is the case with his own myths as well). Only a myth, obviously, would present the gods in human form. The winged souls that govern the whole cosmos are actually incorporeal despite their wings, and the wings are introduced only for the sake of the allegory that follows. Plato

believed, of course, that the souls that were in the heavens did have bodies—the stars, especially the planets that were self-moving. And if these stars were all contained in the cosmos, the latter too would have a body; it is only that which is beyond the heavens that is utterly free from corporeality. But it would be a serious mistake to identify the stars with the gods of traditional worship.[16]

On the general meaning in ancient Greek of *theos* and *theios* (divine), we must note that both can be used adjectivally and substantively. *To theion* can refer to a god in Aeschylus, Herodotus, and Thucydides,[17] though as we have just seen, the adjective can refer to human beings and various kinds of experiences. We can orient ourselves again from an enlightening remark of Wilamowitz:

> When students of mythology and the history of religions look at the winged figures of Nike and Eros—and in fact people still understand those figures pretty well in the form the Greeks gave to them—they often call them "personifications." Even more, they suppose that Laughter or Death, Pity, Health or Wealth, or Fear (*phobos*), Envy (*phthonos,* earlier, the Gorgon) have become "persons" with their altars and their cults. But this betrays a complete lack of understanding of natural religion. These supposed "personifications" were gods because they were great forces whose power people could sense within themselves and in others. Whatever was stronger than human beings, what guided them, what hurt them, what gave them joy, was god. For "god" itself is above all a predicate-concept. When Hesiod says that "Rumor too is a god," when Euripides says "to meet your friend again is a god" (*Helen,* 560), when even Plato allows himself to say "The god of wise men is the law, of foolish men pleasure" (*8th Letter,* 354e), this accords with the kind of thinking by which not only Eros and Nike but also Zeus and Hera became gods. We do not need to sketch their transformation into persons, immortal human beings, but that Justice and Virtue are potent eternal forces raised above everything earthly was virtually self-evident for this kind of thinking. The poets had done it first, speaking of the golden face of Justice (Euripides, frag. 486), or placing Virtue on the highest mountain peak surrounded by nymphs, the very souls of Nature in

---

16. Wilamowitz-Moellendorff, *Platon,* vol. 1, p. 464.
17. H. D. Liddell, R. Scott, and H. S. Jones, *A Greek English Lexicon* (Oxford, London: Clarendon Press, 1940). See also Burkert, *Greek Religion,* pp. 271–72, and 179 ff., with notes.

its purity (Simonides, frag. 58), or had installed Fame to keep watch over the grave of one who achieved glory through dying for the homeland (Simonides, 1) or let Virtue sit mourning on the grave of Ajax (*Aristotelian Peplos*, 7). The artists who then gave plastic form to these poetic images were doing something quite different from a silversmith today who fashions a couple of semi-Hellenic maidens with some attributes signifying Trade and Industry.[18]

Platonic Theology

There are, however, passages from time to time in Plato that could be called philosophical theology, and one of them occurs in the continuation of the dialogue between Adeimantus and Socrates in the *Republic* II. Here, and in other passages, he employs a grammar that must seem puzzling to the modern reader, in which in the same speech he uses a singular noun, *ho theos,* and likewise a plural noun, *hoi theoi,* employing the two of them interchangeably as if it made no difference. We can see this in *Laws* 716–717, *Timaeus* 27c–d, and other places too. We shall look at the *Republic* passage, 376e–383c, which forms the conclusion of book II.

Adeimantus has found (362d–367e) that the usual indoctrination of the young corrupts them, for it praises justice only for its rewards, and it places high reputation above authentic goodness. How should they be educated instead? Socrates points out (376e–377a) that children have to hear stories, and for that reason alone what they hear is false in the sense that the stories are fables or myths. Yet the stories contain some truth or at least can contain some (377a). Therefore, parents, nurses, and teachers must not be allowed to tell them just anything: the little stories told to children, and likewise the great epics of the tradition, must be made appropriate (*kalon,* 377c, i.e., excellent or edifying), especially in what they say about the gods. Hesiod's obscene legend about the castration of Ouranus by Cronos, for instance, is a false story (377d); it is like an inaccurate picture (377e); it is a lie (377e). And the story of the quarrel between Cronos and Zeus should not be told either. Regarding this story, Socrates adds that it should not

---

18. Wilamowitz-Moellendorff, *Platon,* pp. 348–49. The predicative concept of divinity is one of the themes of Wilamowitz's great work, *Der Glaube der Hellenen,* 2 vols. (Berlin: Weidmann, 1931–32).

be told "even if it were true" (378a2), and further that, if told, it should only be told in secret (378a3–6). But this remark is not intended as a suggestion that the story might be true after all; the point, rather, is that the telling of stories is guided by two criteria: the stories must be true, and they must be *kalon*. After more examples of bad stories—in both senses—Socrates gives Adeimantus his "principles for theology," which will render a god such as he is in truth (379a).

1. 379b–380c: A god is good and therefore cannot be the author of evil and harm.
2. 380d–381e: A god is strong and therefore not changeable, not assuming many guises and shapes.
3. 382a–383a (not differentiated from [2] in the text):   A god is truthful and therefore does not deceive us or trick us.

What concerns me at the moment is not the content of these principles, but rather the words that I have translated as "a god." Throughout these pages, Socrates uses most often the singular noun with an article, *ho theos*. This can be translated "the god" when some particular god, Zeus or Apollo, is under discussion, as in 378b4, which refers to Zeus. In the passage as a whole, however, Socrates is concerned with the presentation of any and all gods. He is undertaking to correct the errors of traditional poetic theology by speaking generally and eidetically, about what pertains to a god as such. But since he continues to assume the plurality of gods, *ho theos* is best rendered "a god." Further confirmation of that translation is the fact that the Greek definite article can be used in other situations in a sense that is best rendered in English by the indefinite article, for example, *ho anthrōpos,* "a man." Socrates is exploring that single character (*idea*) that marks a god as being a god, in the style of a philosophical discussion. If we review the way principle (1) is expressed in 379b–380c, for instance, we find that the singular *theos* (usually, but not always, with the article *ho*) occurs at 379b1, c2, c7, and 380a7, b1, b3, b5, b6, c8. But the reference is plural, *hoi theoi,* at 379d1, e5, and 380c6. Indeed, at 380c6–9 occurs one of the sentences that use singular and plural at once, so in his translation of the *Republic* Grube writes: "This then is one of the rules and guidelines about the gods within which speakers must speak and poets compose, that the god is not the cause of all things but only of the good." "A god" rather than "the god" would have been clearer.

Toward the end of the discussion, at 382e6, Socrates employs yet another phrase, the neuter *to theion,* in a sentence which might be literally rendered, "So then that which is demonic *[to daimonion]* and that which is divine *[to theion]* are in every way free of falsehood." That being admitted, he concludes, "So a god *[ho theos]* is entirely simple and true in word and deed." There had been little if anything said about spirits, *daimones,* here, and I too have little to say about them. It could be, however, that these neuter terms serve as generalizing, eidetic terms in this passage, signifying that which can be said about the divine (and demonic) as such. The term serves well in the concluding step of Socrates' reasoning. It would be overreaching the evidence to invoke here an *idea* of divinity, the divine, perfectly parallel to *to kalon,* the beautiful, *to dikaion,* the just, and so on, but the neuter phrase does at least mark a way of speaking about what is divine in general.

We should note that the words *ho theos* (with the definite article) function as a proper name in the New Testament, in the Septuagint, and in the Greek-language writings of Christian theology. In the translation of these texts, we are right to use a proper name with a capital letter and no definite or indefinite article, "God." But in Platonic translations into English, this term is misleading if it carries a suggestion that this fourth century Greek philosopher had a prophetic understanding, some kind of anticipation of biblical religion. That is the effect, sometimes, of the exuberant use of the name *God* by the Victorian Jowett (see, e.g., his *Timaeus* translation). The use of this term might be justified in certain contexts of Plato, where suggestions of the Bible can be kept at a distance, and this certainly is the case, for instance, in the translation of Aristotle's *Metaphysics,* Book Lambda. But nothing in the *Republic* II, warrants this use of the divine name, nor does anything in the *Phaedrus.*

To go back and forth from gods to a god, and likewise to the impersonal divine, *to theion,* is a linguistic practice that undermines a strict difference between traditional language and the language of philosophy, between *mythos* and *logos.* Moreover it blurs any line that might divide "monotheism" from "polytheism." It is not just Christian commentators who find monotheistic discourse in Plato—it is there, though it is fused with polytheistic discourse in passages such as these. It is clearly wrong to be transfixed by a quantitative criterion in interpreting Plato: one god or many gods? He will never renounce the gods, yet he always has the other terms too.

Could we proceed further on this basis into philosophical theology?

The multiple discourse of Plato's writing, accepting of myth along with dialectic, worked to free him of the puritanical disgust about the gods to which Adeimantus gave expression in the *Republic.* We have to recognize, however, that he always subordinated his gods to truth, to true being—the theme announced in the *Euthyphro* and expressed in the *Phaedrus* in the doctrine, 249c, that it is to the vision of true being that the gods owe their divinity. We might be inclined to wonder whether a Greek god, or a Platonic god, could ever fulfill our notion of divinity, based as it is on biblical writing and Christian creeds. We shall take up that question in the concluding section of the chapter, but here it will be well to note an oddity in Hackforth's commentary.[19] He asks how it is, at 249c, that Socrates can call a god, *theos,* godlike, *theios.* Hackforth reads the latter term as the predicate "god-like." He understands the god-like as that which imitates the subject *theos.* But that is not the force of this adjective. It is used here, and in so many other occurrences, to mean what *constitutes* a god. Indeed that is the sense of the later term *Gottheit* in Meister Eckhart and its English equivalent, *godhead,* whose original use has been effaced by centuries of misunderstanding.

The Divine

When we ask about "the Greek gods" or "Plato's gods," we still generally retain the memory of Christianity, so it is hard to use the term *theology* in a Greek sense. Being influenced by two thousand years of Christianity, our own questions are really about God, not the gods. On the other hand, we get nowhere in Plato interpretation if we cannot surmount any of our modern habits and culture. It is for that reason that, here, I shall use the non-Christian term *the divine.* My hope is to clarify what Plato means by a god by way of clarifying what is divine.

We ought to try to see the specific force of *to theion* in Greek life and in Plato. We have to differentiate it from a whole wealth of common anthropological ideas: the sacred (*sacer*), the *mysterium tremendum,* the *kadosh* (holy), the *numen,* and so on. Perhaps we have still not got very far beyond the Cambridge school with its anthropological interpretations of religion. As far as I am able to tell, *to theion* is not an expression of fear, or anxiety or awe. Nor does it have a root in magic, in the hope of influence, the desire to control nature and one's destiny,

---

19. *Plato's Phaedrus,* p. 86, n. 3.

the growth of grain, and so forth. Rather, if I may try to capture both what the term generally means and what Plato makes of it, I would say it springs from exuberance and celebration. To put it into English, I shall try a word of Latin derivation: *majesty*. This word was taken from *majestas,* formed from *major,* "greater," the comparative of *magnus,* great. It signifies unqualified greatness and was applied in the first instance to the gods, then to human beings. This word was taken over later, in English, into a constitutional context, but retains a similar function in that it expresses a degree of greatness. A god is that than which a greater cannot be conceived, *nulla maius,* "nothing greater." Theology, then, is the thinking about what is the highest and the greatest. A civilization that has no theology is not in a position to identify anything that is absolutely the greatest of all—no beings, practices, or experiences that we can call divine or that have divine majesty.

This, then, would be my exegesis of *to theion:* to believe in the divine is to identify what has majesty. But what in fact is highest and best? Here I wish to dwell seriously upon the connection of the theme of erotic love and the theme of prayers and the gods. The Great Speech is introduced by Socrates' act of repentance and it closes with a prayer to the god of love. The first part of the speech introduces prophecy, therapy, and poetry as the forms of a divine madness that are the kin of *erōs.* Love is, for Socrates and Plato, a divine and religious matter. Moreover, our intercourse with the gods, religion we call it, awakens the very powers or the very stratum of the soul that is awakened in sexual love. Like sexual love, religion stands opposed to the dry calculus of benefits: it puts joy and bliss decisively at the head of human goods. Both are the work of the imagination. With the folly of supposing that sexual love is to be subordinated to advantage, the divine is excluded from the calculative thinking of Lysias. The psychological consequence of such thinking is that these erotic feelings become associated with, or attached to, politics and business and the world of competitive advantage, with devastating consequences for the soul. Where these feelings have no art, no religion, no lovemaking, to give them utterance, they are violated (and, as a further side consequence, politics too is violated, being asked to bear psychic weight that it cannot—never more dreadfully exhibited than in Nazism and Fascism). My own suspicion is that the so-called death of God followed upon a death or at least a disorder of the imagination: we have fallen into the sexual disorder that Socrates feared so much, the loss of the dimension that connects us to the life of the gods.

Every part of the soul has its *erōs* as well as an awareness of that which it loves and knows. To suppose that it is only by our faculty of rational calculation that we identify what we love and hope for is the folly expressed, in part, by Lysias. The feelings and longings of the heart are, no doubt, the roots of religion, and its myths are a discourse that calculative reason wants urgently to cast off. But it is the inwardly divided soul, whose reason rejects its feelings, that will be in chaos. Rather, an integration of discourses is required; it is the heart and the desire that learn to accept the thinking of reason, and the reason that learns to acknowledge the urges of the heart and its deep-seated desires, that bring a soul to the truth. The work of the soul is to express in one intention, one thought, all the modalities of its *erōs.* Here it is a follower of a god.

Our own contemporary confusion about gods or God is in part a confusion about what it is to "have a god," to "follow a god," or to "worship a god" (and to change these expressions by using the capitalized divine name, *God,* would not alter the point). For Plato, some follow in the train of Zeus, others after Apollo, and so on, outlined at 252c–253c. This is no mere picturesque detail of the *Phaedrus* myth but a point that is important substantively, which I might express by saying that it is one thing to know about a god, quite another to follow the god. To follow the god expresses a choice that had to be made, often a passionate choice, where the claims of other gods were felt but rejected. This is the human situation in the Greek epics and tragedies (though to be sure, the gods' choice of their human servants usually takes precedence over the human choices). Hippolytus, the adoring servant of Artemis, would not concede the claims of Aphrodite, a tragic error. Agamemnon transgressed against Athena, to his cost.

Knowing about many gods but choosing to follow one of them also expresses the attitude of the Greeks (and other ancient peoples) to the many traditions of the peoples of the world. As we see in Herodotus, for one, the Greeks could understand the Egyptian deities by correlating some of them with their own—and they did the same with the gods of Rome, as the Romans did in return to the Greeks—while granting that some Egyptian deities had *no* Hellenic counterpart. To be a Greek did not bring with it the worship of animal-gods like Anubis, but they would identify Osiris with Dionysius. With his evident respect for traditional religion, Plato would have seen things in just this way as well. If he had known about Israel, what would he have thought about their worship of the Lord, their God? Surely Plato *would* have grasped the divinity of the Lord of Israel, and, if we can in imagination ascribe to him an understanding of Israel's prophets, institutions, and scriptures, he would have understood that the covenant of Lord with his people, and his promise of the Day of the Lord and the Messianic Age, was the incomparable expression of the divinity of Justice. And if, by an equivalent extension of our imagination, we could suppose Plato learning about Jesus Christ and his church, he would have recognized the divinity of Jesus, and understood the story of his life, his message, and his death and resurrection, as the incomparable expression of the divinity of love and mercy. My point is that he would have recognized these divinities; my argument does not reach so far as to say he would have *followed* the Lord of Israel, or Jesus Christ, though to be sure Plato's own followers, in later centuries, usually did so.

On the question of our recognition of the divine, one approach that will help us is through the *Phaedo* doctrine of recollection. If we identify the empirical aspect of human religiousness and the awareness of gods, especially the many gods, the discourse Adeimantus (and Plato) had heard since childhood, it could follow that we also carry within us a primordial memory of divinity itself, an innate idea. It would not have the color, the detail, and the folklore, of local festival traditions. Imprinted on the soul is something more serious. The empirical, then, is supplemented and it comes into a union with something a priori. We can well read *Phaedo* 77c–84b that way. The soul that is by nature like the divine will return after death to dwell with the divine. But this is *to theion* itself, not the varied pantheon as represented in the myths passed down in popular belief.

The Platonic doctrine of true being is also important for theology. We read that true being is invariable and invulnerable. Let us ask here how this issue would play itself out in theology. How might the divine principle be brought together with being? One way is that of Aristotle. At least as Owens interprets him, Aristotle speaks of God or the divine as the eminent sense of being itself—not just *a* being, but the very principle of being.[20] And there is little doubt that Aquinas did the same thing. But Plato does not do this. It is striking that if form is the

---

20. Joseph Owens, *The Doctrine of Being in the Aristotelian Metaphysics,* 2d ed. (Toronto: Pontifical Institute of Mediaeval Studies, 1963).

principle of being in Plato, he nowhere identifies deity with form, or makes forms into gods or gods into pure form—that is, the route of Aristotle.

Another route that beckons here is the Neoplatonic: to assert the equivalence of being with form, to link the two of them with intellect, and then to postulate the domain beyond being, and thus, beyond form, as the first principle of all, which might be spoken of as the One or as the Good. It is then possible for a Neoplatonic theology to insist that the divine should not properly be confined to the level of *nous* or form or being, but rather that it lies beyond being. Such I think would be a Christian Neoplatonism. The theology of Paul Tillich continues this tendency. God is, for him, not a being—"God does not exist"—but, lying beyond everything, God is yet equivalent to being itself. He explains this by way of a device derived from Schelling, the "God beyond God," which itself is Neoplatonic.

I have tried to present a "Platonic" route that is different from these—granting that beings like spirits and powers are legendary and belong to the discourse of myth; beyond them lies, not an Aristotelian or Thomistic being itself, *esse ipsum,* but the divine itself, *auto to theion.*

CHAPTER
SEVEN | The Human Soul
Phaedrus 244a–250c

An exposition of Socrates' Great Speech should start from its account of the soul, *psychē*. This will require reference to other Platonic works that treat the soul and to other books that give a more comprehensive treatment of Plato on the soul. But there is another context still for our study, an even broader one—the entire question of "the soul" understood as a philosophical question, not what Plato or some ancient Greeks might have understood by *psychē,* but rather what anybody at all might understand by soul, *psychē,* or any similar term. Interwoven in this chapter with comments on the *Phaedrus* and other Platonic texts will be discussion of what we ourselves do mean or could mean in speaking about the soul, the mind, and so on. This is in keeping with my expository purpose overall.

The central fact is that the word *soul* has not been used much in philosophical writing or speaking for about two centuries; it has even vanished, largely, from theology. Intellectuals today manifest resistance to such talk. Hegelians subordinated soul to other principles; materialists denied its existence, and "philosophy of mind" in recent times has been mostly materialistic; behaviorists showed it was not needed in experimental psychology; existentialists denounced it along with God; analytic philosophers punctured both the soul and "the concept of mind." In scholarly circles, *the soul* survives mainly as a term of art for translations and for those whose work is essentially exposition of ancient or medieval material or other older material, seventeenth-century metaphysical authors, for instance. Now I do not propose a new translation for *psychē,* nor is it possible to conceive Plato's thought without the soul, but neither is it wise, today, to persist, unreflecting, in the accustomed term of art. The inquiry into philosophers' works can never be purely historical. It must itself be philosophical, so we can never cease asking ourselves in this case, "Is there a soul?" It is not that this philosophical questioning is *foundational,* something to be settled first of all with a scholarly study of the ancient text following afterward. There is a hermeneutical circle, a circle in our interpretation. The exposition of Plato's text will help us to understand what the soul is, but only if we already have some understanding of what the soul is are we capable of expounding the Platonic text. The interaction of historical philology and philosophical thought is a matter of principle, and in practice that means that, at each step in the present chapter, where we entertain some point of Plato's about the soul, we must at once step back to reconsider whether we ourselves can believe the point and accept the terminology in which it is stated.

We can see that a certain range of phenomena was connected in a given epoch with the term *soul* (*psychē, anima*) and that in different epochs quite different phenomena were connected with "mind," "spirit," and so on. The English word *mind,* for instance, has been in popular use since the eighteenth century in locutions that bear upon the function of memory ("keep this in mind"), intention, and purpose. And philosophers began at about that time to be more concerned with memory and intention than with life, breath, and immortality, so they began to speak more and more about the mind, less and less about soul and spirit; the history and connotation of "soul" and "spirit" did not lend themselves so well to those inquiries. In the twentieth century, both popular discourse and philosophy have been concerned more with the self, the ego, and consciousness. If we do not grasp how these different concepts are all correlated with specific phenomena, and become employed by philosophers who are interested in precisely those phenomena, we shall be driven to think that these are all discrete faculties of some sort, squeezed into the narrow space between our ears. We shall have an intolerable lexical overcrowding. I am maintaining here that one should not speak of the soul in isolation, but in connection with the phenomena and the experiences to which a given author or a given tradition linked it. If we can see just *what phenomena* were connected with Plato's *psychē,* these will likely be phenomena that we still know. It was this concept that let the author and his readers *understand* the phenomena. It was the vehicle of their access to them. If we gain access to the same phenomena, then we shall have deduced or re-duced the concept and led it back to its origins, and that will be a justification of the concept, the kind of "re-duction" that brings understanding. Lacking that, we are left today with a debased use of the word *soul,* a ghostly organ, an immaterial thing between our ears.

Our first step in this chapter, then, will be to look at Socrates' use of the term *soul* and see what experiences sustained it. Then we shall do the same thing for the soul of the *Phaedrus,* looking at love, madness, self-originating motion, destiny, and recollection. The doctrine of soul made these experiences intelligible to Plato and his circle, and, therefore, moving in the opposite direction, as it were, these experiences will open up this "soul" to us, give us access to it.

Socrates on the Soul

Although the word *psychē* is as ancient as Homer and earlier, it was only with the emergence of philosophical thought that the theme of the soul was brought into a clear focus, and while the Ionians and Pythagoreans did not ignore it, it was really Socrates and Plato themselves who were responsible for developing and expressing the concept.[1] Here we shall not be looking at the historical Socrates, but we can take our start from the picture of Socrates that emerges in the early dialogues of Plato.[2] Plato's Socrates expresses himself on the soul emphatically in the *Apology*. At 30a–b he says: "I go around doing nothing but persuading both young and old among you not to care for your body or your wealth in preference to or as strongly as for the best possible state of your soul." There is no evidence of Orphic doctrine here, nor is the "care" for the soul to be achieved by ritual or dietary measures. For Socrates, the best state of the soul is the wisdom and the virtue gener-

---

1. Bruno Snell in *The Discovery of the Mind* (Oxford: Blackwell, 1953) called attention to the major role of Socrates, thereby correcting one of the omissions of Erwin Rohde's *Psyche: Seelencult und Unsterblichkeitsglaube der Griechen* (Tüebingen: 1893). Rohde traced the poetic and religious roots of Plato but tended to underplay the impact of Socrates.

2. See T. M. Robinson, *Plato's Psychology,* 2d ed. (Toronto: University of Toronto Press, 1995), for a treatment of all of Plato's writing on the soul. The views of the Platonic Socrates are treated in chap. 1, the *Phaedrus* in chap. 6. Besides that, there are now two treatments of the philosophy of Socrates himself, covering many topics including the soul: Guthrie's *A History of Greek Philosophy,* vol. 3, and Gregory Vlastos, *Socrates: Ironist and Moral Philosopher* (Cambridge: Cambridge University Press, 1991).

ally for which it has been his mission to seek, as he recounts through the whole *Apology*.

In the parallel passage at 36c, Socrates does not even need to use the term *soul:* he can make his point with the pronoun *autos,* self: "I went to each of you privately . . . trying to persuade him not to care for any of his belongings [*tōn heautou*] before caring that he himself [*heautou*] should be as good and wise as possible." In this passage, moreover, where he is responding to the jury's verdict of guilty, Socrates refers to himself repeatedly with the personal pronouns *moi, egō,* and *emauton,* and the other words that he has used, *soul* and *self,* have no other reference than that. Thus, *soul* is a noun that can take the grammatical place that the personal pronoun *autos* can take and that the differentiated personal pronouns, *egō,* and so on, can also take. Like *autos,* the word *soul* permits us to say generally what is usually said individually with *I, you, he,* and so forth. In the *Apology*, Socrates speaks of himself and others as being capable of being wise and good or the opposite. The soul is that which may be wise or good—it is subject to being judged as to its virtue or vice—and where it is wise and good, the self is wise and good, and "you" are wise and good. *The Socratic soul is in fact oneself.*

In our *Apology* passage, the soul or the self is marked off from "the things of the self," *tōn heautou,* which may be belongings or wealth, all one's business affairs, reputation, and political honors. In this very passage at 36b, Socrates recounts his own disregard of "what occupies most people: wealth, household affairs, the position of general or public orator or the other offices, the political clubs and factions." That is what 36c sets in the balance against the self or soul. In this text he compares the soul or self to the city, and he sets in balance the possessions and the business of the city, *tōn tēs poleōs,* versus the city itself, *autēs tēs poleōs,* with the claim that it is the latter rather than the former that must have first claim upon our care, *epimeleia.*

Now the soul or self, that which may be either "good and wise" or the opposite, is one, whereas the things and possessions are many, a point that is reinforced by Socrates' "going to each of you privately," and never confronting people en masse. Being good and wise or their opposites, are attributes that pertain more intimately to that single self that is "me" or "you" than do titles and club memberships, wealth and responsibilities. Even states of the body, and the body itself, are set off against it. At 30a–b he could make the body as external to the soul as wealth is. He is balancing off your wealth and all your affairs, on the one hand, and your body, on the other hand, against your soul. This lets us see the ontological framework most clearly. Because my actions and my thoughts will have an impact upon that subject, me, and not only upon my world, the questions of what I should do and what I should believe become exceptionally important for the care of the self. They are more germane to me than my state of physical fitness or my array of possessions and honors. Socrates expresses in the *Apology* speech the view of the soul that undergirds most of the short discussions of the virtues in the early dialogues of Plato such as the *Laches,* the *Charmides,* and the *Euthyphro.* Courage, temperance, and piety are studied most of all for the impact these qualities have on the one who is the bearer of them.

To conclude this portion, we can interpret the word *soul* thus: Being wealthy or good-looking pales in significance in contrast to being wise and good, but the latter attributes will only apply to us when by virtuous action we have cultivated all our desires, thoughts, and reactions. That which becomes shaped in such a discipline is the soul. Virtue can be predicated of us when virtue is predicated of the soul—the soul is the bearer of those attributes.

This Socratic soul is not mythical—rather it is an item of experience, uniting a group of experiences that we might outline, for a moment, in a modern idiom. "Soul" expresses Socrates' self-consciousness, highlighting his awareness of being good or bad, and his assumption of the responsibility for himself—whether he is good or bad—and, in addition, his awareness of his whole lifetime understood as the allotted time for achieving goodness. To set the highest store by the care of the soul is nothing more than to invest oneself and other human beings with a higher dignity than horses or houses. This Socratic soul is one of the milestones of human thought, and it stands up under the test of reflection. Whoever denies that there is a soul, in this sense of the term, means, "I do not wish to know myself; I prefer to evade responsibility; human beings are no more important than horses."

Divine Madness: *Phaedrus* 244a–245c

Although this framework is still in place for most of the *Meno* and most of the *Gorgias,* there is nevertheless an intrusion of another current in both works—Orphic, as most scholars agree—that invokes the most ancient history of the soul prior to birth (*Meno* 81a–e) and its fate after death (*Gorgias* 493a–d, 523a–527e). Here we have moved into the territory that will be explored in the Great Speech of the *Phaedrus,* leading us beyond the Socratic discourse on the soul, though not revoking any of its discoveries. Here our opening question must be: what sort of experience introduces the *psychē?* Can we gain access to it? The step Plato takes beyond Socrates leads him to appropriate many motifs from Orphic religion and the mysteries. In a purely mythological vein, this opens up to him a vision of primordial scenes in heaven above, but it also leads him to a new appraisal of our terrestrial experience and our self-consciousness. He comes to acknowledge deeper and more mysterious powers at work unconsciously within the soul. Underneath our conscious experience, the "I," the *autos,* the self, with its autobiography and all the responsibilities it has assumed, there is a level at which, for instance, the experience of *erōs* may be aroused. Organized, conscious memory is only on the surface of a darker stratum. In another context, the *Phaedo,* Plato begins his reflection on the soul from the encounter with death, a starting point that led to the doctrine of the separability of the soul from the body and its immortality. But in the *Phaedrus* the topic of the soul arises in connection with love.

The speech of Lysias showed us love as an infirmity, the lover as a nuisance. The first speech of Socrates echoes the indictment, showing, for instance at 239a–d, the ways in which the lover ruins the character of the one he claims to love. The two speeches belong to the domain of social comedy, treating the interaction of lover and beloved humorously, according to typical situations, with the love-besotted lover always spoiling things and the non-lover watching coolly from the sidelines, ready to seize his moment of advantage. But is that the only setting in which one could treat love, a social setting of conventional actions and interactions, seen from the outside? Surely one can talk instead about the very experience, the passion of love as it is felt. Or one can see love, not only in the actions and reactions of the stock character called "the lover," but in a continuing state of character that over many years leads to different kinds of deeds. That is to say, there is certainly a manifold use of the term *love,* either as the comic passion that we laugh at in the stage "lover," or as the deep passion that lyric poetry expresses, for instance, or as the stabilized disposition, *hexis,* of love in its maturity. Socrates introduces his Great Speech by turning away from the exterior and comic characterizations of the earlier speeches, turning to the inward passion and the inward state—a passion and a state of the *soul.* His view of love will then be rooted in a discussion of the soul. Lysias neither speaks about the human soul nor even brings it into view or considers it in his speech. Socrates reaches for the alternative account of love that brings a deepening of view, entering an ontological dimension where social conventions are of little or no account. The utilitarian speech of Lysias could content itself with mere behaviorism. The morality and the reflection of Socrates cannot be content with that.

And this passion of love is introduced as a divine madness (244a). Madness is always despised by the rhetorician and the utilitarian with their calculating intellectualism, and yet madness may not be merely the malfunction of a disordered mind. It may be a gift, a blessing. This is the idea that made the *Phaedrus* famous, though it was not first stated here, nor first by Plato. The philosopher Democritus had already spoken of the divine inspiration of poetry,[3] and the adherents of the Dionysian current in Greek religion had understood their religious ecstasies as *enthusiasmos,* being filled with their god. In the previous chapter, we looked at some of the writings of Guthrie and Burkert on Orphism and its Dionysian background. Of the many writings on the religious tradition of divine madness and enthusiasm, which also estimate the degree of that tradition's impact on Plato, one can consult E. R. Dodds[4] and two influential articles by Linforth.[5]

As Socrates traces it here, divine madness arises in four divisions, which give it an outward, visible expression. The first two of these are evidently Greek religious practices[6]—the mantic gift, or gift of prophesying, and the *telestic* art, which brings purification and healing through prayer and ritual. Socrates' point is that such gifts and arts *can* at times be practiced in a routine way by prophets and priests who remain in an ordinary state of mind, not transported in madness, and that in such cases they accomplish nothing of value. The whole point of religion is to be in an extraordinary state of mind. The remaining two are poetry and music, and *erōs.* Of these the same point holds true—poetry produced in a sane workaday frame of mind is of little value, and the love

---

3. Fragment 21 in the ordering of Diels and Kranz, *Die Fragmente der Vorsokratiker* (Zürich: Weidmann, 1972).

4. *The Greeks and the Irrational.* See especially the chapter "Plato and the Irrational."

5. I. M. Linforth, "The Corybantic Rites in Plato," *University of California Publications in Classical Philology* 13 (1946): 121–62, and "Telestic Madness in Plato's *Phaedrus,"* in the same issue, pp. 163–72.

6. For further background, see, in addition to the literature cited in previous footnotes, Michael Morgan, *Platonic Piety.*

of a so-called lover who remains self-possessed and clear of mind would likewise be of little worth, a truth that will be understood by those who are enlightened (so I translate *sophoi* here), but not by the merely clever, *deinoi* (245c). Through madness, *theia mania,* we have our highest happiness.[7]

What is so striking is that Plato has not only conceived *erōs* as a form of divine madness, but has reconceived *philosophy* too as being sustained by *erōs* so understood—philosophy, supposedly the purest exercise of the rational mind. An excellent article by Gundert has treated this connection—philosophy and madness—making the point that in Plato's early work, he had always set philosophical reason in opposition to divine inspiration.[8] He was now able to surmount that old dichotomy because he could see that his recollection or reminiscence, *anamnēsis,* was a form of enthusiasm or possession (pp. 13ff.). "It [enthusiasm] is a forgetting, but one whose essence is a remembering" (p. 15).

Madness (*mania*), in the form of *erōs* whether divine or otherwise, is a disorientation, or reorientation, of the *entire* soul that affects all the modes of perception and behavior, thought, and speech. It is not just an oddity expressed in one bit of behavior, but a pervasive and enduring condition of the entire person or soul. The other three divine madnesses—prophecy, purification, and poetry—likewise express the soul that has been recharged and reoriented through and through. Being a prophet is not a job but a way of being—and the same for the others. But those who are called sane (*sōphrōn,* 245b4) or clever (*deinos,* 245c2) are closed to this divine dimension of our life and always prefer to seek what is merely advantageous (245b6). Insisting on their sanity and sense, they cannot grasp what is exalted about love or prophecy because they will not take a look into the depth of experience, where they would see the soul and its unconscious life. This life gains release when madness, for example, love, breaks the constraints of convention and everyday calculation.

In the *Phaedrus,* then, the route of access to the soul is love—love not seen comically from the outside, but felt as a passion and lived as a

---

7. In addition to the works already cited, there is a good treatment of divine madness in Josef Pieper, *Enthusiasm and Divine Madness,* trans. R. and C. Winston (New York: Harcourt, Brace, and World, 1964), especially in chaps. 5 and 6.

8. Hermann Gundert, "Enthusiasmos und Logos bei Platon," in Gundert, *Platonstudien.*

disposition. And at 249d ff., love is not only a passion but an activity of the soul. Though we are at first incited to love by seeing someone beautiful, love develops in the soul into a longing for the reunion of soul with soul and for the repetition of our primordial flight with a whole company of souls and spirits through the heavens under the leadership of a god. Love is the stirring of this longing and the renewed effort to fly. This is madness, for it flies against the counsels of prudence and good sense, an imaginative excess that is akin to religious possession, prophesying, and the creative transport of the musician and poet— works of the soul. What Plato observed of the experience of love and the other forms of divine madness disclosed to him a deeper constitution of the soul than had been suspected by Socrates. This soul is the unity of the conscious Socratic ego, to whom virtues can be ascribed, and an unconscious life whose urges are released through love, religion, and art—through madness. It is hard to deny the truth of Plato's view, hard to suppose that human experience is never more than the contrivance of calculation. There is nothing mythical or mad about the doctrine that the soul itself is this unity of conscious and unconscious experience. Of course, the idea is given a rhapsodic and mythical expression in this text, and we shall come to Plato's imagery for the flying soul in a moment.

The Self-Mover: *Phaedrus* 245c–246a

The treatment of divine madness is followed directly, at 245c5, by a tightly reasoned passage of argument in proof of the immortality of the soul. We might have expected Plato to proceed directly with further imaginative flights, but before he does indulge us in that way, he interrupts it to insert a dialectical argument. Why is it located where it is, right before the imaginative allegory of the charioteer and the two horses? It is a patch of the purest dialectic,[9] stylistically out of keeping both with what preceded it and with what follows. It is undoubtedly there just because the deeper thrust of the dialogue *requires* it in this position. It stiffens the spine of the whole; without it we might under-

---

9. It is an argument taken from the very early thinker Alcmaeon, bearing the marks of the archaic, stiff patches of reasoning that we have from the sixth century. See Guthrie, *A History of Greek Philosophy,* vol. 1, pp. 350–51, and vol. 4, p. 420; *Plato's Phaedrus,* ed. Hackforth, p. 68; and Robinson, *Plato's Psychology,* p. 114.

estimate the truth claim of the mythical allegory. Earlier pages made the point that the text of Plato weaves together different kinds of discourse; this passage unites dialectic with myth, and that is part of the pedagogical and therapeutic function of Platonic writing. Plato has wrought the most intimate link between *mythos* and *logos* to test his reader's soul with some severity through the closeness of their juxtaposition. A Platonic education requires us to move among genres of discourse: myth and dialectic, logic and rhetoric.

As I see it, the argument states first of all the thesis that is to be proved, "Every soul is immortal" (245c5), together with a summary statement of the reason, "After all, anything that is forever in motion has got to be immortal." What needs demonstration, then, is that the soul is forever in motion.

Although the soul has been introduced into the dialogue as that which can be subject to visitations of madness, at 245c1–4 Socrates says that the scope of the study has to encompass not only human souls but divine ones too, even though the latter never suffer madness. Such a widening of scope is characteristic of Plato whenever he seeks to probe the nature (*physis*) of a thing and what belongs to the thing as such and hence to every instance of it. This is the principle that will be justified later in the *Phaedrus,* 265d–266b, as the "collection" that must precede every "division," and which we treated in the course of our discussion of dialectic in part 1. The scope intended in the opening lines of our argument, "Every soul is immortal" comprises divine and human souls. "Every soul" is a translation of *psychē pasa* (also at 246b6)[10] in the distributive sense rather than in the collective sense, "all soul." A translation in the latter sense would permit a reading whereby soul was a sort of mass or stuff that permeated the whole universe and permeated ourselves too, so that each person's soul was just a portion of the universal soul, a reading that would treat the word *soul* like the word *air.* The present patch of argument does not require any such unitary mass that would be located by portions in each one of us (despite Hackforth's remark).[11] Moreover, such a "mass-soul" interpretation could not be united with the following imagery whereby each soul is visualized as a distinct entity, the union of a charioteer and a team of horses. The distributive sense of *pasa* is "every," and such a reading is characteristic of

---

10. Versus *Plato's Phaedrus,* Hackforth, p. 64. Griswold, *Self-Knowledge in Plato's Phaedrus,* makes a good analysis of *psychē pasa,* pp. 84–85.

11. *Plato's Phaedrus,* p. 64, n. 3.

Platonic prose generally, for when Plato wants to speak about cities or actions or human beings, he says what is true of them all, each one of them exemplifying a common nature or idea, but never suggests that Athens, Sparta, and Thebes were somehow merged into one continuous megalopolis, or all actions ultimately added up to just one action, or that all humans were merged into one.

Some scholars have supposed that the primary subject of the present argument is the soul of the world.[12] Such a reading could be combined with the "mass-soul" interpretation, and in that case what is true of the world soul would also apply to us, since the world soul, or a piece of it, is in us. But the world-soul interpretation can be stated independently of that. It is the passage at 245d6–c2 that has suggested that reading. The difficulty, however, is that, by itself, the supposed immortality of the world soul would have no bearing on the case Socrates is making for the immortality of each person's soul.

The argument is stated in formidably abstract style, which gives it the effect of a priori truth. In particular, it avoids the term *soul* until the very end, being content with terms such as "that which moves itself," and "that which is an origin." It is in the final passage of argument, beginning at e2, that Plato identifies the *soul* as that which moves itself—the text reads as if he had sensed that it would have been a circular argument if he had called the self-mover a soul right from the beginning.[13] Granting that, I shall still assume from the start that the self-mover under discussion is a soul, and my reason is that I am more interested in what the argument implies about the nature of the soul than in its status as a proof for immortality. After expounding it in that sense, I shall make a brief comment on its status as a proof of immortality.

The central feature of the argument is that it looks back, first of all, to the question of the possible *origin* of the soul. Only after the

---

12. In modern times, this interpretation has been offered by Festugière, in ancient times by Posidonius. The treatment of the whole argument, and of this point of interpretation, by Robinson, *Plato's Psychology,* chap. 6, is very clear and full. Note his defense of the traditional reading of 245c5 with *aeikinēton* (forever in motion) rather than *autokinēton* (self-moving).

13. The argument has frequently been expounded in noncircular, a priori fashion, e. g., Robinson, *Plato's Psychology;* Hackforth, in *Plato's Phaedrus,* ad loc; and R. Bett, "Immortality and the Nature of the Soul in the *Phaedrus,*" *Phronesis* 31 (1986): 1–26.

argument has established that the soul cannot have originated out of something else does it draw the inference: neither can the soul come to an end. Immortality is the consequence of un-generatedness. And from the beginning, this soul must have been for itself the origin of all its own motions.

After the statement of the thesis, the argument moves through six stages, the divisions being signified grammatically by the recurrent copulative *de.* I have separated them into six paragraphs in the translation, and offer here some commentary.

245c5. We differentiate things that are moved or changed through the agency of others from things that move themselves. The former will cease at some time to move, not the latter. In earlier texts, for example, *Phaedo* 98b–99c, Plato spoke of bodies and bodily parts as needing to be moved from the outside, and here at the end of the argument he returns to that point, saying that "every body whose motion is derived from outside is soulless" (245e5). Here the things that receive impetus for their motion from outside also transmit motion to other things, but that is not the important point, not the factor that will explain their own cessation of motion. The salient point is their passivity, their dependence on an external mover. As for the self-mover, since it has no need of an external impetus, it will never cease to be in motion. A self-mover might or might not transmit motion to another—that in itself is not relevant to its own continued motion. It may be that Plato is assuming here that every chain of causally connected motions will in fact cease functioning at some point, but that point is not required by his argument. What the argument demands is only that—unlike the case of self-movers—such chains *can* cease to function. That being alive depends on continued motion is assumed in this argument. But we do find other texts where that point is established, for example, later in the *Sophist* 248e–249b, where the Eleatic Visitor is speaking. But why will a self-mover remain in unceasing motion? The reason is this: motion ceases in non-self-movers because of the externality, the detachability, of the cause of their motion. In the self-mover, Socrates is ruling out a self-alienation in which the active power in the soul of causing motion might somehow become detached from the soul's capacity to be moved. If that were to arise, those parts of the soul would be as external to each other as two bodies are, and at some point the passive part might fail to be moved. This strong psychic unity is reinforced at 246a. Before that, Socrates concludes this first portion of the argument at 245c8–9 by asserting that only a self-mover can be the ultimate origin of all motions, including the movement enjoyed by non-self-moving things. I do not think we are meant to infer directly at the present stage of the argument that all motion originated ultimately from a self-mover. Rather, this is what will be shown in the later passages at 245d3 and at 245d7. Here we should beware the misunderstanding of supposing that just as what becomes moved is dependent on its origin, so the origin depends in some way on what becomes moved, as if, say, the self-mover necessarily had to cause motion in another. Nothing in the present argument suggests that (a point I have been stressing throughout these comments). A self-activated motion may be entirely psychic, as in thinking or desiring, or it may initiate bodily motion; it does not *need* to stimulate motion in another. In Hackforth's presentation,[14] this argument supposes that what is externally moved, *A,* is moved by the self-mover, *B.* So the impetus external to *A* could only be interrupted by a failure within *B,* the self-mover. Hackforth reads c9 as saying that every motion performed by *A* is caused by a direct operation of the self-mover on it. But of course, there are thousands of *A*s, one of them acting on another, this on yet another, and so on, and so the elaborate system of their heteronomous motions can be interrupted in many different ways, not just through a blackout in the self-mover, *B.* Moreover, what belongs to the very nature or idea of *B* is not to bring about these motions in *A,* or *A1, A2,* and so on, but merely to be *self*-moving, autonomous in that sense. I cannot agree with Hackforth that Plato is being arbitrary when he allows that a self-mover might not be transmitting motion to another.[15]

245d1. "Anything that is [truly] an origin [or a beginning] is ungenerated. . . . The origin cannot have a still earlier origin itself." Anything that came to be out of an origin would not really be an origin. This argument does not deny that the motion of one finite body can be the immediate cause for the motion of another one. It does maintain that if it has a further cause itself, it cannot be regarded as, properly, an origin or a beginning. Origin (*archē*) here must be understood in a strong Platonic sense, signified by *truly,* in the line just quoted, as refusing to admit into its essence anything opposed or different, such as "not

---

14. *Plato's Phaedrus,* p. 66, and especially n. 1.
15. Ibid.

being an origin," that is, being derived from an external origin. In this sense, being an origin is now treated as an absolute character, not reducible to the relative role of being "origin of X," where X was, say, the motion of the non-self-mover. In the present argument, the character of the *self-mover,* to be (absolutely) *an origin,* is the middle term from which further aspects of the self-mover are derived.

245d3. Socrates infers that the self-mover cannot be destroyed. This comes about as the consequence of the combination of being ungenerated and being an origin. Given the destruction of the origin, it could not be regenerated itself, for that would make something else the origin for it. Neither could that which proceeds from it be generated or regenerated either, for it, and it alone, *is* the origin of those dependencies. We see the general principle that an *archē* is the sort of thing whose failure could never be repaired. All its dependents would fail, and (more important) there could be nowhere to look to find a way of fixing it. Its being as *archē* rules out its having any auxiliaries. Now this principle is stated so strongly in the text that Socrates needs to provide some kind of evidence for it. That, I believe, is the function of Socrates' sole excursion into cosmology in the lines that follow.

245d7. We suppose one case of an obliterated origin, the obliteration of the origin of the universe. What happens? "The entire universe and everything that happens here would come to a standstill, and there would not exist any point from which motion could be once again originated." The point of this excursion is to offer a cosmic analogy that will help us to grasp the crucial importance of an *archē,* be that in the cosmos as a whole, or be that in the psychic life of an individual. The extreme situation we are imagining, of a collapsing heavens and an annihilated earth, is an illustration of the incomparable role of anything that is an *archē.* We see how profoundly the cosmos depends upon it. The cosmic *archē* does share with the human soul the character of being a self-mover—that is the salient point of the analogy. The point is certainly not that our human souls take on some role in sustaining the economy of the cosmos, nor is it that a world soul plays any role in our lives as individuals. It is likely that we are right to infer from Plato's presentation the further point that the *archē* of the cosmos is a soul. But the argument neither says that nor depends on that interpretation. As far as the validity of the present argument is concerned, there could be a self-mover, and one in the role of an *archē,* and an *archē* of the whole cosmos at that, which nevertheless was not a soul. The point being aimed at in d 3–6, something distinct from the cosmological analogy offered in the excursion, is stated next in the argument, e2–6. It concerns the *human* soul.

245e2. "What we may properly call immortal, then, is that which has the power of moving itself . . . the essence and the definition of the soul consists in this power. Every body whose motion derives from outside is soulless, but a body whose motion derives from itself has a soul." Being a self-mover, then, is the nature and definition of the soul, a fact confirmed by the inertness of a body that lacks one and the readiness of every besouled body to engage in movement. The meaning of this point is that there is no need for the infusion of anything else into us in order for us to move. Whether, however, every self-mover must be a soul or whether there might be some other nonpsychic self-mover is not discussed (I have no wish to impute that idea to Plato!) The argument has reached its goal with a clear focus upon the human being, composite of soul and body. The point is not that humanity must share in a nature more evidently seen in a "world soul."

245e6. This is the statement of the conclusion of the argument: if the soul is that which moves itself, the soul is ungenerated and therefore it is immortal.

One question discussed by scholars is whether the reasoning of this argument would establish the immortality of only some part of the soul, for instance, the rational part, at the expense of other psychic components such as the desires or the spirit of aggression, or whether it would apply to the entire soul. Surely there is no reason to confine the application of this argument to just one part. Any psychic motion can qualify as self-caused, and that is the salient feature. In the allegory of the horses and the charioteer that follows next, the relatively lower parts of the soul are shown to be sources of energy and movement. A related issue frequently discussed in earlier commentaries, whether that which is immortal is really the conscious individual personality of each one of us, what Gaye and Hackforth term "personal immortality."[16] They both believe that Plato did teach "personal immortality" but that the present argument has established something less than that, namely that the soul continuing after death (as far as the conviction of the present argument is concerned) may be something less than the "conscious

---

16. See *Plato's Phaedrus,* ed. Hackforth, p. 65, who refers there in text and notes to a previous treatment by R. K. Gaye in *The Platonic Conception of Immortality.*

personality." But a discussion of this question is best postponed until after the discussion of the nature and composition of the soul (246a–247b). One limitation will be offered by the treatment of transmigration, in which (in accord with Orphic teaching) we read that the soul may become embodied in different persons or in different lives, after the extinction of memories. Such a soul, obviously, cannot be identified with the conscious memory and autobiography we today associate with "person" and "personality." We shall take up the concepts of "individuality" and "personal identity" in a moment—these are questions about the *subject* of immortality.

As for the argumentation that derives immortality from this being's self-motion, I should like to acknowledge an implication of my earlier claim that the self-moving soul did not need to impart motion to another, to a body, for instance. This is a point on which I differ from Hackforth. If Hackforth were right on that point, it would, I believe, strengthen the argument as stated by Socrates. Because I have supposed the self-mover as being free from the need to impart bodily motion, I have allowed it to operate independently of the interconnected chains of bodies that move through heteronomous causes. There *are* purely psychic motions. In this way, self-motion becomes parallel to a principle stated by Kant. Kant argued that where we see causality through natural laws we cannot insert a "causality through freedom," "freedom" in this case referring to self-motion. No self-mover can occur within the chains of interconnected things and events that exhibit regular causality. Motion and change being, in general, heteronomous, self-movers would be an anomaly in nature. But, according to Kant, there is other evidence that freedom does operate causally, outside causality through natural law.[17] And although self-motion, or causality through freedom, cannot be integrated with the natural causality that rules throughout the phenomenal world, reason in its practical employment proclaims to us the reality of self-movement, or causality through freedom, for only on that hypothesis can there be any account of morality. This teaches us the metaphysical limitation of nature, and of the knowledge of nature, indicating the existence of a nonphenomenal reality. My commentary imposes a similar interpretation on the Platonic

---

17. Immanuel Kant, *Critique of Pure Reason,* Transcendental Dialectic, Third Antinomy; also *Critique of Practical Reason,* Introduction.

argument. Self-movers do not belong to the general system of hetero-nomously moving entities, such as physical bodies. The self-caused motion of the soul is not a visible, bodily event, and the ontological structure of the soul is out of accord with the structure of bodies that move. In the soul the "mover" is unified with the "moved" in an indissoluble bond. This comes with the divine intensity of the soul's way of being. By my interpretation, the soul's self-motion and immortality are tied up with the difference of the soul from the chains of contingently connected things. Such a reading, I concede, is probably not in line with Plato's intention, for it sacrifices the physical evidence he wanted for immortality. It would make the immortality a consequence of the *meta*physical principle, derived from other grounds, of the divinity of the soul.

Image of the Self-Mover: *Phaedrus* 246a–247b

At 246a, Socrates introduces the question of what the soul is, using Platonic language, "What is its *idea?*" but, suddenly modest, he says the topic is too great for mortal philosophers. As in the *Republic* 506d–e, where Socrates cannot discuss the topic of the Good itself directly, but only its offspring (*ekgonos*) or its likeness (*homoiōma*), the sun, so here he tells Phaedrus not what the soul is but only what it is like (*eoiken*). The narrative is imaginative and imaginary, belonging to the genres of myth and allegory. It starts from a simile (*eoiketō,* "Let the soul be likened to . . ."), which serves as the seed for a full-scale allegory narrated in language that draws on ancient myths: let the soul be likened to a winged pair of steeds, that, in being yoked together, have merged into the unity of a single power, and their charioteer. The images and metaphors to come are all motivated in some way by the opening simile. It harmonizes this text with the tripartitism of *Republic* IV (439b–441c): *epithumia* (appetite) there is represented here by the black horse; *thumoeides* (the "spirited part") there is the white horse here; and *logos* (reason) there is the charioteer here. Though he introduces the charioteer here, it is only later on (251c) that Socrates indicates that the charioteer too is endowed with wings; wings on each part accords with the *Republic*'s teaching (580d–581d) that each of the parts of the soul has its own desire (*epithumia*) and love (*philia*). What is new in the *Phaedrus,* above all, is the image of the wings. Generally, they are spoken of as belonging to the whole soul, their number left indefinite (249a, 249c, 251b–d). The partitioning of the soul is, if anything, even more pronounced than in the *Republic,* for each psychic power is now represented as a separate organic being (horse or charioteer), and the flight of the soul poses the challenge to the charioteer of harnessing and guiding the two separate sources of power.

The simile is applied no less to gods than to mortals, at points calling attention to their difference (246b–c), but in principle grasping all souls under a common description. So in the economy of the whole narrative, an adequate account of love must not only go deeper than Lysias would, linking love to the profound topic of the soul, but also broader, in that the complete account of love must introduce divinities as well as mortals.

If the simile of the horses and charioteer constitutes the seed of the entire allegory, then the kernel of the seed is the image of the wings. This image of the wing (*pteron*) occurs in many grammatical modes: winged, the winged one, wingless, the less definite *plumage* (*pterōma,* 246e2), broken wings, regained wings, the roots or stumps of the wings, and the bud of a wing. Central to interpretation is the sentence at 246d6–e1: "It is in the power of wings to raise on high that which is heavy, lifting it up to where the race of the gods dwells, and, most of all bodily parts, they have a share in the divine. That which is beautiful and wise and good, and everything of such a nature, is divine." The key implication of this sentence is that we are able to experience even here in terrestrial life the sense of an elevation, the acquisition of a power to go soaring like Pegasus or the driver of the sun, through the sudden drive of an energy released within our soul. We shall explore in chapter 9 the implications of this image for the account of love; here it is apparent that this image brings together the account of erotic love with the intellectual activity of the souls of god and mortals. The simile unifies different parts of experience.

At 246c–d, Socrates offers some cautionary thoughts on the use of images and allegories, a remarkable reflection given that it occurs in the midst of the most exuberant passage of imagery ever written by Plato. So often, says Socrates, we imagine a god in the form of a mortal creature, as having both a soul and a body—absurd, of course, and springing from ignorance, from our not having ever seen a god nor given adequate thought to the gods. We treat the immortal being, not as purely immaterial and spiritual but as a combination of soul with body that would last forever—absurd! The verb for "imagine" here, *plassō, plattomen,* indicates a visual imagination (it could even refer to the sculpture of icons) and recalls passages both in the *Republic* (596c–598d) and the later *Sophist* (233d–236c), where Plato gives voice to his unease with visual images. Yet surely these words are also a warning to Phaedrus and to Socrates himself and to the reader, pointing out a danger that lies equally well within a discursive presentation such as the present speech: it is not specifically a *visual* problem. The problem has arisen because, according to Socrates, our present condition, our human condition as living creatures, *zōa,* is the result of a fall from heaven and our acquisition of an earthly body. This fall has resulted in a fallen form of imagination and thought as well. When we suppose that the gods are like us, just bigger and more beautiful, we exhibit a fallen form of thinking, specifically the fallacy of attributing bodies to the gods, but equally the mistake of attributing bodies to the mortal souls in advance of their fall and incarnation. Socrates is calling on Phaedrus (and the reader) to make use of the horse-and-charioteer imagery in another way altogether, to dematerialize the images when we hear them, especially the image of the wings.

It is not just the horse and charioteer that we have to interpret in a nonliteral way. The same issue arises with the representation of the heavens, the earth, the intermediate zone, and the region "above the heavens." At 247b7 we read: "Whenever the souls that we call immortal go up to the summit of heaven, they go outside and take their stand right on heaven's rim, and as they stand there they are carried along by the rotation and see the things that are outside the heavens. No poet here on earth has ever sung of that place above the heavens, and none will ever do so fittingly. Yet we ourselves must dare to speak about it truly, because our very theme is truth." These souls—and here it is *principally* the gods that are under discussion—are flying forever, and likewise the universe or cosmos is rotating perpetually in circular motion, and everything is in motion with the possible exception of the Earth.[18] But the divine souls who rise up above the outer rim of heaven to see what is above it are able to contemplate there something that does *not* move. This narrative that even opens up a place *above* the heavens

---

18. Earlier dialogues presented the Earth as stationary (*Phaedo* 108e–109a, for instance), and the reference to Hestia here at 247a1 may have that meaning, for this hearth goddess was often identified with the Earth in antiquity (see both *Plato's Phaedrus,* ed. Hackforth and Rowe, *Plato: Phaedrus,* ed. and trans. *ad loc.*). But *Timaeus* 40c describes a rotating earth.

could be interpreted to some extent in cosmological terms, reckoned as a part of ancient astronomy and science generally, for we see some traces of it in the *Timaeus* and in the *Laws* X, and in later works, for instance, Aristotle's *Metaphysics* XII, chap. 7–8, and *Physics* VIII, chap. 10. And yet the principal meaning of this image will become apparent only if we dematerialize it in accordance with Socrates' warning, read it not as a sketch for cosmology but as bearing upon the life of the soul.

In the *Phaedo* 107c–108c, Socrates speaks of the souls going down into the underworld. At the end of the *Republic*, 614c–d, the souls of the dead are shown proceeding either into the earth or up into the heavens after they have received judgment. In the *Phaedrus*, the soul is likened to horses and a charioteer soaring through heaven and even (if they are divine) gazing out beyond it. These texts all separate the soul from the body rigorously—they relate encounters undergone by the discarnate self. So we cannot visualize this "underworld" and this "heaven" primarily in physical or cosmological terms. After all, the idea of justice and other ideas are what occupy this "place beyond the heavens" (see chapter 8). This heaven and this underworld constitute an environment for a purely immaterial soul: they are an imagined heaven, an imagined underworld, and an imagined earth that constitute a sort of location for an imagined soul. We are imagining the heavens we traversed before we became incarnate. Indeed, as the narrative sets these horses and chariots, especially the divine ones, at the rim of the rotating cosmos, we are imagining a rotation that is rapid enough for us to sense it. These heavens, and the things that lie beyond or outside them, are to furnish a background for the explanation of the human experiences of love and knowledge, toward which Socrates is making his way in the narrative, experiences that befall the human beings in their location here on earth. It is noteworthy that much of the recitation of the myth takes place in the present tense (e. g., 246c–249b). But at 249b–250d, where attention has turned to the experiences human beings have during their lifetime here on earth, the mythical material is presented in a retrospective style, by way of the philosopher's recollection of those supernal scenes, and those scenes are narrated in the past tense, the aorist.

The flight of the souls takes place in an imagined space. When Plato treats the creation of the world in the *Timaeus*, he conceives an earthly space or a material space, a Receptacle (*hypodochē*) and a Space (*chōra*)—see 49a–52b—where bodies can be extended, and that is governed by the main polarity of heaven and earth. But in the *Phaedrus* the imagined space has now been expanded out into a place *beyond* the heavens. And the space imagined *within* the heavens allows for the cyclical rotation of all the chariots, interrupted, though, by the confused tumult of the mortal chariots in their confused struggle and their eventual fall.

This story also runs on through an imagined time. It was untold eons ago that our souls were soaring on high in that happy company; and then chaos and confusion arose among the mortal chariots. Then the decree of destiny was uttered (248c): that all should enter into earthly life in differentiated fates. Plato is able to assimilate the Orphic narratives into his imagined time by virtue of its divided sequences of duration marked by a different tone in each: the primeval adventure of flight, the chaos of competing chariots, the decree of Fate being uttered, and the falling to Earth. The cosmic, created time of the *Timaeus* has no epochs of that sort; it is the "moving image of eternity" carried in the world soul.

The imagined space and time are the dimensions for the adventures of *the imagined soul.* But now we must address the issue of philosophical principle that arises in connection with this imagery for space, time, the world, and the soul. Is it necessary to distinguish the imagined soul of this narration from the actual and true soul, the topic of philosophy? I wish to answer no, and in doing so I shall appeal to the example of both Socrates and Plato. Philosophy is the inquiry into truth that is able to employ and interweave different discursive modes, the mythical, the rhetorical, and the dialectical, taking each of them to be one style or mode for the disclosure of what is. A philosopher of pure reason (Hegel comes to mind) might wish to demonstrate the integrity of the imagined, mythical soul and the real soul, the object of philosophy, by reducing the former to the latter, that is, interpreting the myth by restating its point nonmythically. But there is another route, which I believe is closer to Plato's. It would, as it were, work the other way around, not reducing the mythical imagery to something else, but rather showing that there is a *reason* for our use of mythical discourse, a reason rooted in the nature of the soul. The myth of the soul in the *Phaedrus* shows us a soul whose rational part is in struggle with the other parts, the latter symbolized by the horses, and it shows the limits of vision achieved by this charioteer (more on that point in chapter 8). The human soul, then, is such that it will never be capable of a discourse of pure reason. There is a reason, rooted in our nature, why philosophy must express itself at certain points in myth. It would be altogether too literal, of course, to trace the mythical voice back to the black horse, or the rhetorical voice to the white horse, but we can grant, more generally, that the finite and divided soul is what gives grounding for philosophy's need to employ more than one voice.

Eschatology: *Phaedrus* 248a–249b

It is at 248a1 that the narrative of the special drama of *human* prehistory begins, the struggle in the heavens of the powerful teams of horses, precipitating the first fall, away from heaven's rim. Then at 248c–d comes the doom of fate, the second fall, whereby the souls must descend in a ninefold order into the different human lives (a few are still permitted to stay), for they have lost their wings. Here the vastness of the imagined time opens out, with ten cycles of a thousand years each—and, as far as Plato or the Orphic sources are concerned—the possibility seems open that the drama may be played out again and again in endless cycles of ten thousand years each.[19]

The tragic myth expresses the human sense of walking on Earth but suffering from a primordial loss or a primordial wound; we are crippled inside through the loss of our noblest member, the wings, a loss that is not consciously remembered. The Orphic religion, and its Platonic elaboration, obscurely identifies us as defective from the start, yet the further teaching, in the story of love, will be the restoration of wings. There is the throbbing erotic experience, which offers the promise of a restoration. And yet the human experience of love will never be utterly effective. We may begin the growth of wings, a budding which engenders the promise or hope of soaring again on high—but the restoration on earth is not complete. It is just the preparation of the soul for a return to divinity.

Not only do we return to Earth—we must do it again and again. We have lived before; our soul has had other habitations, and it will have more. This thought indicates a relaxation of identity. Plato is no longer frightened of dissolving the identity of the self, relaxing the firm outline that had at one time stood guard over the particular soul, as in the

---

19. Two classic articles on the eschatological myth are those of R. D. Archer-Hind "On Some Difficulties in the Platonic Psychology," *Journal of Philology* (1881): 120–31, and R. S. Bluck, "The *Phaedrus* and Reincarnation," *American Journal of Philology,* 79 (1958): 156–64, 405–14.

Apology of Socrates. In the *Phaedrus,* Plato permits his soul to be Plato plus Dion plus Alcibiades plus innumerable others and others, dissolving an individual identity into a kind of carnival of identities. First of all, the tripartition of the soul is much more serious in the *Phaedrus* than it has been in the *Republic,* for when the doctrine is introduced here by way of an image, it is the unity of several powers that have grown together (246a). Also, the tripartite soul exists in two utterly different states: winged and wingless. But an even deeper point, disturbing no doubt, is brought by the Orphic dimension of Plato's myth: we shall be living again and again in multiple lives, even in multiple species. The life we live now is neither our first nor our last; the bodies we have now are like so many suits of clothes; this life is one arena of experience, not unique. The experience of the "I" must waver in its identity as surely as the identity of the "Thou." It is this Orphism, perhaps, that was the object of deep fear and fierce opposition among the Christian Church Fathers, motivating the long attack on the Platonist Origen. For them, the biblical doctrine brought not only one God, but one and only one course of history as well, an *Einmaligkeit* (once and once only!) with a serious eschatological import: only one life for each of us.

Here, as in the *Phaedo* (81–83), there is even the transmigration of the soul into other species. Can we attribute this seriously to Plato (and his Pythagorean sources)? As Hackforth says, we have little reason to doubt Plato's seriousness at least at the time of composing this dialogue, though by the end of his life he likely had given the doctrine up.[20] As with other systems of religion that incorporate metempsychosis or transmigration, Orphism brings to expression a sense of the community of all life, perhaps most of all in a spirit of mourning animal suffering, another expression of the relaxed identity, the many "me"'s, the many "you"'s. It is therefore clear that the soul of the *Phaedrus* is a more elementary and primitive thing than what we call the "person," that individual who possesses a name, a sex, a community, a role, a place in history, moral and legal rights, and a memory. Moreover, I should like to argue that being an individual is a kind of substratum, presupposed, I think, for being a person, the ontological condition for it, something more elementary and fundamental than it. Do we have to deny individuality as well of the soul of the *Phaedrus?* If we follow the imagery of the speech, focusing on the preincarnational soul, the pure

---

20. *Plato's Phaedrus,* pp. 87–91.

soul, we see that it is one of a host of mortal souls in communion with a leader-god, and, moreover, that each one is articulated into three members or parts, the horses and the charioteer. This pure soul meets many conditions for individuality. But, in an ontological reversal, this is an individuality without identity. Identity, self-sameness, is a deeper-lying ontological condition in terrestrial experience than is individuality, for no animal or plant can be an individual without being stabilized through time as being the animal that it is, that is, without identity. But the pure soul of the *Phaedrus* can come to being in different lives.

In the *Phaedo,* 79e–81a, Socrates treats, not the preexistence of the soul, but the destiny that awaits it at the end. Since the soul as ruler of the body is the part that resembles the divine—what is immortal, intelligible, unitary, indissoluble, and self-consistent—its destiny is to rejoin everything that is of that nature. "It departs to that place which is, like itself, invisible, divine, immortal, and wise, where, on its arrival, happiness awaits it and release from uncertainty and folly . . . to spend the rest of its time with the gods" (81a). The soul is divine and so is everything that is like it—the gods themselves, the place of their abode, the forms of Beauty and Justice, and the rest. The divine, *to theion,* is of broader extent than the race of the gods.

Recollection

I would like to refer to a text from the *Phaedo* in which Socrates, in discussion with Simmias, appeals to some experiences of memory and perception that Simmias acknowledges readily and that the reader too has little difficulty in acknowledging (72e–77a). The force of Socrates' argumentation is to take us from this acknowledgment to an acknowledgment of a deeper and more mysterious power that operates within ourselves; that is, Socrates shows that lying underneath the familiar experience of conscious life there is the operation of a darker power, a depth dimension on which conscious experience floats. Just this, I think, is the meaning of the word *soul* in the context of mystery religion: we say *I,* meaning to refer to the stratum of organized, conscious memory and perception; but to apply the noun *soul,* in the third person, to that range of experience summons up a preconscious power that first brought into being all the conscious experiences associated with "I." Seeing one friend reminds us of another one, or seeing a cloak or lyre or picture does the same thing, calling the friend to mind. We must have already known that friend, the preconscious condition for being reminded (73c–74a). The general idea of Equality cannot have been first acquired from perceptual experience (74a–75c), but this is what we are remembering when we see things that are nearly equal. That experience too has a preconscious condition. There is always a déjà vu.

A number of factors are at work together in the situation of seeing two equal sticks. There are the two sticks, I myself who am seeing them, and the absolute Equality that I am recalling at that moment. Now I think we must mention here two other points that Socrates does not mention in the very passage, but which he has mentioned just a little bit earlier (73b–74a). Along with the present perception of two equal sticks is the memory of past perceptions of these two sticks. Moreover, there is also the memory of past perceptions of other equal things, other sticks, and also stones, dice, and so on. Next, we learn (75c–77a) of the whole class of absolute ideas: Beauty, Goodness, Justice, Holiness, and many more. They were *all* communicated to our souls before we were born: the whole class of ideas has to constitute a further element in the situation. We do not rely just on one absolute idea, Equality for example, when we perceive equal things, but, being reminded of the one idea, we enter the vista where all of them are at work together: a network. Let me treat Beauty in this connection to illustrate my point. I would say that the sight of a beautiful face induces a déjà vu reaction, the reminder of other occasions of seeing this face, and then the reminder of other beautiful faces; therewith, as other seeings and other faces rise up in memory, they bring the unthematic reminder of myself, the deep stratum of this experience, the soul stratum as I might call it, the unthematic awareness of the self who saw all this on previous occasions. And there is, finally, the awareness that Beauty itself has imprinted my soul and, then, where there is Beauty there is also Justice, Goodness, the vista as a whole.

Some philosophers have argued that Plato's cases do not prove any nonempirical or nonperceptual knowledge at all. I believe they are wrong about this: he provides sound reasoning for there being innate ideas, and we shall explore some of the reasoning in the following chapter. Another group of philosophers have granted the premise of innate ideas, but argue that there are other explanations of them that are more probable than the preexistence of the soul. But I am not sure that any who have offered versions of a priori knowledge have quite succeeded in their account. In that case, it is as well to retain the doctrine, for the time being at least, in its mythical form.

If we assume the usual dating for the dialogues, several works were written between the *Phaedo* and the *Phaedrus* which, though they treat the soul at some length, make no mention of reminiscence. In the *Symposium,* Diotima leads the young Socrates up the ladder of love to a vision of Beauty itself, but this is only at the end of the soul's journey: she has not outlined any prenatal vision of Beauty. In the story she tells about the birth of Eros, there is no hint of our preexistence. Thus a pre-existent soul is not, in the *Symposium,* a precondition for the experience of love. In the *Republic* X, the vision of Er as recounted mythically does imply the preexistence of the soul. But that myth is not referred to during the presentation of the doctrine of ideas in the middle books; nor do those books contain anything equivalent to it. Contemplation of ideas, then, according to the *Republic,* does not seem to hinge on our preexistence. The *Phaedrus* has returned to this doctrine, so characteristic of the *Phaedo.* Perhaps it is because Plato at that point wanted to treat the theme of love with a dignity equal to that of the earlier treatment of death. The unblinking study of death highlighted the soul intensively, and immortality prompted the idea of preexistence. The rival in intensity for death is now love—love, no mere spirit, but a god.

The following chapter will examine the treatment of *anamnēsis* more closely. As we conclude the present chapter, however, it might be a good place to return to the question of myth and myth interpretation. In chapter 1, we looked at Hegel, whose method of interpretation we contrasted with Schelling's. We sought to profit from an interaction between Hegel's intellectualism and a more pluralistic hermeneutical theory in Schelling, one more open to different discourses and systems of meaning. At this juncture, it is helpful to note that Hegel has an interiorized, or spiritualized, interpretation of the Platonic *anamnēsis* which we shall do well to ponder as we examine more of the details of Plato's treatment of knowledge and love:

> Plato's ancient saying is . . . that we learn nothing but only recollect something that we originally bear within ourselves. Taken in an external and non-philosophical way, this means that we recollect a content that we have known in a previous state. That is its mythical presentation. But its implication is that religion, right, ethics and everything spiritual in human beings is merely aroused. We are implicitly spirit, for the truth lies within us and the spiritual content within us must be brought to consciousness. Spirit bears witness to spirit. This witness is spirit's own inner nature. It involves the important specification that religion is not mechani-

cally introduced into human beings but lies within them, in their reason and freedom generally.[21]

Hegel's reading of Plato's doctrine illustrates his whole method of elevating mythical "representations" into "conceptual" comprehension that we looked at in chapter 1. This quotation should make it plain that his method is sustained by his entire philosophical system. The spiritual meaning of the myth is that right, knowledge, and religion are themselves inward; they are attributes of spirit itself, not inculcated from the outside. But Hegel's term *spirit* always has a double meaning and more. The individual human being is spirit in its subjective form, but subjective spirit is sustained by objective spirit and absolute spirit. Hegel is able to elevate Plato's mythical representation into conceptual form only because subjective spirit is comprehended by spirit in its fuller scope. Right, knowledge, and religion are not part of the *individual*'s own inner nature, and if they are attributes of spirit itself, this is because of the vast scope of objective and absolute spirit. Such is the Hegelian process of *Aufhebung,* in which an item expressed in myth becomes elevated and converted into a dialectical meaning. But in the following chapter, I shall attempt a different approach to *anamnēsis.* I shall not merely "let it be," remaining in the fabulous form of the text's Great Speech, but neither shall I eliminate its mythical statement through a conversion or *Aufhebung* into dialectic. Rather, I shall observe the conjunction between the mythical statement and the rhetorical and dialectical discourses that accompany it.

---

21. Hegel, *Lectures on the Philosophy of Religion,* pp. 160–61.

| Truth
Phaedrus 247c–250c

We have explored something of the destiny that awaits the human soul. Yet the *Phaedrus* differs from the *Phaedo* in that its focus is less on the ultimate fate of the soul and more on the life of the soul in advance of incarnation. Socrates maintains in the *Meno* and *Phaedo* that we had an acquaintance with ideas in an earlier existence. But there Plato had not ventured to put into words a description of the primordial, prenatal encounter that the soul had with the ideas. This encounter is detailed for us in the central pages of the *Phaedrus.*

Plato's metaphysical texts are often read as early exercises in physical science, charting the structure of the heavens and the earth. We must grant that although Plato's own final picture of the universe becomes codified in authoritative form in the *Timaeus,* there surely is a world picture contained in the *Meno* and the *Gorgias,* the *Phaedo* and the *Republic,* and the *Phaedrus.* Their mythical passages sketch the Earth, with its rocks and seas, grottos and caves, and Tartarus, the underworld; then, above the Earth, the winds and clouds of the sublunary region; again above that the bright upper air and *aithēr,* where the heavenly bodies circulate; and, special to the *Phaedrus,* the outer rim of heaven and even the "place beyond the heavens." Parts of this "meteorology" certainly replicate the Orphic cosmologies. And yet, whether we are reading the old Orphic texts or the text of Plato, treating the arduous journey of the soul to the places of its purification, its return to Earth, or its ultimate release, we cannot suppose them to be manuals for a space flight. As I noted in the previous chapter, when we read, "the souls that are called immortal mount up to the summit of the heavens and see the things that are outside," this is an imagined soul flying through an imagined heaven and an imagined space and time. We have to dematerialize the account and grasp its cosmology in relation to the main theme of the myth: the origin and fate of the soul itself.

At 249b–c, and restated at 249e4, Plato establishes a general condition for becoming human: the soul must have seen truth, *alētheia*, because a human soul must be able to grasp things according to the idea. Recollection makes that possible, as we shall be seeing in detail. Thus the mythically stated journey of the soul in and beyond the cosmos, in the company of the god and a select group of companions, proves to be the condition for the possibility of characteristically human awareness. Stated mythically, it is a prenatal vision, a story of how being and truth are infused into our souls, a prenatal encounter of the soul with being, truth, justice, and the like. And the topic actually has to be treated to some extent mythically, for it is an effort to express in words the ground of the possibility of dialectical reason, an account that cannot be conducted only in dialectical terminology. Its value is not diminished by its mythical form of statement.

We are making not a cosmological reading, then, but a reading focused on the grounds for having a self and knowing oneself. In fact, the whole dialogue has already been convincingly expounded as an exercise in self-knowledge by Griswold.[1] Griswold is able to treat all three rhetorical exercises as being animated by the question of self-knowledge.[2] It is in the teaching of the supernal life of the soul that Socrates achieves the self-knowledge he has been seeking. Even the account of the heavens and what lies beyond the heavens continues the same course of inquiry into the self or soul, for what this speech opens up is the eternal homeland of the soul. Self-scrutiny and self-knowledge have not been left behind at the point at which the *Phaedrus* becomes most metaphysical, because that metaphysics contains the truth about the soul.[3] It was possible for ancient readers of the *Phaedrus* to take the Great Speech of Socrates, and parallel texts from other dialogues, as essays in cosmology. But we cannot do so. We must interpret them as the elaboration of self-knowledge.

---

1. Charles Griswold, *Self-Knowledge in Plato's Phaedrus.*
2. Ibid., pp. 45–51, 57–59, 74–137.
3. Griswold makes this point well in ibid., pp. 3–4, 92–99, 105–8, and 114.

The Ideas

Moreover, the *Phaedrus* offers a general account of all that which belongs together with the soul in its primordial, preincarnational state, the domain of its original being. In this account, it is offering a general ontological theory, a theory that must be clamped together with psychology, for the soul is not something that can be isolated from its true milieu. We shall have to consult the *Phaedo, Republic,* and *Symposium* first of all to give the appropriate direction to our exposition.

If we look back to the *Phaedo,* 72e–77b, we find Socrates' argument that all knowledge is achieved through recollection, and his case is that we can recognize two sticks as being equal only because we have a prior acquaintance with Equality (74a). The same point illustrated by this case, he maintains (75c–d), will also hold true for what is greater and less, for the beautiful, the just, the pious, and, as he puts it, "all the rest of them." No other members of the array of ideas appear in this particular passage. We should note a strict line of demarcation: it is our sense experience alone that makes us acquainted with the sticks and stones themselves, that is, the things that exhibit equality. They are marked off sharply from the equality that they embody, because it seems that no recollection is needed for us to recognize them as sticks and stones. Later pages of the *Phaedo,* 99d–107b, devoted to a critique of the mechanical explanation of events, expand on our list by including the Good and the Even and Odd. Given the whole thrust of this later argument, it might be permissible to include the soul, and life and death, in this array, and perhaps fire, and the Hot and Cold too.

Already in the *Phaedo,* if not earlier, Plato used the terms *idea* and *eidos* to refer to all members of this array in general terms. It is at 102b and 103e, I think, for the first time in the *Phaedo,* that Socrates speaks of them as *eidos,* and at 105d as *idea.* Wilamowitz offers an economical explanation of these words, which can launch our inquiry on its way.

> One guideline for us is the language that Plato took over, and another is the people's accustomed manner of thinking, from which even the sharpest and most original mind will free itself only gradually. *Idea* and its equivalent *eidos* are named after seeing, and the words retained that suggestion. With things, and especially with people, *idea* meant the outer appearance. But it had become common to speak of the many variety or types of something as its many *ideai,* its ways of appearing, just as we would speak of its many forms. When Isocrates taught rhetorical logic and topics, he

taught the different *ideai* that went to make up a speech. Democritus believed his atoms were all of different shapes and thereby prescribed all the shapes that could be realized in nature, so he called his atoms *ideai,* shapes. Now it was the Socratic question whether virtue was one or many that led Plato to see that each single virtue was one appearance of virtue itself, and also to gather together the different instances that manifested a single virtue under one *idea.* What appeared in everything that was just, so as to make it worthy of that predicate, was that which could be "glimpsed" in each one, the *idea;* it gave to each one the aspect or form that we call "just."
. . . What was specifically Platonic and unexpected, however, was to grasp as something concrete what we suppose to be merely abstracted out of the empirical, so that being would pertain precisely to the *idea* and not to the appearances that people tended to call real, and that the attributes manifested by an appearance were actually owing to this *idea.*[4]

Although the *Phaedo* postulates *anamnēsis,* it offers no images for the prenatal soul or for its encounter with that which it would later recollect—it only postulates some sort of experience. But now this is brought before us in the *Phaedrus* as flying, feeding, and seeing. The divine madness of love is realized in Plato's imagination as flying, soaring. Why is it that the human soul is open to this possibility of madness? It is because the love experience restores to us, below the conscious level, the memory of primal scenes from the soul's ancient past. Love causes the soul to take flight, thus resuming its original heavenly activity. There are two kinds of soul—divine and mortal—and their flight in formation through the heavens gives a more graphic realization of that affinity of our soul with the gods than that expressed in *Phaedo* 81a; their primordial kinship is *shown.* We must note that a strenuous activity of flight was needed before the mortal soul descended into a body—justice, temperance, and the other ideas cannot merely "imprint" a soul in a passive state. Moreover, throughout the description in the *Phaedrus,* there are references to the soul's feeding upon the ideas—a metaphor for living creatures that recurs in the *Phaedrus*'s account of the wings of the soul, even here on earth, throbbing and bursting with new growth—a fusion of language, as Ferrari has shown,[5] that combines human sensations with other cases of vitality such as the bird's growth of feathers on the

4. Wilamowitz-Moellendorff, *Platon,* pp. 346–48.
5. *Listening to the Cicadas,* pp. 150–67.

wing. The exercise of flight, along with nutrition, accompanies the pre-natal experience of seeing. No mere unsituated or passive imprinting but an active acquisition, seeing is the principal experience recounted in the myth, and that is because Plato is leading up to an explanation for experiences of seeing that the incarnate soul has in this lifetime, the awakening of *erōs* through the seeing of beauty, and, likewise, the cognitive recognition of truth here on earth. Plato's device is to prepare an account of embodied seeing by postulating a condition for it: a supernal seeing. In the reactions of love and knowledge here on earth, there is an awakening recollection of another seeing.

On Truth: *Phaedrus* 247c

The principal metaphysical passages of the *Phaedrus* do not rely mainly on the terms *idea* and *eidos*—there is a different tapestry of terms that requires attentive study. As we read at 247c3, "No poet here on earth has ever sung of that place above the heavens, and none will ever do so fittingly. Yet now we ourselves must dare to speak about it truly, because our very theme is truth." The soul had a primordial experience of seeing, and that which it saw has several names in the *Phaedrus,* first of all, truth, *alētheia.* Speaking as a philosopher, Socrates is saying that he wants to go further than any poet has ever done, and his warrant for doing so is that philosophy assumes an obligation to speak the truth, to "speak truly." He asserts that it is especially important that the words we are to utter about the place above the heavens be true. This cannot refer back to 246a4–5, where Socrates apologizes for failing to state what the soul *is* and resorting to an image for it; far from renouncing imagery at this point, he becomes ever more emphatic about using it. The meaning, rather, is that we have to be bold and not fainthearted, not stop short of the complete truth, a maxim, I think, to justify the use of any and all modes of discourse: myth, rhetoric, and dialectic. The lines we quoted give the reason philosophy has to take special pains in this case to speak the truth: it is because the present theme *is* truth. In fact the term *alētheia* recurs so frequently (247c8, d4; 248b6, c3–4; 249b6, d5) that it should be the primary name we use for Socrates' theme throughout these pages.

Peri alētheias legonta, "speaking about truth," means exploring that which sets a standard by which all discourse is measured. Everyone in some way aspires to truth, even in mythical and rhetorical discourse, and we are now going to identify, within the present thought and speech, that which is to guide all human thought and speech. We can infer that if this philosophy were not true itself, measured by the true measure, its claim to be a guide, a revealer of the measure, would be ludicrous.

Truth serves in this passage as a collective or general term for all that which the soul saw above the heavens, including the things that become specified a bit further on: justice, temperance, and so on. Truth is not one member of this group but the general character of the group. It would not be correct to translate *alētheia* here as "*the* truth." What the soul has seen is not some true doctrine, but rather that which makes for the possibility of any such doctrine and for all possible true doctrines even if there should be an infinity of them.

We have encountered this principle of truth already in the *Republic,* especially in 509d–511e, the Divided Line, and 514a–519d, the parable of the Cave. In both those passages, Plato's special focus was on degrees of truth—in the Divided Line, Socrates speaks of different degrees of truth as degrees of clarity, *saphēneia,* 509d9, 511e3; in the Cave the degrees of truth (515c2, 515d7; 516a3; 517c1–5) are correlated to different kinds and degrees of light and shadow. What is implied by both accounts, although not stated in so many words, is the discovery of a pure truth at the climax of the ascent of the soul (517c1–5 makes the idea of the Good, the last thing to be seen, the source and cause of all lesser kinds of truth). It is especially the *Phaedrus* that focuses on the soul's vision of pure and unalloyed truth.

A bit later on, at 249b5–c6, we read: "For [a soul] that has never seen truth will not enter into this [human] frame. For it is by way of an *eidos* that human beings comprehend something that is said, something that comes out of many perceptions and is gathered into one through reasoning." Here Plato is tracing human reason itself, that which achieves knowledge by way of the idea or form, *eidos,* back to the recollection of truth, that is, of "those things that at one time our soul saw as it journeyed with a god." Plato would be correcting a common view that human knowledge arises from merely terrestrial experience or from the mere learning of language. He is reinforcing his commitment to the doctrine of recollection. There have been different ways of construing and translating this passage,[6] but when considering any of

---

6. See *Plato's Phaedrus,* ed. Hackforth, p. 86, and de Vries, *Commentary on the Phaedrus, ad loc.*

the interpretations, we cannot miss the primordial exposure to truth and to that which truly is, as contrasted with the exposure to what most people call reality. Moreover, Plato is establishing a specific connection between the constitution of the human being and the practice of philosophy. Having seen truth makes us human. But remaining close in memory to truth makes us philosophers (249c5–6). The philosophical life is just a further increment to what it is to be human. And in both ways we have an affinity to the gods, for they too enjoy a vision of the ideas. That is already implicit in the *Euthyphro*, in fact, where Socrates argues that the gods discerned and loved the pious, *to hosion*. But the *Phaedrus* alone proposes the audacious idea that the gods owe their divinity to their beholding the ideas. That thought is introduced at 247d, with the reference to nourishing, and it comes to be stated explicitly at 249c5–6.

Being: *Phaedrus 247c*

We shall make our approach to the next *Phaedrus* text by quoting from the *Republic*, Book V, 474–80. Socrates, having proposed his program for the rule of philosophers in his city, must now explain what makes a philosopher. It is someone who loves all wisdom and all knowledge. At 476e, Socrates establishes that the object of knowledge is that which is, *on*, rather than that which is not, *ouk on*. Concerning that which is not, there can be no knowledge at all—only ignorance—but there is an intermediate faculty between knowledge and ignorance, namely opinion, *doxa*, 477b, and that suggests to Socrates that the object of opinion could be something midway between that which is and that which is not, 477b–478e. He now identifies this as that which *appears* to be just or beautiful, all the many objects of our perception, 479a–c:

> My dear sir, of all those many beautiful things, is there one which will not also appear ugly? And is there one of those just actions which will not also appear unjust? and of pious actions, one that will not appear impious?
>
> Not one, he said, for inevitably those beautiful things will appear ugly under certain circumstances, and so with the other things included in your question.
>
> What about the many things that are double? Are they any less half than double?
>
> Not one of them. These things too are ambiguous and one can-

not know for certain either that they are or that they are not, or that they are both or neither.

Well, I said, have you any better way of dealing with them? Can you put them in a better place than between being and non-being? [Grube translation]

In this *Republic* text, as in others, Plato characteristically brings together two phenomena: relativity and mutation. Part of his point is that what we discern around us may depend upon where we ourselves are located, or who we are, or what other information we have brought to bear. Thus our opinion would be relativized to us; with equal justice a person situated differently could affirm the opposite. The other part of his point is that changes are always occurring in the things themselves: what is beautiful now is becoming ugly, and so on. Both the *Cratylus* 439a–440e, the conclusion and climax of the dialogue, and the lengthy study in the *Theaetetus* 152a–157e bring Protagorean relativism together with the flux philosophy of Heraclitus. (See especially *Cratylus* 439d–e and *Theaetetus* 152d–e, 157a–c.) Plato invokes the principle of being as his response to this circumstance, with terms such as *to einai* and *ousia,* for instance, which appear at the end of the *Republic* quotation just given.

We have to realize that Plato is not talking about what we call existence. He is probing the contrast between some *x* that really is beautiful and some *y* that just seems to be beautiful at the time or that happens to be so for a moment, only to lose its beauty soon enough. It is a contrast between an *x* that is *F* and a *y* that seems *F* but is not. For Plato, there is no bare or pure *being* but always *being-F,* or *being-G,* that is, being wise, or being just. His terms for being are always tied to predicates of form, shape, or definition, so a thing that manifests being is one that is what it is—it has a nature *F* and it fulfills that nature completely.

In the *Republic,* too, just as in the *Phaedo,* these things receive the name of *idea* and *eidos.* When the *Republic* treats the just, the beautiful, and the good as the objects of our love (474d–475c) and knowledge (475c–e), it groups them all as *eidē* (476a5) or *ideai* (479a1), marking them off from the variety of sights and sounds and things that may exhibit them (476a–b). The *eidē* and *ideai* are the objects of knowledge (476d) and the things that *are* (476e–477b), while the latter, objects of mere opinion, have only a partial hold on being (478d–479b).

Now we turn to the *Phaedrus,* 247c6. The key statement opens thus: "Far beyond all that is colored and all that has shape and all that you can touch, there is being that truly is. It is glimpsed only by the charioteer of the soul. And that is the place for the things that become known by the only kind of knowledge that is worthy of the name." A bit later, 247d3, Socrates says that the souls behold that which is, *to on,* and become nourished by it, and later still, 247e2, he describes it as that which has true being, *on ontōs.* The substantive term *to on,* grammatically a gerund formed from the neuter participle *on* and prefixed by the definite article *to,* means "that which is" (plural, *ta onta*). When it is modified at 247e2 by the adverb *ontōs,* it signifies "what really is, what truly is," and this is a phrase that draws a contrast. We can see from 247e1 that the contrast is with the domain "that people today call the real, *ontōn.*" However, although the gods and the discarnate souls are enjoying the display of *to on ontōs,* the contrast between what they see and what most people see is not being drawn by them but by the narrator Socrates, speaking for Plato. It is the philosopher, not the divine or the discarnate soul, that compares the heavenly and the earthly experiences, for the gods and the discarnate souls do not take heed of what human beings experience on earth, though their not making the comparison does not imply that they are unaware of the status of what they see. They recognize truth and true being without needing to draw a contrast with a lower order of things.

What the gods behold, the full array of what truly is, becomes further specified, as the passage goes on, 247d6-7, as "justice itself" and "temperance," then "knowledge," and a number of others that will be named further down in the text. Most mortal beings here on earth, on the other hand, confront a very different array, including the objects of ordinary perception. Socrates singles out for his focus the conviction of mortal beings that the things they interact with daily are real, that they have being (*ontōn*—247e1). And this gives us a lead for the further interrogation of this passage. On what grounds, we may ask, do most people rest their conviction that the things they have dealings with in daily life *are* real? *Why* do they think that the objects they touch and see are real? What does the term *real* mean to them? If we can clarify this everyday, ordinary conviction of reality, the next question concerns its grounds and conditions. Where do people derive their awareness of being? From what source or paradigm did the concept of being spring? What is the source of that concept, a concept most people find fulfilled by the everyday objects of perception and practical concern?

To go by the present *Phaedrus* text, the answer to this question is

(a) that everyone who believes in the reality of the everyday environment has maintained some recollection of what truly is, enough to have the conviction that the proper object of the mind is the real, that which is. But (b) this person, in applying the recollection to everyday objects, is at fault in the belief that such things fulfill this criterion or standard, that is, are truly real. That arises because of the interruption of the supernal contemplation. One might remember, though perhaps only dimly, the norm of true reality. But the continuity *within* the memory itself has been broken; there is no trace of a memory of the personal exercise of real knowledge. When the bond within the memory itself is broken, the person just does not remember what it was like to have real knowledge.

Justice and temperance, we have seen, deserve the title *on ontōs*—they are what they are—whereas the objects of our daily perception do not possess that status. They are not declared a zero, an outright nullity, but they lack the emphatic and veritable kind of being that justice and temperance have. As the philosopher, Socrates is able to draw that contrast because he is able to see a single common mark or character in all that supernal array (justice, etc.), and a common mark in the ordinary terrestrial array, the objects of our daily encounters. This is what he expresses with the emphatic words we quoted as the key statement and to which we turn now, *ousia ontōs ousa,* translated as "being that truly is." As first stated at 247c7, these words have a formidable emphasis, which to an untutored ear could sound something like "the beingly being being." Now I hope to clarify that expression.

Being is like truth in that it is one of the collective characterizations of what these gods and mortal souls are seeing. It is not one particular item standing among the others, but the general character of everything they behold. Note first of all that *ontōs,* an adverb, does not modify *ousia,* a noun; as if to say this were a true being. Rather, it modifies the participle *ousa,* so whatever is *ontōs ousa* is not only something that *is*—it *is* in a special way. It is a certain kind of being, or a way of being, exemplified by justice, temperance, and other such objects of divine vision, namely, being what they are. The *ousia* modified by *ontōs ousa* betokens that by which the *ontōs onta* are what they are. It is the mode of being or way of being by which something is not just an entity, *to on,* but something that truly is, *ontōs on.* These things are encompassed in a place, the supercelestial *topos,* defined by this *ousia* itself. What occupies this place is the array of entities or things that have in common this particular way of being. Socrates says that this *ousia ontōs ousa* can only be seen by the charioteer. To possess such being, *ousia,* is to have no color or shape or tangibility; thus, since we have eliminated what sight and touch are good at detecting, such things can be viewed only by reason, *nous,* the charioteer of the flying soul. The unique way of access to what truly is is by virtue of the unique way in which it is. The charioteer who could raise his head—and it seems that not all the mortal ones could—was able thus to come into the abode where the things that truly are have their actual residence.

We are calling attention to the difference between the entity or entities, *to on* or *ta onta,* and the being that is proper to them, their *ousia.* Though Plato was aware of this difference, he did not call special attention to it, and it is only recently, through Martin Heidegger, that it has become discussed in philosophy under the name of the ontological difference.[7] In saying that the *ousia* itself is *ontōs ousa,* Plato does not mean to make it into one more existing entity side by side with justice and temperance. Rather, he is singling out the power that is found in all the beings that have this way of being—to be genuine and true beings. Just as the philosopher must differentiate the entities of the supernal order from the kind of being they have, so too, in the terrestrial or visible order, it is necessary to differentiate the existing, visible entities (house, tree, etc.) from the being or the mode of being that pertains to them. In the *Republic,* especially in the Divided Line, Plato gave a lot of attention to the different modes of being found in the ordinary things of perception; mutation and relativity are two marks of such a way of being, as we have already discussed. The way of being of these sensible objects must be differentiated from the objects themselves, just as, on the supernal level, there is a difference between the *onta,* on the one hand, for example, justice and the like, and the *ousia* that belongs to them and constitutes them, on the other hand. It is only because the philosopher grasps the character of the supernal *ousia* as distinct from the character of terrestrial being that he can differentiate the two classes of entity, showing how the beings that truly are are distinct from what most people think of as real. Differentiating the supernal from the terrestrial entities is a characteristic action of the philosopher, not of the gods and discarnate souls, but, though they do not contrast what

---

7. See my article "The Ontological Difference," *American Philosophical Quarterly* 33 (1996): 357–74.

is supernal with what is terrestrial, they are aware of the supernal ontological difference.

In view of this difference between *ousia* and *ta onta,* we can say that the *Phaedrus* has moved away from a doctrine characteristic of the *Republic.* At 509b, Glaucon is trying to obtain from Socrates a statement about the highest object of human thought and human desire, the idea of the Good. Though Socrates is unable to satisfy Glaucon's urgent demand, he does venture one thought that seems to Glaucon audacious and amazing: if the Good is the cause not only of knowledge but of being and *genesis* too, Socrates says, it follows that the Good is beyond being, *epekeina tēs ousias,* beyond it in age, dignity, and power. But the *Phaedrus* has abandoned that doctrine. Here the things that truly are are beyond the heavens (and there was some anticipation of this in the *Republic* 508c, 509d, 517b, where the ideas are located in an intelligible place, *noētos topos,* different from the visible heaven where the sun and stars are located), and their being, *ousia,* is the true kind of being, *ontōs ousa,* the kind of being that guarantees that these things truly are, that they are *onta ontōs.* To this extent, the *ousia ontōs ousa* that constitutes the *onta ontōs* as true, lies outside them or beyond them. But there is nothing further that could lie beyond being; these beings and their being are already beyond in a place that no poets have ever sung or could ever sing. Those who, like Emmanuel Levinas,[8] have sought to build upon the doctrine of the "good beyond being" ought to rethink their position in view of Plato's more mature reconsideration of the doctrine. The consequence drawn by Levinas, that ethics rather than ontology ought to be reckoned as first philosophy, is, at any rate, not Plato's own final view. In fact, the *Phaedrus* does not refer at any point to the idea of the Good, although, of course, there is much about beauty, *to kalon,* which we shall be discussing in the following chapter.

Superintensity: *Phaedrus* 247d

Let us investigate further this way of being, the *ousia* that deserves to be called genuinely real, *ontōs ousa.* In the *Phaedo,* equality is introduced at 74a with the term *auto to ison,* equality itself or "the equal

---

8. Emmanuel Levinas, *Otherwise than Being, or Beyond Essence,* trans. Alphonso Lingis (The Hague: Martinus Nijhoff, 1981).

itself." Wilamowitz notes that "in *Menexenus* 245b he calls the Athenians *autoi Hellenes* [*Hellenen selbst,* in Wilamowitz's words] to signify that they are purely Greek. In Homer already, a master thief is called *autolykos,* that is, wolf-itself, arch-wolf."[9] Socrates uses a similar construction in the *Phaedo* 75c–d for the just and the pious too, *auto to dikaion, auto to hosion.* The *Symposium* deals principally with beauty, *to kalon.* At the climax of Diotima's address, the lover comes to see a wonderful beauty that always is and never changes, that is not just in some respect beautiful, or beautiful only to some people (211a), that does not inhere in some face or body but is *self-sufficient and by itself and of one form and everlasting (auto kath' hauto meth' hautou monoeides aei on,* 211b). This is beauty *itself* (*auto to kalon*), unalloyed, pure, unmixed, and divine (211d–e). See also *Republic* 476b10, which contends, "those who can attain to beauty itself [*auto to kalon*] see it as itself [*kath' hauto*]."

Now I am interested in the line from the *Phaedrus* 247d5–6: "As it [the soul or the god] soars through its cycle, it looks out upon justice itself [*autēn dikaiosynēn*], and it looks out upon temperance, and it looks out upon knowledge." The term *autos,* or its accusative form, *autēn,* is pervasive throughout Plato's discussions of truth and true being. What does it mean to see justice *itself?* This is the same sort of intensive pronoun that Edmund Husserl used to characterize the complete and fulfilled act of knowledge as distinct from merely adumbrative, relatively empty intentions.[10] If I hear a train whistle, I may posit a passing train, but if I go to the station to see the train, this is the optimal epistemic situation, and it is characterized phenomenologically as the fulfilled intention that "gives me the train *itself.*" Yet a perusal of Plato's text shows us that this characterization cannot be the context for his term *autos.*

To confine our discussion for the moment to one case, justice itself, we see that in the present text it is not being contrasted with something like *signs* of justice or *evidence* for justice as the visually present train might be contrasted with a train whistle. If there is a contrast before Plato's mind at all, it would be between justice itself and what he later in the text (250b1–3) calls "the likenesses down here" on earth, *homoiōmata,* of justice, temperance, and so on. He might be thinking in

---

9. Wilamowitz-Moellendorff, *Platon,* p. 347.
10. Edmund Husserl, *Logical Investigations* (in German) (Tübingen: Niemeyer, 1968), vol. 2, part 2, sec. 16–23 (pp. 64–84).

that passage of the laws passed in civic assemblies or the judgments rendered in human courts. At *Republic* 517d–e, for instance, in explaining the parable of the Cave, Socrates indicates that the philosopher who has seen justice itself (*autēn dikaiosunēn*) would not willingly enter into courtroom disputes that were guided only by "the shadows of justice." Plato's earthly "likenesses" and "shadows" of justice itself do not function for most people as indicators or signifiers of justice itself, as in Husserl's phenomenology; rather, the earthly likenesses of justice have usurped the place of justice itself.

There is another contrast in the present text that is of still greater importance than the contrast of justice itself and its likenesses. Line 247b6 makes reference to the "immortals," and 248a1 makes reference to gods, both indicating that immortals and gods behold the things that are above the heavens and take delight in them. At 247d1–4, however, some mortal souls too imitate this divine contemplation, "as many of them as care to take the right nourishment," seeing what truly is and being content. There is a profound difference between the divine and the mortal experience, and the lines beginning at 248a1 show what profound conflicts and shortcomings there are in mortals' experience. But we must grant that mortals do share to some degree in the divine vision.[11] Though even at best a mortal soul sees truth, true being, or justice itself only imperfectly, there is no denying that many have seen something, and this is repeated often: 248a1–3: some nondivine souls can raise their charioteers' heads into the place above; 248e3–4: some nondivine souls having seen truth are able to remain on high for a further period; 248d2–3: the soul that has seen the most becomes incarnated in a future philosopher or lover; 249d5–7: having had some such vision is a condition for being incarnated in human form; 249e 4–250a1: every human being must have seen *ta onta*. In fact, it is evident that the entire topic of recollection, which forms the mainspring of Socrates' account of love, depends on this hypothesis. The mortal souls have had to endure a harsh and violent struggle up in the heavens (248a–b), struggling with their rivals, sustaining injuries to all the parts of the soul but particularly to the wings, the most divine part, some of them

---

11. Hackforth's note on p. 78 in *Plato's Phaedrus* is too restrictive, claiming that 247d–e as a whole refers only to the gods. But gods and mortals are both under discussion up to 247e4. Lines e4–6, on the other hand, concern the gods alone, and that is what is confirmed at 248a1: "Such is the life of the gods."

in their eagerness to see true being blocked by others, never gaining a view of it.

This passage contrasts the perfect vision enjoyed by the gods with the imperfect vision enjoyed even by the best of the mortal souls. Yet both have seen justice itself (247d5–6). We cannot suppose, then, that the pronoun *itself* functions here in a Husserlian way to signify that which is apprehended from the most favorable standpoint, the optimal epistemic situation. Though mortal vision is partial and subject to chaotic interruptions, that which they have seen is equal to what the gods have seen. Though the seeing of mortals is partial, that which they see has no parts and no temporal phases. If you have seen justice itself at all, then you have seen all of it. Even if you were to imagine some "part" of it, such a "part" would be equal to the whole of it—what does not admit of parts or degrees is the infinite.

Earlier, I mentioned relativity and mutation as two marks of the things that fail to have true being. Here, I shall mention a third, which emphasizes their contrast with justice *itself.* Where true justice is self-contained, it is concentrated and intense, but its earthly likenesses are divided or dispersed. Justice appears only in part in this deed or that law, which will always need to be balanced off by some other deed or some other law that captures some other part of justice. The division between what is concentrated and what is dispersed becomes ever more central in Platonic ontology, and it appears as the key category of the *Timaeus,* for the prototypes for creation are not only everlasting but contain in a concentrated unity everything that will appear seriatim in the creation. The different species of animal life, for instance, are all contained in the archetypal animal. Here is the context for Plato's theory of time. Where the true archetype has eternal being, the created things such as created animals are born, age, and die, realizing seriatim the different stages of life that are all contained in concentrated unity in the eternal prototype. Indeed, time itself was created precisely in order that the different creatures would be able to imitate, in their different ways, different aspects that are all contained in the prototype. The creatures are, as it were, moving images of the eternal, and for that reason the *Timaeus* calls time itself "the moving image of eternity" (37c–d).

But if gods and mortals have seen exactly the same thing, how could we account for the superiority of the gods over mortals and the superiority of the gods' *seeing* over mortal *seeing?* The difference is not to be traced to the actual moment of seeing—justice itself is disclosed

perfectly to anyone who can get any view of it at all: such is the superintensity of everything that has true being. But the composition of the
divine soul differs from that of the mortal, so while the disclosure
of justice itself was always perfect, our constitution, inferior to theirs,
makes us the prey of other desires (the black horse), jealous of position
and place (struggle with others). In short, we lack simplicity and clarity
in our relation to the truth, we lack purity of heart. When we are incarnate on earth, we seek to make judgments about the justice of deeds,
laws, institutions, and persons, and the judgments we make reflect our
own character and constitution. In the supernal world, where the basis
for our judgments is found, there is no judgment but a seeing of justice
itself, but we are nonetheless imperfect mortal beings.

Do we have any clear consciousness, ourselves, of our own imperfection? Does it show up in earthly life, as some aspect of our recollection of truth? That is Plato's theme as he moves closer to a description of the earthly experiences of love and knowledge, in the passage at
Phaedrus 249e4–250b1.

> According to what was said, every human soul, by nature, has
> seen the things that are, or else it would not have entered into this
> creature. But it is not easy for every soul to be reminded of them
> by the things that are here—not for those who then saw what
> was there only briefly, or those who by some misfortune were cast
> down here and through keeping bad company have committed un-
> just deeds, quite forgetting the holy things that once they saw. Just a
> few remain who still retain a sufficient [*hikanōs*] memory, those who,
> whenever they see here a likeness of what is above, are amazed and
> lose control of themselves, in a passion they cannot understand be-
> cause their discernment is not sufficiently [*hikanōs*] clear.

Socrates is describing the consciousness of the embodied human being,
calling attention to differences between two broad groups: those who
are lovers and philosophers and those who are not. The special stress of
the passage is the imperfection that continues to haunt the philosophical life. We are stirred by beauty, and yet the memory awakened taunts
us with its obscurity; just as it can grow more clear, it can also grow
more urgent and passionate. There is the suggestion that we possess
sufficient (*hikanōs*) memory, and yet at the same time that it is not sufficient—the sufficiency of it reaches just so far as to make us aware of
its insufficiency. The Orphic-Platonic idea is that of a double fall. The
first fall took place in heaven itself when we lost our wings. The second

fall, in consequence of the first, is the descent to earth, where we come to occupy a body. Where Plato describes the prompting of recollection, one of the key elements brought home to us is the reality of the first, celestial fall. But now this memory is not treated in narrative mythical style, not as a sort of theological postulate. Now it is treated as a living experience of the incarnated consciousness. We have the memory that what we saw we saw only briefly, and only in part, and that we have suffered losses at the very origin of our being. This is the awareness that although we have a recollection, there is more that is concealed from us. Justice and moderation were "above the heavens," the myth says, and they were seen and feasted on by the gods. Although we have the memory of a fragmentary witnessing of their joyful life, it was clear to us, and is clear to us, that we were just the followers and the observers of their plenitude and that we fell away. We could not stay at heaven's rim. And it is especially the philosopher who preserves the consciousness of this failure that lay within the original condition. Our memory of seeing includes the memory of a not seeing.

This awareness is especially potent in the consciousness that accompanies the life of the philosopher (and the lover)—the knowledge of our own ignorance, our own lack. The question can be raised, Is that awareness also a part of the human consciousness as such? Does everyone maintain that sense of ignorance, lack, and fault? How indeed would the philosopher ever become aware of his or her ignorance and fault if there were no trace of such an awareness in human life as such? The answer of the *Phaedrus* would seem to be that normal embodied experience is guided by the conviction that the things we encounter here are solid and real, a conviction whose roots I discussed a few pages ago. This complacent belief-system rests on a recollection of true being without any recollection of the *knowledge* of true being. But what can arise in everyday life is the encounter with beauty, an awakening of *erōs,* that prompts a longing not only for the *idea* of beauty and the other *ideai,* but for the intimacy with it, the activity of flying, a longing to do something long forgotten, sharing in the soaring flight of the heavenly host. Where it is merely the object of the original knowledge that I remember, I proceed confident in my confinement to earthly experience. But where I recall the *experience* of original knowledge, I want to repeat it and I become discontented. This awakens me to the memory even of what I lost at the origin of all things, that is, I remember the difference between gods and mortals.

Knowledge of Knowledge:
Phaedrus 247e

To return to the *Phaedrus* 247c, we can link its account of knowledge to what is said about truth and being: "and that is the place for the things that become known by the only kind of knowledge that is worthy of the name." A bit later, at 247d5–e2: "as it soars through its cycle, [the soul] looks out upon justice itself, and it looks out upon temperance, and it looks out upon knowledge, but not the kind of knowledge that comes to be, that which, always varying in some way, stands within the domain of the variable.... No, this is the knowledge that belongs together with that which has true being." We see here that knowledge itself is treated as one of the array, something that the soul sees: knowledge is standing there side by side with justice and temperance. The particular point of the reference is that this knowledge is *directed to* justice and temperance even as it stands in their midst. On the other hand, belonging down with change, and so forth, there is the improperly so-called knowledge. The journeying soul has *seen* genuine knowledge even as it has seen justice and temperance, and this seeing is true of the gods as well. Their seeing is itself a knowing, for it is certainly genuine knowledge that the gods and souls attain. So knowledge sees itself, be that human or divine knowledge. Genuine knowledge is also knowledge of knowledge. Their seeing sees itself: it sees seeing. And Socrates contrasts the knowledge that is genuine, which is knowledge *of* the genuine, with that which people call knowledge, a changing "knowledge" devoted to what changes and that lives in the midst of change. Notable in this account is that the supernal seen knowledge is the criterion for anything that is to count as knowledge. It is by reference to the supernal seen knowledge that the shifting knowledge of that which shifts is defined as less than ideal. Socrates says (e1–2) that the only branch of knowledge that can count as knowledge properly speaking, *to tēs alēthous epistēmēs genos,* will be knowledge concerning such being as this. What truly counts as knowledge, real knowledge, will be concerned with that which truly is, whereas it is shifting opinions, as in *Republic* 477–78, concerned with shifting things, that most people cling to. Here Socrates is postulating the *idea* of knowledge itself. Earthly experience is not adequate to that *idea,* and therefore the *idea* did not derive from such experience. It has been seen supernally, and it plays a role in making earthly experience possible, just as truth and being do.

We rely on this *idea* to dignify our experience even as the experience falls short of it.

My earlier claim, in chapter 3, was that the practice of dialectic depends on our exposure to the ideas—it does not account for our awareness of them. Though we undertake dialectic under the normal conditions of everyday life—it is one form of discourse like rhetoric, one way in which we encounter one another through speech—the condition for our attaining truth through dialectic lies in our having been exposed to the ideas in advance of all experience and all dialectic. But now that we have reviewed the Great Speech, we are in a position to address a new question. Could there be a dialectical treatment of the preconditions for dialectic? Or was it inherently necessary for Socrates' account of the soul and its vision of the ideas to be mythical? For we must grant the mythical character of the Great Speech. To answer these questions, I think, we can pursue another thought we developed in part 1. I made the point that Plato is prepared to speak about the gods and the soul in a mythical as well as a rhetorical and dialectical fashion. There is no rule that divides one mode of discourse from another in Plato's writing. *No normal mythical narrative, this Great Speech is in fact a mythical-rhetorical-dialectical address.* And that gives the reader every right to ask about the meaning of these pages, to pursue the matter dialectically, and to ask about the meaning of the story of the soul's circuit with the gods around the heavens before its incarnation (I have already sought to set a cosmological interpretation aside) and the meaning of the soul's glimpse of the things beyond the heavens that truly are.

The most remarkable feature of the speech is not the presence in a mythical address of souls and gods—many mythical narrations prior to Plato encompassed the soul and the gods. The unexpected here, given that it is a mythical narration, is the discussion of true being, the ideas of justice and of temperance, beauty, truth itself—the central themes of philosophy. Only philosophical thinking can encompass themes like that, yet here they are couched in a mythical narration. Some scholars have even supposed that because Socrates treats the ideas in a mythical discourse, there is something not quite respectable about them, from a philosophical point of view. That is the hypothesis I have been opposing all along, and my reasoning can now be made more plain.

For us to recognize beauty in the here and now and to respond to it with love depends on our preserving the memory of a prenatal encounter with perfect beauty, and, as in the *Meno* and the *Phaedo,* it is a similar recollection that accounts for our most important cognitive achievements. It seems that Plato himself never attempted a nonmythical, dialectical treatment of the preempirical formation of the soul. On the other hand, if we look to later centuries of philosophy, we find different routes taken to validate a Platonic doctrine by dialectical means. There is the Neo-platonic doctrine of the procession of the soul from *nous,* the Leibnizian preformation of the monad, the Kantian a priori, the doctrine of the Absolute in Schelling and Hegel, and Heidegger's "preontological understanding of being." These later variants are a part of the *Phaedrus's Wirkungsgeschichte:* the history of its effectiveness; they illustrate the depth of its influence in Western thought, and they counteract any tendency in the reader to dismiss the mythical account as a mere fairy tale uninteresting to philosophers. They are all worthy interpretations of Plato.

There is one further way in which we might interpret Plato. You recognize beauty and respond to it with love; you recognize the equal or the just in your experience. The mythical narration recounts a composite soul in flight and seeing great things beyond the heavens, and specifies the seeing as one that took place long before our current terrestrial seeing. The precondition for a current seeing is an earlier seeing. But what is mythically described as an earlier seeing, occurring before current seeing, can also be grasped dialectically. The dialectical language tells us what the soul sees: justice itself and all that has true being. But it is not just the objects of vision that possessed true being and superintensity—the supernal seeing had the same character. The "earlier" seeing narrated in the myth is, dialectically speaking, that seeing that alone corresponds to the superintensity of the ideas, a seeing that is itself superintense. Such a seeing is not experienced in bodily form on earth, but is recollected in the course of our terrestrial seeing and knowing. Dialectic, then, incorporates the knowledge of knowledge: it focuses on the *idea* of knowledge, and that focus incorporates the whole mythical content of the Great Speech, the content of the idea of knowledge. I do not intend this interpretation as a substitute for the mythical narration—rather it expresses the mythical doctrine of *anamnēsis* that we find in the text and all the later variants of Platonism to which I referred. Normal seeing and knowing are or can be infused with a sort of memory of superintense seeing and knowing, the very perfection of seeing itself. Such an awareness does inhabit or can inhabit normal seeing and knowing, being present within normal knowing in the form of an *anamnēsis.* I think that this constitutes an objective self-interpretation, in dialectical form, of the Platonic myth, though not a complete exegesis of it by any means.

I shall conclude this chapter with an observation on the later works of Plato. This chapter has sought to show that the theory of ideas is present in the *Phaedrus* as a doctrine of truth and true being. This is an aspect that should not be forgotten in the debates about the later Plato, particularly the question of whether Plato later on abandoned the theory of ideas. That opinion is perhaps even an orthodoxy now: "Plato no longer accepted the theory of Forms as it is presented in the Great Speech"—not even as he was writing it![12] Partly this rests on setting the dialectic of collection and division against a doctrine of ideas and especially against a doctrine of recollection—ventures we explored in our earlier chapter on dialectic. The other grounding usually offered for this opinion is the critique of the theory of ideas offered in *Parmenides* 130a–135c, viewing that critique as if it had demolished the theory.[13]

But we can now, perhaps, acknowledge that the opening part of the *Parmenides* is hardly a refutation of the theory of ideas. The criticisms stated there fail to grant the teaching of the *Phaedrus* that the ideas do not merely have being, *on,* but exemplify true being or superintensity, *ontōs on.* The arguments brought against Socrates early in the *Parmenides* put the ideas again and again into a common class with things, mere *onta,* which is precisely what should not be done, as nobody knew better than Plato. Thus when Socrates maintains that an idea can be shared among many individuals, 131a, Parmenides asks him wickedly if it is like a sail spread over the heads of many persons—a *material thing,* one part of it touching each person. Or, turning to the "third man" argument: if the idea expresses something we see in many individuals and is something in terms of which we compare the individuals, then must we not also compare the individual to the idea itself—*in exactly the same way!*—invoking thereby in this further com-

---

12. Nehamas and Woodruff, introduction to their translation of the *Phaedrus,* p. xlii.

13. Gregory Vlastos helped to shape this widespread interpretation through his treatment of the best-known of the *Parmenides* arguments, the "third man" argument; see his "The Third Man Argument in the *Parmenides,*" in *Studies in Plato's Metaphysics,* ed. R. E. Allen (London: Routledge and Kegan Paul, 1965).

parison a further idea under which our first idea must be ranged along with the various individuals; and so on ad infinitum? But the *Phaedrus* would teach us that there can be no such second comparison. Instructed by the *Phaedrus,* then, we would read the *Parmenides,* Part One, as a cleansing of the ideas from the inadequacies that had gathered round them when they were conceptualized with inadequate attention to the truth and the true being that constituted them.

| Love and Beauty
Phaedrus 250b–257b

In the section from 250b to 257b Socrates explores the true inner nature of love, stating his reply to the earlier speeches, in particular that
of Lysias. In this way, we can see the speech, not only as an exercise in
rhetoric, but as dialectic too, as it comprises the considered exploration
of love and the refutation of the preceding inadequate views of it. We
shall follow Socrates' treatment in this chapter, linking it to some other
Platonic texts, in the hopes of formulating some points about what is
called Platonic love. These pages of the *Phaedrus* are not difficult in the
way that some of the preceding pages may have been, and where Plato
discusses the reaction of sexual arousal, the prose sizzles—at times, I
am sure, humorously. These pages do not require much explanation, but
they raise many issues on which the reader may welcome some discussion.

In the early pages of this section, 250b to 253c, Socrates shows how
the experience of erotic love depends on the inner nature and constitution of the human soul, and how it explains in particular our response
to beauty. In the first part of this chapter I shall show how love and
beauty are connected in our visual experience.

The second half of the section, running from 253c to 257b, details
many of the lover's passions and experiences, and my discussion in the
second part of this chapter will try to make clear the ethical character
of Platonic love and its relation to other ideals of love.

When Plato treated the immortality of the soul in the *Phaedo,* he
did not give much attention to any of the soul's powers other than cog-
nition: the recognition of resemblances, for instance. Certainly the *Republic* treats appetite (*epithymia*) and spirit (*thymos*) as major forces in

the soul along with our cognitive *logos,* and yet the *Republic* seems still to manifest the kind of puritanical ethic we have already seen in the *Gorgias:* through rigorous intellectual control of *epithymia* human beings will fulfill themselves. These sources of energy need above all to be controlled by their governor. The *Symposium,* probably written a bit earlier than the *Republic,* gives more recognition to the nonrational elements in the soul, for the Diotima speech assigns tremendous importance to *ta aphrodisia.* Just as, objectively, there is a ladder leading from the first object of our sexual desire—a beautiful body—through moral and political practices, to *auto to kalon* at the end, so the *aphrodisia* within our own souls bring about a subjective kind of continuity reaching from our immediate sexual response to the highest of our intellectual acts, a ladder within the soul as well, with intellectual love at the apex.

The *Phaedrus,* in the Great Speech, gives a greater place still to the nonrational elements of the soul. The *Symposium* does not express directly any doctrine of the divisions of the soul. The *Republic,* in contrast, clearly affirms its tripartition, but the *Phaedrus* goes further in this direction by visualizing the three parts as three distinct creatures: two horses and a human governor. In keeping with this development the sexual ethics of the *Phaedrus* is more indulgent than the *Phaedo,* the *Symposium,* and the *Republic,* and its doctrine of sublimation less rigorously puritanical. Plato is not only ready to describe our sexual feelings more graphically, but he is more welcoming of them, treating them as substantially good. I do not deny that the soul of the *Phaedrus* is a unity, but that unity encompasses a far greater variety of experiences than exists in the preceding works, and passion and feeling are allowed greater scope. That change means that the unity of the soul is not accomplished in the *Phaedrus* primarily through the rule of reason, or *logos.* Rather, *logos* is one power within a whole range of powers of the soul. This dialogue expresses an opening of Plato's mind to a wider range of feelings and experiences deep within the soul, and this opening up appears to permit the soul to take flight to heights even beyond those sketched in the *Phaedo,* the *Symposium* and the *Republic.* In this way, Plato in the *Phaedrus* is something like Hegel, for Hegel postulated *Verstand,* intellect, as one power within spirit, *Geist,* one that had to be kept from insisting on its own primacy. The barren intellectualism of Lysias's address, devoid of *aphrodisia* and indeed all forms of *erōs,* would signify the deviant situation in which the soul as a whole was overshadowed by, subordinated to, *logos.* Applying divine madness as the corrective to such intellectualism, we see the liberation of a soul that is genuinely whole and integrated.

Beauty, Seeing and Love: *Phaedrus* 250b–253c

Plato's intent was never to make his reader despair of the human condition by freezing the great divide between reality and appearance or damning the imagining soul to an eternity of illusion. The early *Ion* and *Apology* offer a way of release through Socratic questioning; the middle *Republic* offers a pathway leading upward toward the sunlight; the late *Sophist* offers its own species of dialectic. But how does the soul first get started on its way? We know of the sting, the shock, the goad administered by the Socratic gadfly, and yet the dialogues are true to life when they show that Socrates' elenchus produces resentment far more often than it initiates conversion. The *Symposium* and the *Phaedrus* give a more believable story on how the soul gets started on the journey to the truth: it is love that seizes the soul in the first place, and the influence of love, step by step, draws the soul on high.

The *Phaedrus* shows the essential condition for this conversion: there was the primordial seeing of beauty in advance of our experience, and it perseveres in the form of an unconscious memory. So in advance of our empirical encounter with beauty and our experienced love, there was a preempirical encounter with beauty, a precondition for the response of love. All beauty has a luster, not only in its absolute presence but in its earthly embodiments too, and that awakens the soul, starting it on its way. Such is the bond of beauty to love. This account is profoundly at odds with most of the treatments of beauty we know from eighteenth-century philosophers, Shaftesbury, Burke, Kant, and their descendants. They proposed beauty as a matter for *judgment* and *taste*. Kant, the most important of them, had it perhaps as his main purpose in the *Critique of Judgment* to deny the reality or objectivity of beauty. He argues that it is the faculty of judgment in us, exercised by a mind that is conscious and free from carnal urges and obscure desires, that pronounces on beauty. Beauty is not something that can disturb the mind's sovereignty. Beauty is found, first of all in "nature," which includes the human form along with tulips and sunsets, and second in the art that renders nature. Though we experience these objects with our sensory apparatus, the beauty itself is not perceived but judged by the mind in its freedom, and the basis of the judgment is the activity awakened in our sensibility and imagination by this object. The beauty does not "belong" to the object—the body or the picture—but in a certain way is supervenient upon the object and its constitutive qualities; it is a transcendent quality or is judged to be one. Our encounter with beauty is accomplished by reflective judgment, a self-consciousness of our own responses. Beauty, then, must be rigorously differentiated from what is sexual or erotic in a body, a statue, or a painting, just as it is distinguished from the historical elements of a work of art, who is being represented, and who made the work. This is the theory that Gadamer has called "aesthetic differentiation."[1]

For Plato, on the other hand, beauty as seen in this world, and as seen transcendentally in our preempirical being, is genuinely there in the bodies or the works of art and not differentiated from its power to arouse us erotically. Love is awakened by beauty that we *see*. At 250b, beauty is discriminated from justice and moderation, for the latter have no brightness, *phengos*, whereas beauty and its likenesses shine out most clearly of all. Moreover, the organs we possess for discerning justice and moderation, and the likenesses of justice and moderation, are by no means as powerful and sharp as the faculty of sight by which we behold the likenesses of beauty.

We know how deeply Plato's vocabulary is penetrated with visual terminology; terms like *eikasia* (illusion) are indeed names for whole ways of being in the world. The *Phaedrus* is rich in examples of such terms, and we shall look at a few of them. It is on account of your seeing somebody that your wings begin to grow. "When somebody sees beauty here, he is reminded of true beauty, and he becomes winged" (249d5–6). The particular experience described at this point is a visual variant of recollection: I come again to remember (*anamimnēskomenos*, 249d6, 250a1) the true beauty, and my wings begin to grow. This refers retrospectively to what we had beheld while we were soaring on high in the company of the gods: now there is the return of the primal vision in the form of memory. The passage refers retrospectively to a blessed vision we enjoyed while soaring on high in the company of the gods, and now there is the return of the primal vision in the form of memory.

Some who here on earth can see a likeness (*homoiōma idōsin*,

---

1. Hans-Georg Gadamer, *Truth and Method,* trans. G. Barrett and J. Cumming (New York: Seabury, 1975). See part 1, I, chap. 3, "The Retrieval of the Question of Artistic Truth."

250a6) of the things above are moved to amazement; those fresh from the gods' pastures may see godlike beauty in a face or a bodily form (251a) and revere it as if it were the sight of a god (*prosorōn hōs theon sebetai*). Socrates says that when we are in the transport of love, we look upon our beloved the way we do the image or statue of a god (*agalma,* 251a6, 252d7).

The primordial vision beyond the earth was enjoyed in a greater or lesser degree by different souls: at 247b, some were distracted by the black horse; at 248a, some could see only part of the display; and at 250a, some saw it only very briefly. Now here on earth, some have forgotten the holy vision owing to their unrighteous living under bad influence, but there are a few who preserve a sufficient memory of it (*hikanōs*). It can happen that one of them will see a likeness of the holy vision (*homoiōma idōsin*)—and then, when he does, he is utterly dumbfounded, he loses control, and he does not know what it is or what has hit him. All this, Plato says, is because he cannot see clearly enough (*hikanōs*). This whole sentence stresses his puzzled amazement. It is a seeing experience he has: but there is some further power operating in the seeing, the power of some déjà vu. We do not know why we are so stirred.

Having brought us inside the perplexed soul of someone who sees with the eyes of love, Plato takes us out again, 250b, to narrate *what* that memory contained that the lover did not understand. It has two parts. First, he speaks of the holy (*hieron*) and blessed (*makarian*) vision above, meaning the entire scene that includes beauty along with justice, and so on, but he stresses the character of beauty in particular and its contrast with justice and moderation. It is special both in its eternal being and in its embodiments in this life: it shines, it glows, and it has luster and radiance, and this gives beauty alone the awakening power in its earthly exemplars. As the second component of this memory, Plato evokes the character of the prior life above, not only the sacred objects of vision, but the happiness of our previous life together there, indeed the holiness of our life: "and we ourselves were whole then as we made our celebration . . . " The memory is not only of something seen, but of a state of our being, a memory, therefore, of being with the one we now see. Plato, in seeing Dion, remembers the previous fellowship of their souls up in the company of Zeus. Yet this memory, as lived through by us, is unconscious.

Plato treats vision often—at *Republic* 507e–508e it is made the model for *nous, Timaeus* 45 treats the physics and physiology of it, and so on. But close reading of scattered passages, especially in the narrated dialogues, reveals accounts of specific ways of seeing, visual experiences differentiated by their occasions: seeing in the early morning (*Protagoras* 310) versus seeing at noonday (*Phaedrus.* 230); seeing with erotic arousal (*Charmides* 154–55) versus seeing with fear and alarm (*Republic* 336d); and so on. Seeing is really a family of many kinds of experience, all of which afford the seer a certain degree of insight, but it could be that one sort of seeing could open up more for us than any other. Seeing with the eyes of *love* is, for Plato, not foolishness or the self-deception of the fond lover, but rather is seeing the deepest; it is the most enlightening and most true.

What is the response of the soul to the promptings of beauty? Love brings an impetus. Yet it is not at all correct to think of love as a power that seizes us and carries us forward, ourselves purely in the passive condition of being carried, as if all power of movement belonged to love—Empedocles seems to have believed that. The focus of this speech is evidently upon the *activity* of the soul, flying under its own power. Central to the *Phaedrus* myth is that it is prefaced by a non-mythical argument in proof of the soul's immortality at 245b-e, which proceeds from the soul's attribute of being itself the cause of its own motion. Self-movers, needing no impetus from another, will not start or stop motion and will therefore move eternally and exist eternally. Self-motion, indeed, is made the very *ousia* and *logos* of soul. And yet it would be wrong to make the soul so self-sufficient in its self-motion that it would have no need of the promptings of love. Love must set the soul to flying, yet love does not carry the soul; the soul has its own wings, flying under its own power. The soul is a self-mover—and yet before love seizes it, it cannot fly because its wings are atrophied. Eros himself is winged, we know from 252b8-9, and Eros awakens the wings within our soul. But those wings themselves *are* not Eros; they are an organ proper to the soul itself, not a power coming from without. Eros is not a part of our soul, but a god, a power that awakens this part or this power of our soul.

The stunning novelty of this image, over the tri-partition of the *Republic,* is the presentation of the threefold soul in its two utterly different states, one devoid of wing in every part and one endowed with wings in every part. The possibility of the loss of wings—and again the gain of wings—also puts the *Phaedrus* quite beyond the viewpoint of the *Phaedo.* What Plato sketches for us at 249d–250d and 250-51, is the means of this new growth of wings. We are able to experience even here in terrestrial life the sense of an elevation, the acquisition of a power to go soaring like Pegasus or the driver of the sun, through the sudden drive of an energy released within our soul. It is a sexual love experience. We imagine the very transition between a life without sexuality and a life with sexuality. Puberty in modern times is experienced as a stage in the development of our organism, but Plato's growth of wings is under the influence of a seen beauty. An influence calls the wings forth. It is on account of our seeing somebody that our wings begin to grow.

The first description of this growth is at 251a–252a, and the prose is extraordinarily graphic, capturing the sexual response in a language that fuses animal and vegetable metaphors, and with touches of comedy that seem to echo the descriptions of the possessed lover we heard in Lysias's speech and in Socrates' first speech. There is a second description of the interior struggle of the soul at 253e–254e, which we shall look at a bit later.

We quoted in the previous chapter some lines from 249c. After first saying (249b) that every human being must have seen truth, Socrates proceeds to single out the philosopher: "Hence it is right that the mind of the philosopher alone should regain its wings, for it remains eternally close in memory to those things the proximity to which gives to a god his very divinity." Socrates continues on from this to invoke a picture of the heaven-struck philosopher, gazing upward, scorned by the multitude, ruled by a memory, *anamnēsis*. We have encountered the picture of the abstracted philosopher in earlier texts, such as *Phaedo* 64a–67e. But we wonder how that picture is going to function here. Will Plato be able to merge this picture somehow into the figure of a man smitten with erotic love? He does manage it, I think, and his solution turns on a difference in kinds of seeing and degrees of seeing at 249d: "When somebody sees beauty here, he is reminded of true beauty and he becomes winged. With new-grown wings, he would eagerly fly again and yet he cannot." Here Socrates is not describing someone who is contemplating abstractions, bringing his mind to bear on mathematics, and so forth, but rather on someone who is utterly and completely taken with what he is seeing and yet made to feel the presence of an unnamed mysterious power. In this smitten lover, the memory of the primordial scene is completely unconscious. He does not know of what the likeness is a likeness, nor know even that it is a likeness. This is the aspect of truth, philosophy, and poetry that lies within anyone's erotic experience, and at the same time it expresses the erotic seedbed of art and philosophy.

It is a very particular experience that Plato has described here in forging the connection between sexual desire and philosophy, and though his extravagant gifts as a literary artist could have allowed him merely to imagine and create this account, it is far more probable that he is writing about what he had experienced himself. The soul is driven by the powerful sexual urge symbolized by the black horse, and yet, in approaching the beloved one, another part of the same soul, symbolized by the charioteer, is so smitten with the beauty of the face that it is reminded of the *idea* of beauty, where it is enthroned alongside temperance, and the *idea* sets a constraint on the sexual urge. This experience is a powerful one, and powerfully described, but we should not suppose that Plato intended to make it a necessary condition for any recollection of the ideas. To suppose that only by way of such *erōs* could one make an approach to the truth would be to rewrite the earlier and later dialogues altogether too radically—the *Phaedrus* is describing one powerful experience of the truth, not the only possible experience of it.

In a further exploration of Plato's description of *erōs*, we must also pose the question of whether the experience is inherently a homosexual one, as it must surely have been in Plato's own case. In an earlier chapter, I sought to show a literary parallel, drawn from Jane Austen's *Persuasion,* to the ethical issue posed by Lysias and the first speech of Socrates. Can we then imagine modern, romantic equivalents to the account the palinode offers of erotic experience and its philosophical outcome, and would the substance of *erōs* be the same if it were realized in settings of heterosexual love, or would such an adaptation efface it? One thing we can say here is that the *metaphysics* of Plato present no barrier to a heterosexual adaptation of *erōs,* for what we have seen in the previous two chapters is a preexistent soul encountering the idea of beauty and the other ideas—a soul that is not a person with a definite name or family and that does not have a fixed identity as male or female. Plato says little about women in the *Phaedrus,* but no reading of the text would support a view that all supernal souls are male and that all incarnations of the souls are male. If there is a male and homosexual privilege in matters of *erōs,* that is not metaphysically grounded. We shall return to this question after looking further at the description of the lovers' earthly experiences.

Platonic Love: *Phaedrus* 253c–257b

Previous pages have taken us inside the soul of the lover in describing the onrush of desire and love. But at 253d–254e, we are made witnesses to the inner struggle of the lover, as he is driven by wanton desires and yet conquers them. Socrates gives some characterizations of the white horse, the black horse, and the charioteer, that are close parallels of the tripartite division of the *Republic*, 439b–441c. We must note that although the horses have different characters they are nevertheless both horses, whereas the driver is a human figure. Thus, the horses differ in character from each other, but they are represented as pulling the chariot side by side, both with the same task, then, to be the source of power, even though they might at times pull in different directions. Moreover, though all three are attracted by beauty in the terrestrial love-experience, 253c–254e, only the charioteer can recollect the original idea. Wilamowitz captures well the character of this text:

> The *Symposium* showed a Socrates who mastered sensuality without effort: it could seem all too easy. Here we are to learn of the hard struggle that it requires. That is the reason for the two horses, although in treating their nature and temperament Plato is also able to indulge his love for the animals and show us the thorough knowledge of them that he had acquired in his cavalry days—one is tempted to search in the Parthenon frieze for these horses. He shields none of his deepest feelings as he lets his Socrates describe the paroxysms of sensual passion and the agony of self-overcoming. But self-overcoming is necessary: without it, the soul cannot philosophize, cannot regain its wings, cannot follow in the heavenly flight to the full vision of the eternal, and come to its resting place in heaven. We know the strict discipline of self-mastery that the *Republic* imposed upon lovers—the *Laws* will do no less.[2]

Plato continues on from this point to describe the life together of philosophical friends at 255a–e. In the self-consciousness of each, there is certainly a struggle with the unruly horse. But Plato also describes the interaction of the two friends—one usually the older, the *erōn,* and the other younger, the *erōmenos*—in a way that brings out the spiritual and ethical meaning of their philosophizing together. The lover who has at last secured the control of his passions will come to feel a genuine concern and affection for the other, and make known by his deeds the kindness that he bears toward the younger man. And now, the latter, coming to see for himself the goodness of his lover and teacher, will dismiss the doubts and criticisms he may have acquired from society at

---

2. Wilamowitz-Moellendorff, *Platon,* p. 468.

large and respond in kindness to the other's kindness. As this feeds the flame of love again in the lover, the beloved will be further touched and there will be awakened in him as well the emotion of love, though he may not recognize it. This description, 255a–d, should certainly be compared with the speech of Alcibiades in the *Symposium,* for Alcibiades says that he had seen the inner soul of Socrates and its beauty in just this way, although, alas, his speech confesses that he did not have the courage to persevere with Socrates in the way Plato is describing here. Plato's account in the *Phaedrus* undertakes to show how the conventional ideal of love is capable of being extended, transcended, and transformed. We may put it this way: united initially by *erōs,* the two lovers persevere in *philia.* Plato himself uses the word *philia* at one crucial point: "They may live a beautiful and happy life, bound together by love, *erōs,* and persevering in friendship, *philia*" (253c4–5).

In 256 and 257 Socrates continues to describe different possibilities that arise in the life of friends, and in particular he recognizes that they may not always be as strict in their self-control as perfect cynics or stoics might be. Wilamowitz comments with some surprise on their tone:

> Plato as teacher must be stern. Hence we are surprised at first when he says here [256a–d] that the consequence of an indiscretion is only that one does not attain to the very highest level of achievement. A pair of friends who may lose their self-control in the heat of their passion are not condemned. It may be that their wings will not mature, yet they have begun to sprout and so after their death they are not banished into the darkness of the underworld. They can hope that their continuing friendship will lead in time to their being completely endowed with wings. Rarely has Plato written anything so personal as this concluding remark, personal because it goes against his system, and manifests his deep knowledge of human character and rich experience.... Where else does he show consideration for the weakness of the flesh? It is particularly fine that he lets the heavenly judges be less stern than he himself is in his role as law-giver. Here his system breaks down. Pure justice knows no such forgiveness. Where would Plato have been led if he had followed this path further? Here the experience of life and a milder spirit and his own hopes have prevailed over the cold demands of reason, just as in the *Phaedo* the transmigration of souls that the rational argument required was supplanted at points by a hope for individual survival that he could not banish from his heart. This, then, is Platonic love. Passion, the

pleasure of the flesh, is certainly not unknown to him, nor does he underestimate its power. It belongs to nature, therefore it is permitted and it is good as long as it is constrained and ruled by the ethical will. What a ridiculous fuss has been made about the so-called "Platonic love!"[3]

Let us then say a word about this famous or infamous concept. Let us realize that love itself reaches one of its pinnacles and one of its fulfillments in *seeing*. Love is realized not only in vision but as vision, an embodiment no less complete than the conduct of sexual intercourse. I am not going to defend the celibacy doctrine of Plato, but rather try to show one of its grounds, that love can be fulfilled in seeing and is not incomplete at that point, needing to proceed to sexual intercourse. In the very presence of the beloved, there is already the momentous thing. The narrative can move on from this joyful moment to a joyful sexual consummation; but it can take at just this point another turn and proceed by a deepening of contemplation, realizing the love itself *as* vision, a realization that can become expressed in a painting, a drawing, or a poem or that can also inaugurate a philosophical journey to the stars. The actualization of love *as* seeing permits several outcomes, and I shall try to ponder the experience recounted in the *Phaedrus.*

One should not identify Plato's celibacy doctrine too closely with Freud's concept of sublimation. Freud conceptualized the entire soul as a single network of forces or energy, and proposed that the energy required for self-discipline and repression was borrowed, as it were, from the instinctual power of the unconscious.[4] Sublimated sexuality was a displacement in another direction of the instinctual energy that had originally been sexual in aim. But the Platonic experience stresses far more strongly the independence of that part of the soul that is symbolized by the charioteer. Although in the allegory all three parts of the soul can see the boy, the charioteer alone can see something else, beauty itself, and does not wish to be interrupted or distracted by further sexual actions from its contemplation of the idea, for it is in a state of perplexity, trying to remember the idea, not quite being able to, urgent to bring it into focus. Moreover, in the interaction with the beloved, the wish of the charioteer is to remember the god in whose train it had once been soaring and to re-create in the beloved the image of

---

3. Ibid., pp. 468–69.
4. See, for example, Sigmund Freud, *Civilization, Society and Religion,* vol. 12 of the Penguin Freud Library (London: Penguin, 1991), pp. 39–40.

the god, a creative work of pedagogy that is analogized to sculpting. Plato is far from believing that the contemplative part of the soul receives its energy on loan from the black horse.

In general, it is difficult to bring Platonic celibacy into any connection with later and modern doctrines of sexual fulfillment or indeed modern doctrines of marital love. One cannot seriously entertain a doctrine of celibate marriage, and thus one is forced to the question of whether, on a Platonic view, marriage and indeed sexual unions of any sort are simply incompatible with the practice of philosophy. That would seem to be the case *if* Plato had argued that his particular kind of erotic experience was a necessary condition for philosophy—but we have seen in the preceding commentary that that would overstate his case. But the reader is still left to wonder whether Plato's description of *erōs* and its philosophical effects is relevant to those whose erotic life differs from his. This must be tied up with a question of the overall evaluation Plato has made of the practice of sex in human life, an evaluation he did seem to share with the Orphic tradition, the Pythagoreans, and other traditions that seek to detach us from sexual self-expression. Was Plato terrified of sex, or horrified at it, as a lot of popular opinion today would have it? What, actually, is so wrong with indulging our sexual desires, according to Plato?

If we look at the *Symposium* and the *Phaedrus,* we must ask whether they have something dehumanizing about them. Is the love that we mostly experience (romantic love, erotic love, sexual desire) being made the mere instrument of an intellectual's pedagogical program? One overall point of Martha Nussbaum's study of the *Phaedrus* is that in it Plato reverses himself on some of the earlier doctrines that lent him a somewhat inhuman cast.[5] Now he is open to all the contingencies of individuals and their experiences; now he accepts the emotion, the rhetoric, and the poetry, which earlier he had tried to suppress, as Wilamowitz also saw. In particular, in matters of human love, he renounces his earlier habits of calculative rationality, and leaps into the risks of erotic experience. But the issue is not thereby exhausted.

There is no doubting a negative undertone in the appraisal of sexual experience here, and I do not think the modern reader ought to follow Plato too closely in his denunciation of sexual self-expression. The

---

5. "Poetry, Goodness and Understanding in Plato's *Phaedrus,*" in M. Nussbaum, *The Fragility of Goodness* (Cambridge: Cambridge University Press, 1986).

practical and ethical issue would seem to have a fairly clear-cut answer: Plato's dramatic description of the struggle with the black horse is a worthy account of the interior self-mastery we must all achieve, aiming at the conquest of erotomania, self-indulgence, and sexual selfishness, but it does not follow that an outer life of celibacy is the only expression of such inner strength. That interior self-mastery can be realized as well, I believe, in the context of married sexuality and other forms of ethical life.

There is another critique of Platonic love that we have often heard. Often we hear it said that in Platonic love, when it is *you* I think I am in love with, I shall find at the end of the day that it was something else I really loved all along, the Absolute. Does Plato mean that human beings as such are not really lovable at all? Looking at my beloved with love, am I actually stirred by memories of another scene, a primordial scene on another occasion? Though we may speak to each other, is it something else I'm really listening for, without quite knowing it? Gregory Vlastos, for one, has offered a sharp indictment of Plato for failing to do justice to the love for an individual, for the unique person.[6] But in fact one can raise the same sort of question about seeing: is it the individual I see, the unique person, or is my seeing going to be guided toward someone's qualities and aspects, guided too by previous experience focused on other people? In fact, the two lines of questioning will converge, for seeing is profoundly shaped by love, and so it could be that a phenomenology of seeing will offer another response to Vlastos. The root issue uniting both themes is the idealization and the imagination we exercise upon those whom we love, a theme that has been exploited to the full by comedies of the smitten lover and tragedies about the devastation brought by love's blindness. Those topics of drama are supplemented by the moralist's critique of self-centered love and self-indulgent love. My vision is blurred as to the true character of the other: I do not really "see her," I do not "let her be." For Plato in particular, according to Vlastos, "the individual, in the uniqueness and integrity of his or her individuality, will never be the object of our love,"[7] but only the ideal qualities he or she happens to embody. Platonic love makes the individual dissolve into qualities, and only the selected good qualities at that. Moreover, it permits my love for the other to alter, if

---

6. See "The Individual as an Object of Love in Plato," *Platonic Studies,* 2d ed. (Princeton, N.J.: Princeton University Press, 1981).

7. Ibid., p. 31. See pp. 30–34 as a whole.

somebody happens along with greater beauty or charm, and it permits me to detach my love from the other altogether if I come to find greater beauty and charm in music, statecraft, or philosophy.

But Nussbaum has shown that much of Vlastos's indictment of Plato is unwarranted: in the early pages of her chapter on the *Symposium,* she shows that Alcibiades loves Socrates, the individual person, in just the sense that Vlastos was calling for.[8] It gives many indications in Alcibiades' own words of how he is seeing Socrates with eyes of love and in so doing offers ample evidence for Alcibiades' love for Socrates the individual. As Nussbaum shows, Alcibiades is prone to experiencing sudden disruptive appearances of Socrates (213b–c, 216e, 221a). There is another kind of visual experience, too (215a–b), which Alcibiades himself communicates to us in his unforgettable comparison of Socrates with the statue of Silenus, such an unprepossessing shell on the outside, yet full of divine statues inside. I quote his second statement of it, 216e–217a: "But I once caught him when he was open like Silenus's statues, and I had a glimpse of the figures he keeps hidden within: they were so godlike—so bright and beautiful, so utterly amazing—that I no longer had a choice. I just had to do whatever he told me." Alcibiades is in Agathon's house, speaking to the guests but looking again and again at Socrates, the subject of his speech. He is recounting to them the many meetings he and Socrates had, and stresses often how he had looked at Socrates on those earlier occasions, how he saw him (216b, 218e–219a, 221a), glimpses that are repeated and made actual again here and now in the moment of his speaking. There can be no doubt that Alcibiades' love was focused on this unique individual. But in this text, he recurs to a likeness to express *what* it was he was seeing: those popular little holy works of art. This poetic metaphor, the product of his imagination, tells us that it was something *in* the man that moved him so deeply: something godlike (*theia*) and beautiful: divine statues. As he could in the past, Alcibiades can now in the moment of speech discern the vision of divinity within the soul of the one he loves so deeply. By his wonderful speech, Alcibiades can disclose the vision also to Agathon and his guests, and ourselves the readers. The holy objects of vision are not located in a heaven far away but in the soul of the

---

8. "The Speech of Alcibiades: A Reading of Plato's *Symposium,*" in *The Fragility of Goodness* (Cambridge: Cambridge University Press), pp. 218, 225–32.

living master, even, I suppose, in the words of the speaker and of Plato, the writer, and yet they are united with the experience of the concrete individual Socrates.

The Unity of Love

In making his criticism, Vlastos has also invoked the love, *agapē,* of the biblical God, "a Being whose perfection empowers it to love the imperfect, a Father who cares for each of his children as they are, does not apportion affection to merit, gives it no more to the righteous than to the perverse and deformed."[9] I shall not discuss this point in detail, yet it seems a striking case of the faulty application of theology. No human love ever should have that character—that would be trying to play God. Trying to love others in exactly *that* way, the deformed as much as the righteous, would make you, in my opinion, a faulty Christian or Jew or Moslem. Instead, biblical love, as I understand it, invites us to *see* the charm, beauty and power of those we see. We get a kick out of being loved in that way, to know our qualities are appreciated and loved, but no kick out of being loved by the dutiful practitioners of unmotivated *agapē.* Indeed, in a closer study of the Bible, we can find the record of erotic experience and an idealization of it that is not at all excluded by other ideals of love.[10]

The different species and varieties of love is a subject about which there has been just as much fruitless "fuss" as so-called Platonic love, particularly in reference to Greek history, theology, and literature. Undoubtedly there is a range of situations most commonly referred to by *erōs* and its cognates, another range for *philia* and its cognates, another again for *agapē* and its cognates. Sexual passion is no doubt the prime focus of the first word, friendship the prime focus of the second, and good favor the focus of the third. But the words related to *erōs* can be used in reference to family relations; *agapē* can refer at times to the sexual expressions of love; *philia* can be applied to sexual relations or good favor and in many other directions as well.[11] The three words occur to-

---

9. Vlastos, "The Individual as an Object of Love in Plato," p. 33.
10. An excellent treatment is in Samuel Terrien, *Till the Heart Sings* (Philadelphia: Fortress, 1985).
11. See the entries in Liddell Scott Jones, *A Greek-English Lexicon,* under these three words, particularly the references to literary works of the fifth and fourth centuries.

gether in one line of the *Phaedrus,* at the conclusion of Socrates' first speech, 241d1; we already noticed the occurrence of *erōs* and *philia* together at 253c5. The question we are concerned with here, however, is not actually lexical. The statistics of usage one can gain from a lexicon do not bring us far in a psychology or a philosophy of love, and philosophy in particular must be concerned with *the possibility of different states of mind that can become interlinked, one merging at times into the other.* This principle, it seems, is precisely what Plato has shown us: not only an interlinking of the words *erōs* and *philia,* but, judging by the passages that describe human interactions, the interlinking of the things themselves named by these words. We can postulate that *erōs* is a form of psychic energy, the full development of which leads to the mature and fulfilling human interaction called *philia.* They are not different things, however, but one thing. It is an advantage of English, not a drawback, to employ the *one* word *love* for the inner and the outer forms, the root of it and the branch as well. What Plato has described at 255a–d in the life of philosophical lovers is offered to our view in many of his dialogues, in Socrates' affection for Phaedo (*Phaedo* 89a–b) and in his efforts with Alcibiades (*Symposium* 217b–219e), for example. And the *philia* that links Socrates to Phaedrus throughout the present dialogue exhibits the older philosophic man as guide and leader, *psychagōgos,* for the younger man. The opening pages of the dialogue present Socratic education in its gentleness and subtlety.

Moreover, the third word, *agapē,* most famous on account of its steady employment in the New Testament, and the Septuagint, for the love relation between God and human beings, is not to be marked off from the others, and most certainly not when we are thinking of the philosophy of Plato.[12] Plato himself uses the verb *agapaō* fairly often in a sense we might render, "be devoted to" or "be well pleased with" (e.g., *Phaedrus* 253a, *Statesman* 301d), and his account in the *Phaedrus* of the friendship among philosophers does not lack the dimension of benevolence and selflessness that theologians have often praised in the biblical doctrine of *agapē.* Earlier, I maintained that homosexuality, though forming the *context* of the *Phaedrus* speeches, did not constitute its *theme.* Equally so, I think, references to Christian ideals of love—the

---

12. Anders Nygren's work *Eros and Agape* (New York: Harper Torchbooks, 1969; Swedish text published in 1930 and 1937) postulates an extremely harsh separation between Platonic *erōs* and Christian *agapē,* a doctrine that appeared earlier in Søren Kierkegaard's *Works of Love.*

ideals of self-transcendence and attention to the other's needs—should be welcomed in an exposition of the *Phaedrus*. We should not suppose that this text of Platonic philosophy is confined to the kind of love that people intend with *erōs* when they specifically narrow it in to exclude *philia* and *agapē*. But of course we human beings are not capable of an infinite and divine *agapē*, only a human *agapē*, one that has to take its origin from the experiences of our own limited souls, especially from our experiences of *erōs* and *philia*. If it is true that *erōs* in the human soul is fulfilled through developing into *philia*, then we have to recognize it as a psychic disorder when *erōs* does not undergo that transformation: erotomania, some of whose forms were described by Plato in the *Republic* IX, others in modern fiction and psychiatry from the Marquis de Sade to John Updike. And if we make the claim that *erōs* and *philia* find their final fulfillment in *agapē*, then there would not be many of us, I suppose, who could be reckoned as complete and fulfilled persons.

At times, Plato's critics have complained[13] of his *idealistic* tendency, specifically, the tendency to treat interpersonal human love as being in some way the imitation of a higher orientation—the love of the soul for the absolute forms or for the gods—the suggestion that we are not fulfilled by the interpersonal experience as such. Vlastos has appealed to the love for the very definite individual, in protest against a tendency he sees in Plato to regard a human individual as nothing but the reflection of a higher, eternal truth. It may well be that humanists, materialists, and Nietzschean vitalists have sufficient grounds for this reproach. But it is inappropriate for Vlastos to make it while also affirming a Christian view. Christian love cannot stand on the side of humanism or romanticism, that is, doctrines that assert the ultimate self-sufficiency of the love that one human being has for another. A Christian critique of Plato's tendency to the Absolute is most inappropriate. Jesus is reported in the gospels (Mark 12:28–31) as summarizing the entire content of the divine law in two commandments. The first is the one taken from Deuteronomy 6: "You shall love the Lord your God with all your heart, and with all your soul, and with all your mind, and with all your strength." The second is the one taken from Leviticus 19: "You shall love your neighbor as yourself." Jesus gives a definite order of priority of these two commandments, and this is the priority that would also have secured Plato's enthusiastic agreement.

---

13. See Vlastos, "The Individual as an Object of Love in Plato."

Politics

Phaedrus 257c–262c

From *Phaedrus* 257c to the end of the dialogue at 279c, the tone of the text is different from that of the Great Speech in the middle of the dialogue. From the heights of eloquence and speculation we make an abrupt descent into an everyday world. Dramatically, this is accomplished by Phaedrus himself, who can think of nothing to say after the disclosure of this mighty vista except how poorly Lysias would do now if he had to compete in oratory with such a speech. And he begins to converse—to gossip!—about different political figures, how they would feel about Lysias, and about their own rivalries and vanities. I greatly admire the urbanity of Socrates here: having just soared in thought and speech above the heavens, he makes no complaint about Phaedrus's banality, but gets right into the swing of gossip. It is an achievement in art to build *into* a work the transition from the sublime to the everyday. Shakespeare among playwrights is the great master of this, for when, in the middle of the action, the tragic hero has finally seen the desperate fate that he confronts, Shakespeare inserts in the following scene a couple of grooms trading quips. This is the dramatic effect of anticlimax, the rope tossed by the artist to the playgoer, the relief of comedy that lets us absorb the desperate tragedy. Plato is Shakespeare's equal in this art. After the Great Speech, he knows how to let us down. We see this in the *Republic* too: starting from the mercantile home of Cephalus in Book I, we are led through the reform of the constitution to a colossal vision of the forms in the central books, then back down again through the series of constitutions in decline in Books VIII and IX, a literary pathway that is the very image of the route of the philosopher in the allegory of the Cave, who is led upward toward the sunlight and then back down into the politics of the city.

Lines 257c–258d contains a barb aimed at the vanity of politicians, men of stature, men of dignity. Such men look askance at someone like Lysias, says Phaedrus, for he earns his living as a speechwriter. A great man of the city would not fuss with pen and ink (for that he would have a slave), nor would he endure the sordid commercialism of being paid for writing speeches on consignment. Yet Socrates is not so sure. These great men seem to seek the applause of the crowd too; they too like to have writings and intellectual standing attributed to them (Plato may be thinking of his Uncle Critias, who was surely a great man but who loved to put on his tragedies in the Athenian competitions.) Socrates does not refer specifically to the literary works of the great men, but he is alive to the vanity whereby they want to ensure that works of legislation are attributed to them as authors. There is no politics free of rhetoric, and the pretense of the great men to be simple, honest men of the state, and free of the rhetorical love of glory, is nothing more than a pose.

At 259e–261a an argument repeats the classic position of both Socrates and Plato, that the political rhetorician is never able to exempt himself from the demand of truth, a restatement of the doctrine of the *Gorgias* and the *Republic* in a graphic and economical form. Speech without knowledge of the subject matter and of the souls of the hearers is never right. But as I indicated in part 1, chapter 2, Plato does not carry his point to the extreme conclusion he has advocated earlier. In his early works, the argument leads him to the conclusion that there is no legitimate rhetoric at all—only philosophy was legitimate. Now, Plato is preparing to state a position that recognizes rhetoric as long as rhetoric, for its part, does not evade the demand of seeking truth.

Earlier, he had attacked rhetoric tooth and nail, and, since the rhetoricians had claimed to be experts in government, he had to come up with a different solution for government. Some time after the great blast of the *Gorgias,* he set himself to drafting his alternative to the debased and unphilosophical culture dominated by rhetoric—that was his *Republic.* It shows how the philosopher Socrates might constitute in thought a reformed city and city government, contrasting this ideal structure throughout with an acid portrait of the existing Athens (see *Republic* 488a–496e, 555b–561e). Not only is this new city constituted in Socrates' philosophical thought—its central principle is that government should be undertaken by philosophers, trained in philosophical thought (*Republic* 473c–d). That this city is pervaded through and through by philosophical principles is also ordained by the manner in which the discussion begins, for the whole discussion springs from a philosophical encounter in Book I that attempts to define the *idea* of Justice and from the direction set in Book II that one and the same *idea,* Justice, will be found both on the smaller scale in the human soul and on the larger scale in the *polis* (368c–369a). It emerges that philosophers, who collectively pursue the truth without regard for their own advantage, are the genuinely just and happy souls, and a city ruled by such philosophers (who undertake government only out of duty) is the most just and happy city. The contrast between this ideal regime and other existing regimes takes up Book VIII of the text.

If we assume that Plato's *Seventh Letter* is an authentic work, we can see that a profound conflict within him had found some resolution through the writing of the *Republic.* For on the one hand, as I mentioned in the introduction, Plato writes, "when I was young, I had the same ambition as many others: I thought of entering public life as soon as I came of age" (324b). And on the other hand, he writes "I came to the conclusion that existing states are badly governed and the condition of their laws practically incurable, without some miraculous remedy and the assistance of fortune" (326a). Influenced no doubt by the inherited tradition of Athens and his family, but shaped likewise by his own conviction and idealism, Plato had always seen the problem of *politics* as the problem of *government.* His response to the evils and corruption of the years at the end of the war with Sparta, the rise and fall of the Thirty tyrants, and the excesses of the restored democracy, was to ask: How should a city be truly governed? What is the right constitution and regime? This led to his *Republic* and to his thesis that government is legitimized by the knowledge or insight of those who understand the Good and the Just. But the route he followed in the *Republic,* laying foundations for the rule of those who are competent and wise, had some extreme features he was not able to adhere to for long. He had to justify the concealment of truth from the masses of the people, the so-called noble lie (414b–415e). He instituted an extremely intrusive authoritarian supervision of culture (423e–425e). It seems he wanted eugenic measures to secure the best population (546a–547b), though perhaps this was not entirely serious, as Grube suggests in a note to this passage in his translation. These are just a few of the features of the *Republic* that have often given offense, but these days it should be perfectly evident, which it was not in earlier decades of the twentieth century, that Plato himself did not long remain satisfied with them. And in the tradition of political philosophy, beginning with the *Politics* of Aristotle, everybody sought different answers from those of the *Republic*—nobody followed the regime laid down in the *Republic,* though they all followed the *Republic* in practice by engaging in a philosophy of government, writing philosophy so as to be a sort of directive for the praxis of government that was itself directive.

There should be no doubt that Plato abandoned the famous *Republic* doctrine that philosophers should be kings shortly after he finished the *Republic*. We can see its abandonment in the *Phaedrus*. In the great speech of Socrates, 248d–e, there is the ordinance of necessity that leads to the mode of incarnation of the souls that had seen either more of truth, or less of truth, in their procession in the heavens. The soul that has seen the most will enter into life as either a lover of wisdom (*philosophou*) or a lover of beauty (*philokalou*) or a "musician" (*mousikou*) and lover (*erōtikou*). Given his account of beauty, of course, Socrates must make *erōs* and *kalos* come together, and there can be no doubt that these two would converge with the philosopher; the *mousikos* belongs here as well probably owing to the divine madness with which he is favored (see 245a). But there is no political government that will be required of this philosopher! We find that the second level of incarnation will be in a "law-abiding king, or a warrior and ruler [*polemikou kai archikou*]." This king, *basileus,* is made subject to the norm of law, we see, and the other is a figure who combines ruling with making war. At the third level, we have an incarnation as "a politician [*politikou*] or some kind of businessman or merchant [*oikonomikou e chrēmatistikou*]." Differentiating the third from the second level shows that Socrates is putting a lower estimate on the person who functions in a democratic climate such as that of Athens than on ancient and traditional ideas of kingship and war: the Homeric society or, perhaps, the royalty still found with the "great king" of Persia. There is no reason to doubt that if Socrates had chosen to mention rhetoricians, he would have included them in this third group.[1] Readers are often surprised at the assignment of prophets and mystery-priests to the fifth level down, and of poets to the sixth, since the opening of the speech seemed to grant

---

1. To be sure, sophists are included with demagogues at the second-lowest level, the eighth. It is in the light of the treatment of rhetoric *later* in the *Phaedrus,* 268a–272b, that I would separate rhetoricians from demagogues and sophists, and place them, rather, with the politicians.

each of them a "divine madness," but as Hackforth clarifies, the present terminology implies those who engage in these professions *without* the benefit of divine madness.[2] At the bottom of the list, in ninth place, is the tyrant, the one who exercises political rule in the most corrupt form, and this ranking is still in agreement with that of the *Republic*. However, the point of principle is the separation between the philosopher and the king or the politician. The difference between the *Phaedrus* and the *Republic* can be encapsulated by contrasting this series of incarnations with the "myth of the metals" at *Republic* 415a–c, for, in that text, the elite "golden" souls belonged to those who were to exercise government in the city. Now Socrates allows his philosophers to be free from the tasks of government, to pursue beauty, love, and "music." Again, although Socrates links the statesman Pericles to the philosopher Anaxagoras at 269e–270a, he does not merge the two figures into one.

But to differentiate philosophy from government does not imply that Plato now has nothing more to say about government. It is just that he has nothing to say about it in the *Phaedrus*. But in the years that followed he did return to the topic, specifically when he composed the dialogue sequence *Theaetetus, Sophist, Statesman* (very likely after the second Sicilian visit). I referred in chapter 2 to the sharp contrast drawn between the philosopher and the rhetorician in *Theaetetus* 172c–177c. Now we can mention the other two dialogues, for they are consistent as a whole with the *Phaedrus*. The *Statesman* in particular expresses Plato's "residual" concept of government after philosophy has been withdrawn from it. There were to be three dialogues, it seems (see *Sophist* 216c–217b and *Statesman* 257a–258b), though Plato did not write the third one devoted to the philosopher.[3] The philosopher would have been shown to be different from both the sophist and the statesman, and from the text of the *Statesman* itself we can see that it is not a philosophical life that makes a statesman (*politikos*) be what he is. In terms of the *Phaedrus*, the statesman's life is either at the second level of incarnation, when he practices a *royal* art, or at the third level, where he is merely a democratic politician (291a–293e).

The *Statesman* does not propose a constitution; instead, it seeks to differentiate that particular human figure, the *politikos*, who must undertake the office of ruling. Adding to the contrasts with the sophist

---

2. *Plato's Phaedrus*, p. 84.
3. The *Theaetetus* cannot be the missing dialogue, as some have suggested, for its aporetic character is out of keeping with the two companion pieces.

and the philosopher that are given with the dialogue's context, the text separates the *politikos* from a series of other figures: various economic functionaries (287b–290e), and then judges, military figures, and others (291a–305e). Though the *politikos* has a science, there is no suggestion in the dialogue of any philosophical wisdom or dialectic in this science. The craft of government is now far more empirical, a kind of "weaving" exercised upon the definite human materials, and other materials, that are available in a given city (305e–311c). The teacher-figure of the dialogue, the Eleatic Visitor, takes pains to clarify that the statesman operates within the realities of empirical history. That is the point of the myth of the Age of Kronos (269a–274d), for that was a time when human beings were ruled by the gods themselves, under the aegis of the wise god Kronus. But Kronus abandoned the cosmos, abandoned his work of guiding the rotation of the heavens and the earth. All things shuddered to a stop and then began to rotate in the contrary direction, and that was how our age began, the Age of Zeus, the age of history, in which we are governed no longer by gods but by other people who are just like ourselves. Plato's earlier philosopher-king had been a special being, and in the *Phaedrus* the philosopher, the lover, and the "musician" were those whose vision of truth had been the greatest. But in the *Phaedrus,* this semidivine or heavenly figure come down to earth, the philosopher, is not a ruler or king. And what the ruler or king of the *Statesman* needs to guide the city is good judgment about human types, to weave his civic web from them, not any eternal insight into the Beautiful or the Good.

Plato's final work, the *Laws,* returns to constitution making and law giving, but it does not repeat the philosophers' rule of the *Republic,* and, differently from the *Statesman,* it institutes a system for the rule of law rather than a rule of the king. To defend the rule of law, Plato institutes a complex and ramified system of safeguards. And these have not, in many cases, sprung from his own brain, but are adaptations of systems of justice that had been worked through in experience in the actual history of Greek cities, notably Athens,[4] so his final political testament is remarkably empirical, realistic, and historically informed.

But to return to the *Phaedrus.* It may not offer a doctrine of gov-

---

4. See Glenn Morrow, *Plato's Cretan City* (Princeton, N.J.: Princeton University Press, 1960), and his 1940 article, "Plato and the Rule of Law," reprinted in *Plato: A Collection of Critical Essays,* ed. G. Vlastos, vol. 2 (New York: Anchor, 1971), pp. 144 ff.

ernment, yet one might still wonder whether the dialogue leans in one direction or another when it comes to actual government. The modern scholar may interrogate the psychology of the Great Speech, or its picture of love and friendship, and seek to draw political "implications" from the text. That is, though it may be apolitical or unpolitical at its core, the scholar may still *insist* on estimating the drift or tendency it may promote, for the scholar may have the desire of estimating the political drift or tendency of *everything*. "Politics" makes its claim on scholarship too. So the reader may be prompted to see in the *Phaedrus* a political import. Griswold acknowledges that its central concerns are not political,[5] but he finds political suggestions in the doctrine of the soul's "care" for things on earth as well as in heaven and in the treatment of justice (pp. 177–81). And when he looks at the doctrine of the self-moving soul and philosophical communication (pp. 181–90), he finds the bonds of a political community that are essentially liberal rather than totalitarian. I believe he does establish this reading capably on the basis of his earlier study *Self-Knowledge in Plato's Phaedrus*. The self-knowing and self-moving soul with an active interior life needs scope for self-directed activity and self-realization. Griswold's interpretation of the *Phaedrus* belongs to a wider family of liberal interpretations of Plato. Kraut, for instance, has made a parallel argument concerning Plato's philosophy of law.[6] The *Crito*, in its strong vindication of the rule of law, is far from a reactionary legalism or legal decisionism, but a bulwark against such tendencies: it defends law itself, not the judges who apply the law.

In wanting philosophers to be kings, the *Republic* expects them to set goals for the city and exercise justice in government administration. But when the theme of politics enters the *Phaedrus*, at 257c, it is not because of issues of administration, good or bad, not because of kingship and government, but because of the contention of rival factions and rival persons in the city. "Politicians" are throwing insults at Lysias. The *Phaedrus* understands "politics" not as government, but as the pursuit of glory, as rivalry, as struggle. This is the conception of politics that is native to rhetoric itself and quite consistent with democracy, whereas

---

5. Charles Griswold, "The Politics of Self-Knowledge: Liberal Variations on the *Phaedrus*," in Rossetti, *Understanding the Phaedrus*, pp. 173–90.

6. Richard Kraut, *Socrates and the State* (Princeton, N.J.: Princeton University Press, 1984).

the *Republic*'s conception of politics as government, or administration, is inherently antidemocratic.

On the other hand, no philosopher can ever escape politics in this rhetorical sense—Lysias was stung by it, and so, of course, was Socrates, later, when he fell victim to the ambitions of the politicians Anytus, Metetus, and Lycon (*Apology* 23c, 24b). Nor could Plato escape politics in this sense, neither in Athens nor in Syracuse. The *Phaedrus* itself cannot escape it either, for even though, by its theme of love and by its dramatic location across the river from the city, it has no concern whatsoever with government and administration—even so, the rivalries of the politicians break in to interrupt its meditations. For although government as a theme may be remote, politics belongs to the facticity of philosophy because it is a part of our humanity. And, finally, there is political struggle even between philosophy and philosophy, just as there is between philosophy and rhetoric. Plato can become the target of a political opposition, as is so common in our own day.

The *Phaedrus* also communicates its sense of politics by putting before us the absolute counterimage of politics in the myth of the cicadas (258e–259d). Socrates imagines that the cicadas chirping in the bush at noontime are looking down on him and Phaedrus and having a laugh at them as if they were two lazy shepherds lying down for a noontime snooze. These cicadas are creatures who sing unceasingly, needing nothing to sustain them, neither food nor drink—devotion to song claims them utterly. And why is that? The story goes that once these creatures were men, but men who took no thought for food or drink or even for preserving their lives, and that came about because they were the generation that was the first to hear the song of the Muses. They were enthralled, so much so that they took to living on music alone. They turned into cicadas. And still their song can enchant us, turn us away from all the thoughts and cares of life, and make us forgetful. But if instead we stay awake and alert, the cicadas can grant us their great reward—if we for our part serve the Muses, or even just one of the Muses, the cicadas will intercede for us with the Muses, who will then bestow their bountiful gifts upon us. If, then, we persevere in the service of Calliope and Ourania, the Muses of philosophy, the intercession of the cicadas will bring us good fortune in the pursuit of philosophy.

Now these Muses, and the cicadas, and their human servants, who make music and dance unstintingly, have no politics and they have no economics, no "food and drink." They are beings of pure leisure (*scholē*), pure art, and unbroken holidays, the opposite of the business of the city and the counterimage of the political. Ferrari is surely right to see in this story a warning to Phaedrus against the aestheticism he is prone to (258e),[7] for surely the cicadas are in some way less than men, their original metamorphosis not a happy one. On the other hand, we must also take the story as an inspiration to "music" and a warning against the completely political life.

The *Phaedrus* holds up the philosophical life as the highest, grasping that politics will have to claim some part of every life, including the philosopher's, but not conceding that politics or government themselves reach as high as philosophy. The *Phaedrus* is among those texts in the tradition that place the knowledge of truth, the encounter with beauty, or the adoration of God on a plane neither government nor politics can reach. It is a Parnassian text, a prototype of the Western tradition of the *vita contemplativa* that played such a creative role in the Latin Middle Ages and of the Hesychasm of Greek and Russian Orthodoxy. It is, at the same time, a prototype of the eroticism of Medieval and Renaissance times, and some varieties of modern aestheticism. A text that firmly elevates contemplation over politics could also be read in such a way as to assert the supremacy of the church over the state. Although that claim of supremacy was overthrown *in practice* by the modern state in all its forms, there is little in the modern *philosophy* of the state that could secure the agreement of Plato, and it is more likely that, on philosophical grounds, he would have supported the Roman papacy in its resistance to state authority and to the lay investiture of bishops. At the same time, he would likely have deplored the authoritarian inner constitution of the papacy and curia itself, especially their undialectical and unphilosophical concept of the teaching office of the church. Socrates the questioner would be honored above all the "Doctors of the Church." Though, for Plato, the philosophical, erotic, aesthetic, and religious lives are higher than a political life, that honor does not require recognition in a *constitution* that grants such supremacy. Philosophical thought, religious devotion, erotic love, and artistic creation can defend themselves through their own free practice, not needing to be institutionalized and recognized by all.

---

7. *Listening to the Cicadas,* pp. 25–34.

BIBLIOGRAPHY

The first part of the bibliography selects some convenient editions of Plato's works and commentaries on them; the second part outlines other literature cited in the present book. With few exceptions, the titles are in English. An excellent current bibliography of Plato can be found in *The Cambridge Companion to Plato,* edited by Richard Kraut, New York: Cambridge University Press, 1992.

Plato Texts and Commentaries

The Complete Text of Plato

Complete Works. Edited by John Cooper, with many translators. Indianapolis: Hackett, 1997. This is the standard text now in use in the English-speaking world.

The Collected Dialogues of Plato. Edited by Edith Hamilton and Huntington Cairns, with many translators. Princeton, N.J.: Bollingen Books, 1969. This earlier edition of the complete works and the Jowett edition below are still widely used:

The Dialogues of Plato. Translated by Benjamin Jowett. London: Macmillan, 1892; reprinted New York: Random House, 1937.

Platonis Opera. Edited by John Burnet. 5 vols. Oxford: Oxford Classical Texts, 1901. This is the most widely used Greek text, and the one on which this translation has been based.

The Phaedrus: *Editions and Translations*

Euthyphro, Apology, Crito, Phaedo, Phaedrus. Translated by Harold Fowler. Cambridge, Mass.: Loeb Classical Library, 1995. The Loeb Classical Library provides convenient editions of Platonic dialogues, with Greek and English on facing pages.

Plato's Phaedrus. Translated by Reginald Hackforth, with introduction and commentary. Cambridge: Cambridge University Press, 1952.

Phaedrus. Translated, with introduction and notes, by A. Nehamas and P. Woodruff. Indianapolis: Hackett, 1995. This very current version also appears in Hackett's publication of Plato's *Complete Works.*

Phèdre. Greek text with French translation by Leon Robin, with an introductory *Notice.* Paris: Edition belles lettres "Bude," 1933, 1985.

Plato: Phaedrus. Edited and translated by Christopher J. Rowe. Warminster, Wiltshire: Aris and Phillips, 1986. Greek text, with English translation and commentary.

Commentaries and Studies of the Phaedrus

Benardete, Seth. *The Rhetoric of Morality and Philosophy: Plato's Gorgias and Phaedrus.* Chicago: University of Chicago Press, 1991.

Brisson, Luc. *Platon, Phèdre.* Paris: Flammarion, 1989.

Burger, Ronna. *Plato's Phaedrus: A Defence of a Philosophic Art of Writing.* Birmingham: University of Alabama Press, 1980.

de Vries, G. J. *A Commentary on the Phaedrus of Plato.* Amsterdam: Hackert, 1969.

Ferrari, G. R. F. *Listening to the Cicadas.* Cambridge: Cambridge University Press, 1987.

Griswold, Charles, Jr. *Self-Knowledge in Plato's Phaedrus.* New Haven, Conn.: Yale University Press, 1986.

Heath, M., "The Unity of Plato's *Phaedrus.*" *Oxford Studies in Ancient Philosophy* 7 (1987): 150–73.

———. "The Unity of the *Phaedrus.*" *Oxford Studies in Ancient Philosophy* 7 (1987): 189–91.

Lebeck, Anne. "The Central Myth of Plato's *Phaedrus.*" *Greek, Roman and Byzantine Studies* 13 (1972): 267–90.

Rossetti, L. *Understanding the Phaedrus.* Sankt Augustin, Germany: Akademia Verlag, 1992.

Rowe, C. J. "The Argument and Structure of Plato's *Phaedrus.*" *Proceedings of the Cambridge Philological Society* 32 (1986): 106–25.

———. "The Unity of the *Phaedrus:* A Reply to Heath." *Oxford Studies in Ancient Philosophy* 7 (1987): 175–88.

Thompson, W. H. *The Phaedrus of Plato, with English Notes and Dissertations.* London: Wittaker and Co., 1868.

White, David A. *Rhetoric and Reality in Plato's Phaedrus.* Albany: SUNY Press, 1993.

Wycherley, R. E. "The Scene of Plato's *Phaedrus.*" *Phoenix* 27 (1963): 88–92.

General Guides to Plato

Adam, J. *The Republic of Plato.* Revised ed. Cambridge: Cambridge University Press, 1963.

Allen, R. E., ed. *Studies in Plato's Metaphysics.* London: Routledge and Kegan Paul, 1965.

Annas, Julia. *An Introduction to Plato's Republic.* Oxford: Clarendon Press, 1981.

Bowen, Alan C. "On Interpreting Plato." In *Platonic Writings, Platonic Readings,* edited by C. H. Griswold, Jr. New York: Routledge, 1988.

Brandwood, Leonard. *The Chronology of Plato's Dialogues.* Cambridge, 1990.

Cherniss, Harold. *Aristotle's Criticism of Plato and the Early Academy.* Baltimore: Johns Hopkins University Press, 1944.

———. *The Riddle of the Early Academy.* Berkeley and Los Angeles: University of California Press, 1945.

———. "The Relation of the *Timaeus* to Plato's Later Dialogues." *American Journal of Philology* 78 (1957): 225–66.

Cornford, F. M. *Plato's Theory of Knowledge (the Theaetetus & the Sophist).* New York: Liberal Arts Press, 1957.

Cross, R. C., and A.D. Woozley. *Plato's Republic: A Philosophical Commentary.* London, 1964.

Dodds, E. R., ed. *Gorgias.* Oxford: Clarendon Press, 1959.

Findlay, J. N. *Plato: The Written and Unwritten Doctrines.* London: Routledge and Kegan Paul, 1974.

Friedlaender, Paul. *Plato: An Introduction.* Translated by Hans Meyerhoff. New York: Harper and Row, 1958. Translated from the 1954 German second ed.

———. *The Dialogues: First Period.* London: Routledge and Kegan Paul, 1965.

———. *The Dialogues: Second and Third Periods.* London: Routledge and Kegan Paul, 1969.

Gadamer, Hans-Georg. *Dialogue and Dialectic: Eight Hermeneutical Studies on Plato.* Translated by P. Christopher Smith. New Haven, Conn.: Yale University Press, 1980.

———. *Plato's Dialectical Ethics.* Translated by R. M. Wallace. New Haven, Conn.: Yale University Press, 1991. First published in 1931.

Grube, G. M. A. *Plato's Thought.* London: Methuen, 1935.

Gundert, Hermann. *Platonstudien.* Edited by K. Doering & F. Preisshofen. Amsterdam: Gruener, 1977.

Guthrie, W. K. C. *A History of Greek Philosophy.* Vol. 3. Cambridge: Cambridge University Press, 1969. Vol. 4 (1975). Vol. 5 (1978).

Griswold, C. H., Jr., ed. *Platonic Writings; Platonic Readings.* New York: Routledge, 1988.

Kraut, Richard, ed. *The Cambridge Companion to Plato.* New York: Cambridge University Press, 1992.

Kraut, Richard. *Socrates and the State.* Princeton, N.J.: Princeton University Press, 1984.

Moravcsik, J., and P. Temple, eds. *Plato on Beauty, Wisdom and the Arts.* Totowa, N.J., 1982.

Morrow, Glenn. *Plato's Cretan City.* Princeton, N.J : Princeton University Press, 1960.

Morrow, Glenn, ed.. *Plato's Epistles.* Indianapolis: Library of Liberal Arts, 1962.

Nettleship, R. L. *Lectures on the Republic of Plato.* London, 1898.

Nussbaum, Martha. *The Fragility of Goodness.* Cambridge: Cambridge University Press, 1986.

Owen, G. E. L. "The Place of the *Timaeus* in Plato's Dialogues." *Classical Quar-*

terly 3 (1953): 79–95. Reprinted in Allen, R. E., *Studies in Plato's Metaphysics.*

Robinson, Richard. *Plato's Early Dialectic.* Oxford: Oxford University Press, 1953.

Robinson, T. M. *Plato's Psychology.* 2nd ed. Toronto: University of Toronto Press, 1995.

Ross, W. D. *Plato's Theory of Ideas.* Oxford: Clarendon Press, 1951.

Ryle, Gilbert. *Plato's Progress.* Cambridge: Cambridge University Press, 1966.

Szlezak, Thomas. *Platon und die Schriftlichkeit der Philosophie.* Berlin: de Gruyter, 1985.

Stenzel, Julius. *Plato's Method of Dialectic.* Translated by D. J. Allan. Oxford: Clarendon Press, 1940.

Taylor, A. E. *Plato: The Man and His Work.* London: Methuen, 1955.

Vlastos, Gregory. *Socrates: Ironist and Moral Philosopher.* Cambridge: Cambridge University Press, 1991.

———. *Platonic Studies.* 2nd ed. Princeton, N.J.: Princeton University Press, 1981.

———. *Socratic Studies.* Edited by M. Burnyeat. Cambridge: Cambridge University Press, 1994.

———. , ed. *Plato: A Collection of Critical Essays.* 2 vols. New York: Anchor Books, 1971.

———. Introduction to *Plato's Protagoras.* New York: Liberal Arts Press, 1956.

Wilamowitz-Moellendorff, Ulrich von. *Platon.* 2 vols. Berlin: 1917.

White, Nicholas P. *Plato on Knowledge and Reality.* Indianapolis: Hackett, 1976.

Other Literature

Archer-Hind, R. D. "On Some Difficulties in the Platonic Psychology." *Journal of Philology* (1881): 120–31.

Bett, R. "Immortality and the Nature of the Soul in the *Phaedrus.*" *Phronesis* 31 (1986): 1–26.

Bluck, R. S. "The *Phaedrus* and Reincarnation." *American Journal of Philology* 79 (1958): 156–64, 405–14.

Burkert, Walter. *Greek Religion.* Translated by J. Raffan. Cambridge, Mass.: Harvard University Press, 1985.

Carey, C., ed. *Lysias: Selected Speeches.* Cambridge: Cambridge University Press, 1989.

Cassirer, Ernst. *Philosophy of Symbolic Forms.* Vol. 2, *Mythical Thought.* Translated by R. Manheim. New Haven, Conn.: Yale University Press, 1955. First published 1925.

Cole, Thomas. *The Origins of Rhetoric in Ancient Greece.* Baltimore: Johns Hopkins University Press, 1991.

Creuzer, F. *Symbolik und Mythologie der alten Voelker, besonders der Griechen.* Leipzig: Heyer and Leske, 1819–23.

Derrida, Jacques. "Plato's Pharmacy." In *Dissemination.* Translated by B. Johnson. Chicago: University of Chicago Press, 1980. The article originally appeared in French in the journal *Tel Quel* in 1968.

———. *Of Grammatology.* Translated by G. C. Spivak. Baltimore: Johns Hopkins University Press, 1976. French text first published in 1967.

Dodds, E. R. *The Greeks and the Irrational.* Berkeley and Los Angeles: University of California Press, 1963.

Dover, K. J. *Lysias and the Corpus Lysiacum.* Berkeley and Los Angeles: University of California Press, 1968.

———. *Greek Homosexuality.* London: Duckworth, 1978.

Foucault, Michel. *The Use of Pleasure.* Vol. 2 of *The History of Sexuality.* Translated by Robert Hurley. New York: Vintage Books, 1985.

Frutiger, Perceval. *Les Mythes de Platon.* Paris: Alcan, 1930.

Gaiser, Konrad. *Platons Ungeschriebene Lehre.* Stuttgart: 1963.

———. "Plato's Enigmatic Lecture *On the Good.*" *Phronesis* 25 (1980): 5–37.

Gill, C., ed. *The Person and the Human Mind: Issues in Ancient and Modern Philosophy.* Oxford: Clarendon Press, 1990.

Graves, Robert. *The Greek Myths.* 2 vols. Harmondsworth: Penguin Books, 1955.

Guthrie, W. K. C. *Orpheus and Greek Religion.* 2nd ed. London, 1952.

———. *The Greeks and Their Gods.* Boston: Beacon, 1950.

Harrison, Jane. *Prolegomena to the Study of Greek Religion.* New York: Meridian Books, 1955.

Havelock, Eric. *Preface to Plato.* Cambridge, Mass.: Harvard University Press, 1963.

Hegel, G. W. F. *Lectures on the Philosophy of Religion. One-Volume Edition. The Lectures of 1827.* Ed. P. C. Hodgson. Berkeley and Los Angeles: University of California Press, 1988.

Jebb, R. C. *The Attic Orators.* London: Macmillan, 1876.

Kennedy, George A. *The Art of Persuasion in Greece.* Princeton, N.J.: Princeton University Press, 1963.

Kern, Otto. *Orphicorum Fragmenta.* Berlin: Weidmann, 1922.

Kierkegaard, Søren. *Works of Love.* Translated by H. and E. Hong. New York: Harper, 1962.

Kraemer, Hans-Joachim. *Arete bei Platon und Aristoteles.* Heidelberg: Winter Universitätsverlag, 1959.

———. *Plato and the Foundations of Metaphysics.* Albany, N.Y: SUNY Press, 1990.

Lévi-Strauss, Claude. "The Structural Study of Myth." In *Structural Anthropology,* vol. 1. Translated by C. Jacobson and P. G. Schoepf. Garden City, N.Y.: Anchor Books, 1963.

———. *The Raw and the Cooked,* Vol. 1 of *Mythologiques.* Translated by J. and D. Weightman. New York: Harper Torchbooks, 1969.

Linforth, I. M. "The Corybantic Rites in Plato." *University of California Publications in Classical Philology* 13 (1946): 121–62.

———. "Telestic Madness in Plato's *Phaedrus.*" *University of California Publications in Classical Philology* 13 (1946): 163–72.

Lysias. Edited and translated by W. R. M. Lamb in the Loeb Classical Library. Cambridge, Mass., and London: Harvard University Press and Heinemann, 1930.

Moors, K. F. *Platonic Myth: An Introductory Study.* Washington, D.C.: University Press of America, 1982.

Morgan, Michael. *Platonic Piety.* New Haven, Conn.: Yale University Press, 1990.

Nicholson, Graeme. *Seeing and Reading.* Atlantic Highlands, N.J.: Humanities Press, 1984.

Nilsson, Martin P. *Geschichte der griechischen Religion.* Munich: Beck, 1967.

Nygren, Anders. *Eros and Agape.* New York: Harper Torchbooks, 1969. Swedish text published in 1930 and 1937.

Price, A. W. *Love and Friendship in Plato and Aristotle.* Oxford: Clarendon Press, 1989.

Pieper, Josef. *Enthusiasm and Divine Madness.* Translated by R. and C. Winston. New York: Harcourt, Brace, and World, 1964.

Reale, Giovanni. *Towards a New Interpretation of Plato.* Washington, D.C.: Catholic University of America Press, 1996.

Robin, Leon, *La théorie platonicienne des idées et des nombres d'après Aristote.* Paris, 1908.

Rohde, Erwin, *Psyche: Seelencult und Unsterblichkeitsglaube der Griechen.* Tübingen, 1893.

Schelling, F. W. J. von. *Philosophie der Mythologie.* In *Saemmtliche Werke* (Augsburg: Cotta), vol. 11 (1856) and vol. 12 (1857); reprinted Darmstadt: Wissenschaftliche Buchgesellschaft, 1966.

Simpson, Michael. *Gods and Heroes of the Greeks.* Amherst: University of Massachusetts Press, 1976.

Sinaiko, Herman. *Love, Knowledge and Discourse in Plato.* Chicago: University of Chicago Press, 1965.

Snell, Bruno. *The Discovery of the Mind.* Oxford: Blackwell, 1953.

Stewart, J. A. *The Myths of Plato.* London: Macmillan, 1905.

Wilamowitz-Moellendorff, Ulrich von. *Der Glaube der Hellenen.* 2 vols. Berlin: Weidmann, 1931–32.

Wheelwright, Philip. *The Presocratics.* New York: Odyssey Press, 1966.

Worthington, Ian, ed. *Persuasion: Greek Rhetoric in Action.* London & New York: Routledge, 1994.

INDEX

PURDUE UNIVERSITY PRESS
HISTORY OF PHILOSOPHY SERIES

Wittgenstein's Thought in Transition
by Dale Jacquette, Pennsylvania State University

1998; 320 pages
Cloth, ISBN 1-55753-103-X;
Paper, ISBN 1-55753-104-8

Aquinas against the Averroists
On There Being Only One Intellect
by Ralph McInerny, University of Notre Dame

1993; 240 pages
Cloth, ISBN 1-55753-028-9;
Paper, ISBN 1-55753-029-7

Augustine's Love of Wisdom
An Introspective Philosophy
by Vernon J. Bourke, St. Louis University

1992; 248 pages
Cloth, ISBN 1-55753-025-4;
Paper, ISBN 1-55753-026-2

Becoming a Self
A Reading of Kierkegaard's
Concluding Unscientific Postscript
by Merold Westphal, Fordham University

1996; 256 pages
Cloth, ISBN 1-55753-089-0;
Paper, ISBN 1-55753-090-4

Confessions of a Rational Mystic
Anselm's Early Writings
by Gregory Schufreider,
Louisiana State University

1994; 408 pages
Cloth, ISBN 1-55753-035-1;
Paper, ISBN 1-55753-036-X

David Hume
An Introduction to His Philosophical System
by Terence Penelhum, Calgary University

1992; 240 pages
Cloth, ISBN 1-55753-012-2;
Paper, ISBN 1-55753-013-0

Edmund Husserl's Phenomenology
by Joseph J. Kockelmans,
Pennsylvania State University

1994; 384 pages
Cloth, ISBN 1-55753-049-1;
Paper, ISBN 1-55753-050-5

Fichte's *Wissenschaftslehre* of 1794
A Commentary on Part 1
by George J. Seidel, St. Martin's College

1993; 140 pages
Cloth, ISBN 1-55753-016-5;
Paper, ISBN 1-55753-017-3

Ockham on the Virtues
by Rega Wood, Yale University

1997; 272 pages
Cloth, ISBN 1-55753-096-3;
Paper, ISBN 1-55753-097-1

Spinoza
The Way to Wisdom
by Herman De Dijn, Katholieke Universiteit,
Leuven, Belgium

1996; 304 pages
Cloth, ISBN 1-55753-081-5;
Paper, ISBN 1-55753-082-3

Strands of System
The Philosophy of Charles Peirce
by Douglas R. Anderson,
Pennsylvania State University

1995; 218 pages
Cloth, ISBN 1-55753-058-0;
Paper, ISBN 1-55753-059-9

To the Other
An Introduction to the Philosophy
of Emmanuel Levinas
by Adriaan Peperzak, Loyola University, Chicago

1992; 240 pages
Cloth, ISBN 1-55753-023-8;
Paper, ISBN 1-55753-024-6

Duns Scotus, Metaphysician
by William A. Frank, University of Dallas &
Allan B. Wolter, Catholic University of America

1995; 234 pages
Cloth, ISBN 1-55753-071-8;
Paper, ISBN 1-55753-072-6

Call 1-800-933-9637 for more information

Tilberg University Press
Books in Philosophy

Exception Proves the Rule
Non-monotonic Logic Via Topology
by H.H. Jurjus
1997, 156 p.
Paper, ISBN 90-361-9608-6

Representing the World by Scientific Theories
The Case for Scientific Realism
by Herman C.D.G. de Regt
1995, 320 p.
Paper, ISBN 90-361-9665-5

The (Non)Expression of Emotions in Health and Disease
edited by Ad Vingerhoets, Frans van Bussel and Jan Boelhouwer
1997, 365 p.
Paper, ISBN 90-361-9528-4

The Scientific Realism of Rom Harré
edited by Anthony A. Derksen
1994, 178 p.
Paper, ISBN 90-361-9974-3

Feminist Utopias in a Post Modern Era
In a Postmodern Era
edited by Alkeline van Lenning, Marrie Bekker, and Ine Vanwesenbeeck
1997, 197 p.
Paper, ISBN 90-361-9747-3

Home Language and School in a European Perspective
edited by Ton Vallen, Addie Birkhoff, Tjalling Buwalda
1995, 146 p.
Paper, ISBN 90-361-9785-6

Religion and Ethics in the Context of the Armed Forces
Exploring the Road to the Renewal of Military Chaplaincy
by Fred van Iersel
1996, 72 p.
Paper, ISBN 90-361-9607-8

Legal Knowledge Based Systems
Foundations of Legal Knowledge Systems
edited by R.W. van Kralingen, H.J. van den Herik, J.E.J. Prins, M. Sergot, J. Zeleznikov
1996, 150 p.
Paper, ISBN 90-361-9657-4

The Individualizing Society
Value Change in Europe and North America
edited by Peter Ester, Loek Halman, and Ruud de Moor
1994, 311 p.
ISBN 90-361-9993-X

Purdue University Press is the exclusive distributor for the Tilberg University Press in the United States, Canada, and Mexico.

Call 1-800-933-9637 for more Information